GORILLA HUNTER

Gorilla Hunter

by FRED G. MERFIELD with HARRY MILLER

FARRAR, STRAUS AND CUDAHY

NEW YORK

To the best pal
I ever had —
my wife

ACKNOWLEDGMENTS

My grateful thanks are due to Mrs. H. B. Powell-Cotton, widow of Major P. H. G. Powell-Cotton and Trustee of the Powell-Cotton Museum, Birchington, Kent, for permission to reproduce so many photographs of my life in the French Cameroons and for advising on the chapters concerning her late husband; to my collaborator Harry Miller, F. Z. S., who was entirely responsible for the style and treatment of this book; and to my wise and gentle friend Laurie Smith, Head Keeper of Primates at the London Zoo, who brought Mr. Miller and myself together and gave us invaluable advice and encouragement.

Contents

Acknowledgments vii

Introduction xi

1. The Great Gorilla of Ambam 3

2. The Maka Cannibals 24

3. Chimps, Chogas and Gorillas 42

4. Big Game Hunters 60

5. L'Inspecteur de Chasse 82

6. The Ghost of the Sanaga Grasslands 102

7. The Woman Chieftain of Cheke 112

8. The Silent City of Rei Bouba 129

9. The Mendjim Mey 152

10. Shootman's Woman 179

11. Jungle Housekeeper 198

12. Good-Bye Gorillas 219

Introduction

It has been estimated that the number of gorillas in the world is not less than a thousand or more than ten thousand. From this we may infer, first, that gorillas are rare animals; secondly—considering the wide disparity between the two figures—that the difficulties involved in studying gorillas must be considerable.

The fact that little is known about the gorilla at first sight may seem strange, for the animal has undeniable attractions for the student of natural history. To begin with, it is by far the largest and most spectacular of the great apes, reaching the prodigious weight of 43 stone (approximately 600 pounds). It is in many ways the most manlike of all animals, for that reason alone meriting our closest attention; and from far back in history its life and habits have attracted the wildest speculation.

The French naturalist du Chaillu brought back to Europe the first authentic description of the gorilla, but for many centuries travelers had told of a giant man-ape, of incredible strength and ferocity, which fought with leopards, belabored elephants with clubs, and abducted village maidens. Gorillas were endowed with a most aggressive nature, and were said to hang by their hands from the branches of trees, using their feet to catch and strangle passing natives. Tales of this kind seeped out of Africa into Europe, the Middle East and Asia, acquiring marvelous embellishments en route, and finally drifting into the folklore and fables of many nations. The inoffensive gorilla may well have been a model for the Ogre of our legends.

Today, the gorilla has been stripped of these fabrications, even in Africa, where hunters and naturalists are so inclined to fiction. But it is still a creature of mystery.

Because of the inaccessible nature of its forest home, its rarity, and strict government protection, few sportsmen have hunted the gorilla, and fewer still have stayed in its territory for more than three or four months at a time. Photography and direct observation are severely limited by the dense forest; and since nine times out of ten young gorillas, caught and caged, will turn their faces to the wall and die of sheer despair, not many zoos have been able to keep them, and they have never been bred in captivity. For years little has been added to our scant knowledge of their behavior.

My own interest in gorillas dates from the period before the First World War, when, as a young planter in the Cameroons, I first heard about them. I lived for a total of fifteen years in gorilla country and it was a lucky chance of friendship with the truculent Mendjim Mey tribe that enabled me to spend four of those years in the Mendjim Mey where gorillas literally were my neighbors, and where the all too common complaint about "those dreadful people next door" had a unique significance. During that time I was able to collect one hundred and fifteen gorillas for European museums, as well as many other rarities. These included the Red Colobus monkey,[1] the Bongo,[2] and the world's largest frog, weighing four pounds six ounces and capable of catching and swallowing whole live rats.

The task of collecting live animals for menageries has caught the public imagination. Much of my work was of that kind, but more of it lay in collecting dead specimens for museums—a less attractive task but equally important. Live

---

[1] *Colobus ferrugineus preussi.* [2] *Boocerus eurycerus cooperi.* [3] *Rana goliath.*

animals in zoos have tremendous popular appeal, but they are of limited importance to the zoologist.

For obvious reasons, it is not possible to study the anatomy of living animals. Although shooting animals is distasteful, the larger part of zoological research would not be possible without it. Zoology, like botany, is still largely concerned with classification, and at present the museum is of greater value than the zoo. Moreover, there are animals which cannot be kept in captivity at all, and many more that should never be in zoos because, in them, their peculiar requirements cannot be satisfied.

This book contains much about the gorilla that has not been published before, but it is not a scientific treatise. I was a hunter, not a zoologist, and in the succeeding chapters I have tried to tell how I entered that strange profession, of the adventures I had, and of the animals, the people and the country I came to know so well during the thirty-five years I spent in the French Cameroons.

Native dialogue throughout the book is in Pidgin English and the reader may be curious to know how this amusing but expressive language came to be spoken in a French possession. The Germans, who ruled this territory before the First World War, made every effort to prevent their subjects from learning German; that, they felt, would be politically dangerous and an encroachment on their privacy. On the other hand, they would not take the trouble to study the many difficult local languages, and since Pidgin English was already the *lingua franca* of the West Coast, they adopted it as a convenient medium of intercourse. The French accepted this situation, but through indolence rather than expediency. Unlike their British counterparts, officials of the French Colonial service in the Cameroons did not take the trouble to learn the vernaculars.

While every effort has been made to preserve the authenticity of Pidgin English in this book, slight modifications have had to be made here and there to make the dialogue intelligible to English readers, for Pidgin is fast becoming a distinct language, evolving a vocabulary and syntax of its own.

F. M.

GORILLA HUNTER

1. The Great Gorilla of Ambam

Before me, the jungle fell away to the east and south, stretching unbroken across hills and valleys towards the Congo and its tributaries. Ebony, mahogany, cottonwood and ironwood trees, with brilliantly colored orchids clinging to their trunks, rose two hundred feet and more above the ground. Around them crowded the struggling jungle, every plant clutching and choking its neighbor in the eternal struggle for light and air.

Where I stood, at the edge of a native plantation, there was a round hole in the undergrowth. I went down on hands and knees and crawled inside, finding myself in a long winding tunnel lit by dim green light filtering through the leaves above.

Swarms of sandflies hurried forward to welcome me, plunging in their vicious little noses wherever my skin was unprotected. A line of bright red ants trickled across my hands, and just above my head a chameleon gripped a branch, one eye fixed coldly and warily on me, the other roving ceaselessly in search of food. It was cool and damp, and the air stank with rotting vegetation. Mingled with this was another smell, faint yet unmistakable; the rank, musty odor of the bull gorilla whose great arms and shoulders had forced this passage through the vegetation.

"You no see 'im, Massa?" asked my guide Nze from outside.

"No, and I no savvy how far this hole go. Leave your brother and come follow me."

A week earlier, news had reached me at Ebolowa, in the French Cameroons, that a solitary bull gorilla was living in this vicinity, just north of the little town of Ambam, and was playing havoc among the natives' tiny plantations of sugar cane and bananas. I had waited years for this opportunity. No white man I knew in West Africa had firsthand experience of gorillas, and while I had long been earning my living as a hunter and collector, circumstances had conspired against my plans to find these apes myself—first, an attack of blackwater fever and enforced convalescence in England, then the Kaiser's war, with two dreary months on the *Hans Woermann*, a German prison ship moored up the Wouri River, and finally service with the B.E.F. in West Africa until the war there ended in 1916.

There were a few gorillas in the Ebolowa Forest, and I had seen them rounded up and killed by the Yaounde tribes, but nothing would induce them to let me take part in a hunt, nor would they sell me the skins and skeletons so badly wanted by the museums. The people of the Ambam district, on the other hand, were not hunters and were terrified of gorillas. They were only too glad that I should wish to free them of the unwelcome guest who supported himself on their crops and ruined so much more than he could eat.

Though they had had little experience as hunters, Nze and his brother Wana were eager to help, and they knew the locality and the habits of this animal. They told me that the gorilla appeared on the plantations every morning. Women and solitary men, he threatened and chased away. If several men appeared, he sometimes made off, but more often he stood up, beat his chest and roared at them, whereupon they deemed it prudent to leave him to breakfast off their bananas. The roar, they said, could be heard for miles.

I was by no means keen on crawling along that tunnel,

where it would be difficult to shoot and impossible to run away. With so little knowledge of gorillas, I had no idea how the animal would behave if I confronted him, and my experience in stalking elephant, buffalo and other big game would be of little use with an animal whose natural history was entirely different.

Would he, I wondered, find me before I found him? And would he attack me if he did? According to reports I had read, which were confirmed by the natives, I could expect to be pounced on and torn to pieces. I did not know then that the gorilla's sense of smell is as feeble as man's. His sight and hearing, however, are probably a little better, and like all wild animals he can correctly interpret sounds that would mean nothing to a man. On the other hand, though a gorilla cannot scent an approaching man, as an elephant does, a man can certainly scent a gorilla. The powerful odor produced by sweat glands in the armpits of the male animal is distinctive, though it is by no means unpleasant.

We had already waited nearly two hours outside the trees before I had decided to go in after this gorilla. Now we had gone about a hundred yards and there had been no sign of him.

We went forward, sometimes on hands and knees, but more often walking in a crouching position, for the tunnel was broader and higher now. Presently I found some droppings which could only have been from the gorilla, but they were stale and I judged them to be at least a day old. Then the tunnel opened into a tiny clearing, and we stopped dead as we saw a slight movement in the bush on the other side. We stood quite still, partly screened by creepers hanging from a tall tree. Slowly and quietly I released the safety catch of my rifle.

Presently, the bush moved again and from behind a shrub came, not a gorilla, but a fine, yellow-backed duiker, a little forest antelope, stepping daintily into the clearing. The duiker stood staring at us for a moment or two, twitching his ears inquiringly in our direction. And then, because we moved not a muscle, he decided we were part of the scenery. He lowered his head and began to browse calmly on the cassava leaves.

He was a lovely animal, just under three feet tall, with short stout horns, a glossy black coat, and a large yellow triangle on his hindquarters. Yellow-backed duiker are plentiful in some parts of the West African forests, and are often audacious enough to invade station clearings by night and plantations by day in search of food. The villagers use snares and game pits to trap them. The flesh is excellent, and in a country chronically short of meat, it is much sought after by both Europeans and Africans.

Nze, unaccustomed to hunting, had been holding his breath, but he could do so no longer, and he now let it out in a long whistling gasp. At once the duiker uttered a bark—a loud "phonk"—and dived into the bush, scarcely disturbing a leaf.

"Sorry Massa," said Nze, deeply distressed. "How you no shoot 'im?"

"I come shoot gorilla, no come shoot bush beef," I told him.

Not only the droppings had convinced me that the gorilla was nowhere about. There were abundant signs that he had used this tunnel many times. Broken plants, empty seed husks, and chewed fragments of sugar cane gave ample evidence of that, but they were at least twelve hours old. Whether, as Nze said, the gorilla had a fairly rigid program of visits I did not know, but if so, something had interrupted it that morning. Africans are rarely confounded by the unexpected, and Nze, as usual, had an answer ready.

"Dis gorilla no like other one. He be ju-ju gorilla an' he savvy you come for kill him, so he hide."

From the plantations outside we heard Wana calling us, so we crawled back as fast as we could. With him was a village woman, carrying a fat, slumbering baby on her broad hips.

"Dis woman," Wana announced importantly, "say gorilla live for him farm."

She nodded vigorously, but her eyes were fixed on the bright colored kerchief I wore about my neck. I asked her whether it was true that she had seen the gorilla that morning.

"Yes, yes, N'gi, N'gi (gorilla)," she said, still staring covetously at my kerchief. I promised I would give it to her if the information was correct, and we set off for her plantation.

This was only a quarter of a mile away, but when we got there we found nothing but damaged sugar cane and banana plants. The gorilla had certainly done a lot of damage. More than a dozen banana plants had been torn to pieces, but he had eaten only a little of the pith from each stem before discarding the entire plant in favor of another. The sugar cane had suffered even worse. Enough had been pulled down to keep a village family supplied for a week. I picked up some of the pieces and examined them. They could not have been broken that morning, for the ends were dry, with no oozing sap.

"You talk for true you see gorilla dis morning?" I asked the woman.

She admitted now that she had not actually seen the animal, but had taken her damaged plants as evidence that he was there.

I felt like crowning her with her own bananas, but she had brought me there with the best of intentions, so I took off the kerchief and handed it over. She wound it round her head delightedly and hurried off to the village to parade before her envious neighbors.

By now the sun was high and there was no chance of the gorilla turning up at that hour, for they do not move about outside the forest except in the early morning. I decided to abandon the hunt until next day, and returned to the village, where the chief had put a hut at my disposal. Joseph, my cook, was waiting for me with a meal of boiled fowl, yams and pineapple, which I ate after a quick bath in tepid water

from a kerosene tin. Afterwards I relaxed in a deck chair outside the hut, smoking quietly and trying to think out a plan
against the gorilla.

Presently, a native man came walking up the village street
towards me. He was dressed in tattered khaki shorts and shirt,
which was unusual in a land where men wear only the briefest
of loincloths, and women's costume is just as simple, consisting of either a few leaves or a tiny triangle of cloth supported
by a string about the waist. The gentleman approaching could
therefore be considered rather overdressed for village life,
and he was remarkable, too, for his stiff military carriage. He
walked straight up to me, came smartly to attention, and
saluted.

"Stand at ease, sergeant," I said.

He stared at me in surprise. "You be Englishman, sar?" he
asked, for there were very few of us in that French colony.

"Yes, and I'll bet you are from the Nigerian police," I said.
Nowhere else could he have learned such discipline.

"Damn right you are, sar," he replied, astonished and delighted, "but I only corporal, sar, not sergeant."

He told me that during the 1914–18 war, when British
troops came to Ebolowa, he had been recruited as a carrier
and had so much liked the British that he had gone with them
to Nigeria, where he afterwards joined the police. He was
now on leave, and would be returning to his post a few days
later.

I remarked on his tattered shorts.

"These are my play clothes, sar," he said. "We have big
Pra-Pra tomorrow."

"For goodness sake," I said, "what's a Pra-Pra?"

He explained that it was a wrestling tournament between
villages, and seemed to be of the opinion that anyone who
had not witnessed a Pra-Pra had missed the very cream of
man's experience. The village chief, he went on, had sent him
to invite me, and would be grateful if I would come and dis-

cuss arrangements both for the Pra-Pra and for the gorilla hunt. I told the corporal to say I would be along shortly, and when I had finished my pipe I strolled off down the village.

There were about forty huts, with walls of bark and roofs of palm thatch, on either side of the bare street, some fifty yards wide.

Behind them were banana and plantain trees backed by tall palms from which the people extracted oil and kernels for sale in Ebolowa. Wandering about were small naked children, undersized fowls and a few sheep and goats. Halfway down the street stood a crowd of villagers, who opened their ranks respectfully as I approached, revealing the chief sitting on a deck chair outside his hut.

He uttered the greeting "M'Boolu," took my right hand in his, and grasped my forearm with his left, the customary salutation in that part of Africa. Then we both sat down, he on his deck chair, I on a carved wooden stool decorated with the figures of leopards, crocodiles, antelopes and a man and woman. I remember it as one of the most uncomfortable seats I have ever encountered.

The chief drew his soiled and colorful cloth firmly around his ample belly and called for mimbo, a liquor made from the fermented sap of palm trees. Meanwhile the corporal had reappeared. His woolly hair was greased and carefully parted at the side and he now wore a clean, well-pressed uniform. Again he came to attention and saluted. I was glad he was there, for I had only a sketchy knowledge of the local language, and the chief did not know much Pidgin.

One of the chief's women produced an old, heavily scratched glass tankard, evidently a relic of the German occupation, and at his direction she filled it with mimbo and offered it to me. I never drank while on a hunt, remembering the time when I had narrowly escaped being savaged by an elephant "the morning after," so I declined the offer as gracefully as Pidgin would allow.

I now mentioned the problem of the gorilla. I suggested that each plantation should be watched by groups of two or three villagers, including a boy to run and fetch me if the gorilla appeared. I would wait in the village for news and from that central point I could reach any of the plantations within fifteen minutes. If the men kept quiet and out of sight there was no reason why the beast should make off before I arrived. The chief readily agreed to the plan—but not to get it under way until Pra-Pra had ended in three days' time. No argument of mine would stir him from this position. Pra-Pra was sacred and inviolate. Until it was over the gorilla could do what he liked with their bananas.

Next morning the drums started soon after the sun was up, beginning with a subdued tapping that mingled with the excited chatter of the people, and increasing in volume and tempo as the drummers warmed to their task. The wrestling arena was a space in front of the chief's hut, where the earth had been loosened and then beaten into a fine powder. Competitors from other villages were already arriving, bringing with them their wives, children and older relatives. The little street was packed to suffocation and there was a general air of festivity and bubbling good humor.

Women shouted gossip at each other, ignoring the children who bawled for their attention or the babies who hungrily sought their breasts. Gray-haired old men squatted in the shade, telling of bygone Pra-Pras in which they had astonished the countryside with great feats of strength. Young men, in threes and fours, oiled one another's gleaming backs and legs or pranced about doing handstands to loosen their tough, lean limbs.

It was surprising that the chief's cough, announcing his arrival, should have been heard above this racket, but then it was an important cough, and everyone had been waiting for it. A respectful hush fell instantly over the gathering as he strode majestically from his hut, followed by his eight wives. Painful memories of the ornamental stool had prompted me to bring my own deck chair, and with a truly regal wave of his hand he invited me to set this up beside him. When we had both settled ourselves comfortably he clapped his hands for the Pra-Pra to begin.

The men now formed about us in a circle, squatting on the ground, while the women and girls stood behind them. Another gesture from the chief and the drums broke out into a terrible din, sending the crows and hornbills in nearby trees into frenzied cackles of alarm. One of the young wrestlers, eager to prove himself, jumped into the arena and walked around, his outstretched right hand inviting a challenger. He soon found one and the first bout began.

Pra-Pras take place only in the Ebolowa district of the Cameroons, and only once again, some years later, was I lucky enough to attend one. The bout opens, without preliminary dodging and sparring, by each contestant putting his left arm round the other's waist, with his hand in the small of the back. As in European wrestling, the bout is won when both shoulders of an opponent are forced simultaneously into contact with the ground.

The two lads I was watching clasped each other in the approved fashion and shuffled about, seeking a hold with their free arms. Then one tripped his opponent and fell with him heavily to the ground. Lying there they whipped into a clinch with the speed and vigor of pythons, so that it was difficult to identify individual arms and legs.

The challenger was on top, putting all the power of his fresh young limbs into the struggle. Muscles strained, sinews cracked; there were grunts and groans. Then his opponent's resistance cracked, and both shoulders submitted themselves squarely to the dust. When the loser rose there was a coating of dust across his back as visible proof of his defeat. The victor rubbed his hands down his sturdy thighs, grinned modestly but proudly in my direction and ran round the circle again, calling for a fresh opponent.

My corporal rose and accepted him. He wore neither his clean uniform nor his old "play clothes," but only a simple strip of cloth tied tightly to his waist-cord. He had a magnificent physique; a broad, hard muscled back, narrow hips and long, brawny legs. I was not surprised when he upheld the honor both of his village and of the Nigerian police by defeating the young challenger and three other stalwart opponents in rapid succession.

For a long time afterwards he could find no one else to take him on, but presently a big man, who had been squatting silently near me, got up and walked towards him. The crowd howled approval as the two men clasped each other and carefully tested their strength with experimental holds. For a moment or two they looked as if they were about to waltz, until the corporal, moving like a flash, locked the big man's arms and neck in a hold that would have worried a rhinoceros. They stood swaying and gasping, with the sweat trickling down their shining bodies, and then the big man gave a tremendous heave.

He moved so quickly that I could not see how it was done, but the corporal was off his feet, losing his hold and falling heavily to the ground. He fell skilfully on one shoulder, turned a somersault and was up again in an instant. They re-engaged, and again there was a stalemate as their trembling limbs struggled for mastery. Neither side gave way, and at last, by silent and mutual consent, they parted and sat down for a rest.

It was getting on for one o'clock so I slipped away for lunch, which I had to get myself, for Joseph was glued to the ringside and I had not the heart to tear him away. When I returned the two men were still at it, though I learned that they had rested several times during my absence. The chief now intervened to announce a draw, and the wrestlers, delighted with each other as only well-matched men can be, retired to be fussed over and applauded by their families.

The wrestling continued during the afternoon and all the next day. On the third and final day there was a change when elderly women took the place of men in the arena. To my surprise they wrestled ably and the bouts lasted longer. In most cases they fought with dignity and good humor but two or three of them lost their tempers and began scratching and pulling hair. They were quickly parted by the men and ten minutes later were all smiles again. I never managed to discover which village won the Pra-Pra, though I tried hard. The final situation was amazingly confused, but the people seemed content and went off to their homes well pleased with the whole affair.

I waited yet another day, so that the villagers could recover from the excitement of the Pra-Pra, and filled in some of the time overhauling my guns. It was wise to clean and oil them every day, since they would quickly deteriorate in that humid climate. Shotguns were vulnerable to another and more peculiar danger. Masonflies, so called from the rock-hard nests they build, abound in West Africa and are attracted to any kind of deep hole. They build rapidly, and a shotgun, laid aside for a day or two, can get choked with a nest as solid as concrete. It might be thought that this could not go unobserved, yet I know of more than one accident which occurred because a careless sportsman tried to use a gun in that condition and it burst when fired.

My own shotgun was a two-barreled 12-bore. Loaded with buckshot, it could be depended on to stop a charging leopard, lion or gorilla at close range. For big game I used a 9 mm. Mauser, with a Mannlicher of the same calibre in reserve. The Mauser was highly accurate and could be depended on to bring down elephant, rhino or buffalo at up to three hundred yards. Many hunters use heavy, double-barreled elephant guns, 400, 450, or even larger, but it is cleaner and more effective to place a comparatively small bullet in a vital spot. For monkeys, small antelope and other lesser game I kept a small .22 rifle, and in later years I carried a .45 revolver when after gorillas in heavy forest.

Meanwhile, the gorilla had been having a whale of a time in the plantations, where he found food much more conveniently placed and plentiful than in the forest. Before dawn on the day appointed I had my little groups of men in position on the plantations, concealed at some distance from every game trail or tunnel I thought the gorilla might use. Satisfied that they understood their instructions, I returned to wait in the village, where Joseph kept me supplied with good black coffee, for the jungle is a cold and damp place in the early morning.

Nothing happened. Towards nine o'clock, with the sun soaring high and hot above the palm fronds, the men came drifting back looking worried and frustrated. The gorilla had not appeared, and this, they felt, was because he knew what we were up to and had made himself scarce. I thought it much more likely that he had spotted the waiting men and had become suspicious, but even this guess was wrong.

Before lunch time a runner reached me from a village over five miles away with news that the gorilla had turned up there. A woman who had intended to gather plantains had almost walked into him, and when she fled, screaming, he chased her and wounded her with his great nails. He had not, however, followed up the attack, the runner added, and the woman had returned to her home with a badly lacerated back.

When I got to the village, as I did with all speed, I found that as usual the facts had been exaggerated. The woman looked badly shaken and she insisted that she had been chased by the animal, but she had certainly not been hurt. I decided to go at once to her plantation, but instead of using the regular paths, I pushed straight through the forest in the hope of finding either the gorilla or at least a recent track which I could follow up.

During the past few days, Nze had been given detailed theoretical lessons in hunting by that incorrigible old humbug, my cook Joseph, and he now insisted on leading the way. Whenever he saw, or thought he saw, a movement in the undergrowth, he ducked down as native trackers are trained to do, so that in an emergency the hunter can fire over their heads. On wider trails, made by elephant or buffalo, the tracker can sometimes slip to one side. I never liked this positioning of hunter and tracker, for it had once involved a close friend of mine, whom I shall call Gilbert, in an appalling accident.

Gilbert was a hunter and trader who had a perfect wonder of a tracker named Esumba. Once or twice, when his master was on holiday in Europe, I was able to employ this man myself, and I never ceased to marvel at his extraordinary powers. He could follow any kind of game over even the hardest ground, often when the trail was several days old. Every twig and blade of grass yielded a message to him. He would handle a leaf as though it were fragile porcelain, and by comparing the amount of dew on it with that on neighboring leaves, judge how long ago it had been disturbed by a passing animal. Gilbert himself was an excellent hunter and a dead shot; a great bond of friendship and mutual understanding had grown up between the two men, and together they made the perfect hunting team.

Esumba's end was tragic. He and Gilbert had been tracking a big tusker through elephant grass for some days, but the animal was old and wary and they could not get within range. At last, by exercising their skill to the utmost, they came upon it feeding quietly in a clearing. Esumba indicated silently that a shot might be tried, and then bobbed down out of the way. Gilbert raised his heavy 400 elephant gun, took aim carefully, and squeezed the trigger. At that instant

Esumba sprang to his feet, right in front of the muzzle, and most of his head was blown off.

Why he should have moved at all at that last, fatal moment will always be a mystery. Gilbert was brokenhearted and never hunted again. When he got back to Yaounde he sold all his rifles and afterwards he could not bear even to look at a gun.

I was glad, therefore, when we came out onto the plantation without having encountered anything more formidable than a pair of flying squirrels, which chattered angrily at us from a tall tree. The damaged plantains were all fresh, and on the tilled soil around them were the tracks of the gorilla. There was one perfect impression of his foot, thirteen inches long and nine inches wide, showing the widely separated big toe. Gorillas walk on the flat of the hind feet and on the knuckles of the hands, which are fat and heavily calloused, and there were abundant knuckle marks in the soft earth. I did not hope to track the animal by these signs, however, for a soft-footed beast leaves no impression on the leafy forest floor.

There was a newly made gorilla tunnel near at hand, and I decided to sit within range of it early next morning. Meanwhile, a hut was again put at my disposal in the village.

A thin strip of bush, projecting a few yards from the forest edge, offered ideal cover, and long before dawn Nze and I were crouching there in the damp, with the mist swirling about us. Soon, the forest began to wake up. Mona monkeys quarreled noisily over their breakfast, parrots squawked and stretched their vivid wings, and in the distance we could hear the cracked voices of the village roosters.

In that dim light, we watched the entrance to the tunnel until our eyes ached. Once I thought I saw a movement just inside, and I brought up my rifle, but nothing emerged. When we had begun to think that we were out of luck again, out of the corner of my eye I spotted a sudden disturbance in the bush on the far side of the plantation, where there was no game track or tunnel. I took out my binoculars and examined the spot. There was certainly something there, but for a moment or two I could not see what it was. Then two great hands parted the foliage, a head leaned out between them, looked suspiciously around, and the gorilla stepped out into the open.

He was certainly an enormous beast, far bigger than the few I had previously seen in the Yaounde forest. His long, shaggy coat was so grizzled with age that from where we were it looked almost white. He stood for a while on all fours, with his huge shoulders hunched forward and his tall, crested head turning inquiringly from side to side. Then, to make sure he was alone, he reared up on his hind legs and looked about him. Even at that distance I could see that he was taller than an average man and twice as broad as my strapping corporal friend. He seemed satisfied that he was safe, for after a close scrutiny of the plantation, he dropped down again, walked forward and began stripping away the leaves of a plantain, to reach its succulent pith. Then he sat on his bottom, crossed his bandy legs and began munching it. He looked for all the world like an old gentleman enjoying an apple.

Although he was well within range I could not risk a shot, for there was a lot of vegetation between us. If a bullet nicks the stem of a plant it can be given just sufficient deflection to miss the target. Moreover, I wanted to study the gorilla's behavior, for this was my first opportunity of doing so, and I began working my way, as silently as I could, along the edge of the forest towards him.

Whenever he looked up I froze against a background of leaves, and he did not see me. At last I got to within one hundred fifty yards and found an outlying bush, behind which I could hide and watch him. I needed both hands to steady the binoculars, so I laid my rifle on the ground. It was bad luck that the rifle should have caught in the binoculars, causing them to rattle faintly against the muzzle. At once the gorilla looked up, stared straight in my direction and then crashed back into the forest out of sight, coughing angrily. There was no need now for concealment. Calling to Nze to follow me, I ran across and, with more foolishness than courage, burst into the undergrowth where the gorilla had gone. Once I was inside the trees caution prevailed, and I stopped to look around.

At this point the forest was thinner than I had supposed, perhaps because of shallow soil beneath. The gorilla had gone straight through, pushing saplings and bushes aside in his haste. Nze came up behind and looked at me expectantly. I hated the idea of going any further, for I imagined that the gorilla might be waiting for me in the nearest cover, as a buffalo will, and his ability to launch a surprise attack at a few yards' range seemed to put the whole situation in his favor.

Nze and I looked at each other.

"Carry on, Nze," I said firmly. "We must follow him. You go before and hold dem shotgun."

Nze was no fool. "Yes, yes, Massa, we follow him," he agreed, "But *you* go before."

Following the track was at first an easy matter, for the gorilla had broken through everything in his path, but presently it joined an old gorilla tunnel in thick jungle, and once again we had to proceed in a crouching position.

After about two hundred yards we came to three subsidiary tunnels, beyond which was a narrow game trail. The gorilla could have taken any of these routes, and though there were signs that something had just passed along the game trail, they might easily have been made by a duiker or a bushbuck. There were no marks at the entrance to the tunnels, so I decided in favor of the game trail, half hoping all the time that the gorilla was not there, for I still preferred to face him in the open.

We pushed along, sometimes bending to avoid hanging
lianas or climbing over fallen trees, until we came to a stream,
winding away through the trees. In the soft mud at its edge,
slowly filling with water, were deep knuckle marks of the
gorilla. In later years I learned that gorillas will never cross
water, even streams that are only a few yards wide. In the
present case, the animal had gone along the bank.

Further along we found more tracks and I fully expected
to see the gorilla round any of the bends, but I suddenly lost
the trail altogether. I went back, picked up the tracks again
and found that the gorilla had turned off into the forest,
where the thin canes of a plant called *Aframomum danielli*,
which has no popular English name, had given him an easy
passage and had closed back smoothly without appearing to
have been disturbed. The red fruits, shoots and pith of this
plant provide gorillas with their staple food.

Eagerness and excitement had quite banished my nervousness now, and I slipped through the canes after him. We had
gone only a few yards when Nze poked me in the back and
when I looked round he sniffed to show me that he could
smell the gorilla. My less sensitive nostrils picked up the scent
further on. It was slight at first but suddenly became very
heavy. We were quite near the animal, but I could not hear
or see him.

In dense forest of this kind, where visibility is restricted
to a few yards and sometimes to a few feet, there is a trick
enabling a hunter to see a good deal further. The first few
inches of plant stems are bare of leaves, and by lying flat it is
possible to see as far as twenty-five yards through them. I have
often spotted elephant by this means, where otherwise they
would not have been visible at all. Making as little noise as
possible, I therefore first knelt and then lay down on the
ground, and looked through the stems. About five or six yards
away I could see something black, and I stared for fully half

a minute before it dawned on me that I was looking at the feet of the gorilla.

He made for me as I started to rise, and when I looked up he was towering above me, stretching his great hairy arms above his head. He opened his mouth, showing long, yellow, canine teeth, and let out the most terrible scream I had ever heard as he brought his arms crashing downwards, sweeping the canes with them, and striking me heavily on my left side as I flung myself out of the way. I pulled the trigger of my rifle at the same time, with no attempt at taking aim. An agonizing pain shot through my leg, and then he rushed past and disappeared in the undergrowth.

When I got up I found my leg was so stiff and shot with pain that I could hardly use it. Blood flowed freely from a gash across my thigh, where the gorilla's nails had sliced through skin and flesh. I took off my kerchief and bound it up as well as I could, bawling for Nze at the same time. At first there was no sign of him, and I could hear nothing but the parrots and a troop of chattering monkeys somewhere among the trees. When I heard a quiet rustle in the bush I thought the gorilla had come back and slid another cartridge into my rifle. But it was Nze at last. His head poked through the leaves and he stared at me with bulging eyes.

"Where the devil have you been?" I demanded, forgetting my Pidgin, "I've been shouting for you for hours."

"Yes Massa, I hear you, but I live up for stick (tree) and fear dem gorilla bin catch you."

With Nze's help I limped, hopped and crawled back to the village, choosing the easiest routes, no matter how devious they seemed, and hoping that the gorilla would have chosen some other way to wherever he wanted to go. We arrived safely, and with Joseph's help I stripped off my blood-soaked pants and examined my injuries. I had a deep flesh wound across the high, but it was not as serious as I had thought, for nothing vital had been severed. The rest of the leg, however, was badly bruised down to the calf and was very sore. Joseph swabbed the cut with iodine and bound it up with clean bandage from my first-aid kit. Afterwards I lay down to rest, with a glass of whisky beside me.

Meanwhile the village was in a turmoil. According to Joseph, all sorts of stories were being circulated. The gorilla was as big as an elephant and had torn off one of my legs, said some; the white man has made him very angry and now he will take revenge on us all, killing us and ruining our crops, said others. I did my best to stop these rumors, calling in the village headman and lecturing him soundly. But the damage was done, and for the next few days the women would not leave the village. This upset the village economy, for no man would dream of doing agricultural work. When the stiffness had left my leg and the wound had begun to heal I therefore called Joseph and told him to fetch Nze, so that we could try again for the gorilla.

Joseph's eyes popped. "You sick for head Massa? You no know this ju-ju gorilla?"

I told him not to talk nonsense and sent him off. He returned half an hour later to say that Nze was not to be found, and no one else in the village would come with me. I remembered the corporal and sent a runner off to fetch him, but he had returned to his post. I decided to go alone, but before I left the hut an elderly man turned up and said he was ready to come with me. Joseph was shocked.

"Better you no go with him, Massa. Dis ol' man no savvy bush."

But the old man was better than no one, and together we set off. If we had been going to our executions the villagers could not have been more upset. The men stood staring and looking frightened, while the women mourned as they do at funerals, blowing through their hands and crying the lament that sounds like "Wey, wey, wey."

As we reached the end of the street the headman came running up. He grasped me by the arm and tried to turn me back, saying, "Massa no go. We no want you for die." If I did get killed there would be an official inquiry, with corrupt native soldiers coming to frighten and bully the villagers, and I guessed the headman was more concerned about that than about me. I didn't want "for die" either, but I didn't think that likely, so I shook him off angrily and continued.

At the plantation we found a trail of my own blood, and the old man pushed ahead of me into the bush with surprising agility and confidence. We reached the place where I had been attacked and found that there was a second trail of blood leading off in another direction. I released the safety catch of my shotgun and, pointing it straight in front of me, followed the new trail, intending to blow the gorilla to bits if he appeared again, but before we had gone twenty yards we found him lying flat on his back, stone dead.

When he attacked me I had fired my rifle from the hip, with no time to take aim, and the possibility that I had hit him at all was so remote that it had not even crossed my mind. The heavy, soft-nosed bullet, however, had caught him in the side of the neck, flattening out as it did so, and smashing its way through the jugular vein. He must have died on his feet a minute or two after hitting me, which was why I had not heard him moving about afterwards.

The carcass had already received the attention of ants and other insects, and decomposition was advanced, but I estimated the gorilla's weight conservatively as between 570-90 pounds. The abdomen was enormously distended, partly by a great quantity of vegetable matter in the intestines and partly by putrefaction. There was a very high crest—a bony ridge rising across the back of the skull, joined by another from the center of the forehead. These crests are found only on adult male gorillas and, in less pronounced form, on the adult male black-faced chimpanzee. No one knows whether they serve any purpose. The short legs, long arms and hands twice the width and thickness of my own were other features of the gorilla I was able to examine closely for the first time.

My gorilla's skin was already spoiled, but I secured the skeleton and eventually sent it to the University of Texas, where the zoologists estimated that in life the animal had stood just over six feet tall. It was really a remarkable case of beginner's luck, for this was the largest gorilla I ever found. Only one other time was I knocked over by a gorilla.

While I was examining the dead animal, I sent the old man back to the village. He returned with Joseph, a crestfallen Nze, and a crowd of young men. We tied the gorilla to saplings and with four men at each end carried him back to the village, where the women stood around laughing and poking fun at the monster. Joseph was explaining that, had he not been so busy, he, instead of the old man, would have taken me into the forest. He tapped poor Nze importantly on the chest.

"I no tell you my Massa be big shootman?" he asked triumphantly.

A week later I was back at Ebolowa. I had found only one gorilla at Ambam, and there were few in the Ebolowa district, yet I knew there must be regions where they were more plentiful and I was now more determined than ever to find them.

2. The Maka Cannibals

The exact distribution of gorillas is still uncertain, for there are vast regions of mountainous, virgin forests which have been only superficially explored. In my early days as a gorilla hunter, I had nothing to guide me but vague reports from traders and natives, but at least they confirmed my belief that there were places where gorillas were relatively abundant. With no clear ideas in mind, I locked up my house in Ebolowa and rode to Sengmelime, fifty miles further east, where I sought the advice of Lieutenant Pennant, the District Officer, who was an old friend of mine.

"Try the country due east," he suggested. "I don't know it very well, but the forest extends from here right across to the Congo and beyond. There are no European plantations and no maps that you can depend on, but provided you stay this side of the Dja River, you'll be all right."

"What's wrong with the other side of the river?"

"Good God, man, don't go there. That's Maka country, with as wild a lot of savages as you'll find anywhere in the world. They're the most die-hard bunch of cannibals we've got in the Cameroons. The Germans tried to stop their cannibalism, but they only drove it under cover, though they made it possible for a few traders to live there for a while. Then the war started and all control over them broke down. Now they are as bad as ever.

"You understand," he added diplomatically, "that we French have only just taken over the administration and it will be a long time before we get things straightened out and put a stop to cannibalism. My own control ends at the Dja River, and we are not likely to get beyond it for years yet."

Earlier, I had had a word with George Latimer Bates, another close friend, who lives at Betche. Bates was an ornithologist and a world authority on the birds of West Africa. He, too, warned me against the Makas, but only casually, for he could think of nothing but the prospect of my returning with new birds for his wonderful collection. He was particularly anxious that I should search for the black guinea fowl, a rarity that existed, so far as he knew, in only a few coastal regions. If I found any I was to send them in wicker baskets with all speed, and if I could not take them alive their skins would at least confirm their existence in the interior. I promised I would do my best, but as it happened I was lucky to return with my own skin in one piece.

The next few days were spent in making preparations. I had two horses: Corney, a tough, thickset native pony, and Charley, a half-bred European three-year-old I had broken and trained myself. Charley was the best horse I ever had, a fine jumper and a great pet. He was excellent for forest work and would not flinch if I fired from his back. When in later years I stayed at the hotel in Yacounde, he would follow me into the bar for a bottle of beer, which he loved. He knew all my friends, had many more of his own, and was immensely popular all round.

Joseph my cook, six carriers, and Johnny, a stouthearted horse-boy, made up my human retinue. Johnny had served in the Maka country under Major Dominick, a German officer who was everywhere renowned for his ruthlessness and energy in dealing with rebellious tribes. I had heard a great deal about this man. The natives believed he had a powerful ju-ju, protecting him from their spears, and many stories were told of his miraculous escapes from death. Naughty children were warned that Major Dominick would come for them if they did not mend their ways, and for years after his death the natives were always careful to salute when passing his statues. There was one at Yaounde and another at Kribi.

With this little expedition I spent a fortnight exploring the hilly forests between Sengmelima and the Dja River without finding a trace of gorillas. There were chimpanzees, monkeys of many species, bushbucks, duiker, pottos, bush-babies, squirrels, civet cats, genets, leopards and many other animals, but no gorillas. Neither could I find the black guinea fowl that Bates was so keen about. Disappointed, I rested for a few days on the bank of the Dja River, looking across and wondering if there were gorillas on the other side. I had a word with a village chief.

"Dem Maka people be plopper bad for true?"

"Dey be bad people too much, sar."

I wondered whether this was really true. After all, I had already been wandering about the Cameroons for nearly ten years, and I had mixed with a lot of pretty tough people, but I never got into difficulties with them. I knew several native languages, and I had found that a little tact, fairness and a touch of humor were sufficient to establish the most friendly relations. Were the Makas, then, so different? I doubted it. Tall tales are as common among Europeans in Africa as among natives, and there was every likelihood that the Makas were victims of the usual exaggeration. I told my men that we would cross the river next morning, and they received the news in silence. I tried to encourage them, but their faces were long and they refused to answer me.

Excitement kept me from sleep for hours that night, but at last I dropped off. I awoke with a start and an immediate feeling that something was wrong, for it was broad daylight and Joseph should have woken me for breakfast long ago. I pulled my shirt and trousers on and went outside. Johnny, my horse-boy, was sitting alone beside the fire.

"Hello, Johnny, what's the matter? Which side all dem carrier gone?"

Johnny looked at me sorrowfully. "Dey all done go, Massa," he said. "Dey fear you go take dem other-side and dey make chop for Maka people."

To be deserted by one's carriers is a blow at the best of times, but perversely it made me even more determined to carry on and enter the Maka country. I looked at Johnny.

"And you, Johnny? You go follow me?"

"Me, I fit follow Massa any place," he answered simply. "I no do fear dis kin' people." And he jerked his thumb contemptuously in the direction of the Makas.

Together we made breakfast, and then put our minds to the problem of carrying our equipment. Much of it could be left in the village, where it would be quite safe until we returned, and the rest could be carried on the horses.

After a great deal of trouble we got the villagers to take us across the river in their canoes, while the horses, held by their bridles, swam alongside. When we got out of the canoes on the far bank the paddlers flung our baggage after us and departed so hurriedly and with so little dignity that Johnny and I burst out laughing.

Stuffing the saddlebags and our pockets with cartridges, I gave Johnny a rifle and the shotgun to carry, taking the other rifle myself. We strapped the equipment on the horses and led them along the bank until a game trail gave us access to the forest. After walking for about a mile and seeing no sign of human habitation, we came to a bare rocky barrier rising steeply for perhaps two hundred feet. Getting to the top was difficult, for the horses kept stumbling and their loads were constantly slipping from the saddles, which were not designed for packs. Eventually we unburdened them, led them to the top and made several return journeys to bring up the equipment ourselves. It was hard, hot work, but well worth it, for the top of the escarpment afforded us a magnificent view of the country ahead.

We were looking down on the tops of trees that stretched away in many shades of green as far as we could see. Here and there the Flame of the Forest blossomed out in great scarlet patches. Parrots, touracos, and other gaudy birds croaked and quarreled in the tree tops. Monkeys of several kinds peered through the leaves at us as we descended, and then hurried off to warn their families. In the distance we could hear a troop of chimpanzees working themselves up into hysterics, as they are always doing over some domestic trifle.

For four hours we marched along a difficult trail, fording small streams and stopping at intervals to slash away hanging branches and lianas so the horses could get through. Then abruptly we came to a village. It was much like any other West African village: a huddle of mud and thatch huts, with bare, hard earth between and the jungle pressing in around them. But although we shouted and searched everywhere there was not a soul to be seen. It often happens that all the men of a village go off on a hunting trip, but they always leave their women and children behind. Smouldering fires and pots containing half-cooked food showed that the villagers had left hurriedly just before we arrived, but though we looked in every hut, the only sign of life we found was a brace of scraggy fowls.

All along I had been on the alert, and though I did not expect to make an easy conquest of the Makas I had banked on a palaver of some sort. But wit and charm are a fat lot of good if your savage refuses to come near you. Johnny, too, was anxious.

We sat down and talked things over. Turning back was out of the question, for neither of us was willing to admit defeat. Moreover, it would take another four or five hours to return to the river and it would be dark long before then. If the

Makas really wanted to kill us—and I had still to be convinced of that—what better chance could they have than to follow and ambush us in the forest? We decided to stay.

Picking a big, sturdy hut, which must have been built by one of the German traders, we put the horses inside and set about cutting grass for them from the edge of the forest. There was a little water in some of the huts, but no more near at hand. Although every village is sited near a stream, I did not care to look for it just then. Johnny, reconnoitering around the village, reported that he had seen Makas hiding in the bush, and they had disappeared when he tried to speak to them. I had no wish to get a spear in my side before I could open my mouth, so I stayed where I was.

We caught one of the fowls, wrung its neck and made a meal of it. When darkness fell the Makas were still absent, so we joined the horses inside the hut, blocked up the door, checked our rifles and sat there smoking, waiting for something to happen.

By now Johnny was convinced that we were to be attacked. If only Major Dominick had been there, he kept saying, they would not dare to touch us. For three or four hours there was silence, save for the usual forest sounds, and then towards midnight a single drum clattered into life outside in the bush. It was answered by another from the opposite direction and then a third and a fourth, until there seemed to be scores of them banging away all around us.

We looked out at the deserted, moonlit village, Johnny through a crack in the back wall, I through another in the door. The drums got noisier and noisier and then suddenly a crowd of Makas burst out from the shadows and began dancing round our hut, shrieking, howling and waving their spears. Spears began falling on the roof, but the walls were of iron-hard mud, 18 inches thick, fortified against just such an attack by its last European tenant, and there was no fear of them breaking through that.

My first idea was that we should open the door and rush out, firing as fast as we could, but Johnny, who knew their tactics, thought that this was just what they hoped we would do. We could never have got through them alive, and while we would certainly have killed a few of them before we went down ourselves, so much the better from the Maka point of view, since that would mean more meat for the pot. They were by no means above eating each other. Our best chance, it seemed, was to stay in the hut, where we could defend the narrow doorway without difficulty.

Johnny did not think there was much chance of their setting fire to the thatch, because of the danger to the other huts close by and to the whole village. In any case, he said, they preferred their meat boiled to roasted, and they were much more likely to try and starve or frighten us out.

Whilst the din outside went on, we put our few boxes and blankets on top of my camp bed and lay down underneath it, so that we would have some measure of protection against spears that might come straight through the roof. As Johnny predicted, the Makas did not fire the hut, and though spears kept thudding on the door, no attempt was made to force it. The horses behaved very well. They whinnied and shied a bit when the noise began, but afterwards stood quietly nuzzling each other against the wall, only starting a little when a spear landed on the roof near them with a loud "whump."

Africans can keep up their frenzied dances hour after hour, with no sign of fatigue, and the Makas were no exception. There were a few lulls, when they withdrew to chatter among themselves, and then the drums again and out they came howling, waving their spears and making great leaps into the air as they danced round the hut.

An hour before dawn they disappeared. We lay listening, half dead with tiredness, but we could hear no more of them. When it was light we opened the door and with rifles ready walked slowly towards the forest. We kept in the shelter of the huts as long as we could, pressing ourselves against the walls, but when we reached the last one we were met with a shower of arrows. Luckily we were just out of range, and they fell harmlessly in the ground a few yards in front of us. When we made as if to walk forward again there came a second volley, but this time we were ready for them and we both fired rapidly at the dark skins we spotted moving among the bushes. I saw a Maka rear up from behind a shrub and fall backwards, clutching at his chest. He screamed and thrashed about for a bit and then was suddenly still. Johnny claimed two, but from the row they made you might have thought it half a dozen.

There was obviously no chance of our getting through, for there must have been a hundred of the tribesmen surrounding the village and arrows greeted us whichever way we turned. We went back to the hut, which Johnny cleaned out while I kept watch. Very little water remained, and we gave most of it to the horses, making do ourselves with a mixture of whiskey and tinned milk—an interesting but not very refreshing beverage. Most of the grass fodder was gone and we could find no more growing out of range of the arrows.

For the rest of the day we sat outside the hut, keeping ourselves amused and encouraged by exchanging stories of past adventures. Johnny told me of German expeditions against the Makas in which he had taken part. He had been promoted to the rank of sergeant, he said proudly, because he had killed so many of these savages.

The soldiers severed the right ears of dead Makas, threaded them on strings and showed them to their commanding officers as proof of the number they had killed. Captured Maka women and girls were shared out among the victors. Johnny himself had so many that he was able to sell several to his friends. He still had four at home in Sengmelima, but they were getting old and he thought he would sell them now. They would not bring much, for they all had several children, but their price, together with the wages I would pay him for this trip, would be enough so that he could buy a nice young virgin.

Wives are freely bought and sold in the Cameroons, and at that time anyone could buy a young girl for a hundred francs, a few machetes, a couple of goats and a dog. Aging women are either resold or given to young boys, who learn the art of love-making from them before buying young girls themselves. However revolting this may seem to Europeans, it must be remembered that it has satisfied both the men and women of these primitive races for countless generations, and any attempt to alter the custom suddenly would be disastrous, as indeed it has already proved to be in some parts of Africa.

The time purchase of wives has been the only serious fault with the system. Amusing as it may seem, it is common for a girl to be bought for a down payment and a promise to pay the balance in instalments. Unfortunately, no written agreements are made, and disputes over what has or has not been paid for a girl are common. During the Second World War, when I become a police inspector at Bafang. I was always being called upon to settle cases of this kind.

I didn't think much of Johnny's chances of getting a new girl at that time, for our position had not improved when darkness fell and once more we barricaded ourselves inside the hut. By now this looked like a giant porcupine, with arrows and spears sticking out all over the thatch. I pulled one of the spears through and broke off its head, which I have with me still. It is a narrow blade of iron, with a number of barbs on the ferrule. My two sons sometimes play with it.

At midnight the Makas returned and the dancing and the shouting began again. In the morning we were still surrounded but still alive, though we were getting weak from lack of sleep and food. The horses, too, were in a bad way, and the inside of the hut stank with their dung and urine. There was no doubt now that the Makas were trying to starve us out.

Johnny was gloomy, in the fatalistic way of the African. My own nerves were weakening hourly under the strain. I could not see how we could escape, for we were kept at bay by arrows if we tried to move out during the day, and at night our jailers kept up their noisy vigil with increasing fervor. This continued for another day and for a third night and I do not mind admitting that throughout this time I was very much afraid.

Why we waited in the hut at all I do not know. I kept making up my mind to try to shoot my way out, and then changing it again in favor of waiting to see whether the Makas would tire of their sport and give us a more favorable chance. But that was a forlorn hope.

On the fourth night the moon rose late, but soon the Makas were howling around us again. Knowing we must be very weak, they were getting braver, thumping on the walls and jeering at us. Johnny, who had learned a little of their language from his wives, translated some of their jibes, and they did not serve to cheer me.

In spite of our weariness we found it impossible to snatch even a moment's sleep, though we took turns trying, for we thought the Makas might assault the door at any time. They had returned after a lull, or perhaps they were a new lot sent to relieve the others—I was too tired to wonder—and had started yelling and dancing when we heard a shout of a different character, and the noise outside died off raggedly. I hurried to the door and peered through the crack.

They had gathered in a little group around a newcomer, who was talking excitedly. They seemed to be arguing about something, but finally they came to a decision and they all went off together. They did not come back that night, and when the sun rose Johnny and I emerged from the hut and reconnoitered again. There was no sign of them anywhere, and when we approached the forest there was no shower of arrows to send us scurrying back to the shelter of the huts.

Suspicious, we fired several rounds into likely-looking bushes, but there was no one behind them. We went deeper into the jungle, rapidly gaining confidence. At first we could not believe our senses, but for some reason the Makas had left us. Incredibly, we were free, at least for the present, and there was certainly no time to be wasted in wondering why.

Running back to the hut, we got out the horses and saddled them. We took our guns, water bottles and first-aid kit, some tobacco and matches, but abandoned the rest of my equipment. Water was our first requirement, and after casting about a bit we found a stream. The horses were terribly weak, but they revived astonishingly after a drink. I did not think it wise to use the route we had come along, for if the Makas were to search for us that would certainly be their first thought. Instead, I hoped to get through to the river in another direction. This was a mistake, as we soon found out, but at the time we were too ill and distraught to be capable of clear thinking.

We pushed on as quickly as we could, but it was a nightmare journey, for every plant along the trail seemed to wrap itself around our limbs and try to drag us back. Precious minutes were wasted hacking them away. At any moment I expected to hear sounds of pursuit and our efforts to get through became feverish. In the late afternoon we were lucky enough to find a broad, clear elephant track, which must have been used by the animals for centuries, and there we rested a while to have a smoke and a drink of whiskey and water. We also took some quinine, for the prospect of fever in our weakened state was a real and terrible one.

It got dark early that night, for there were heavy storm clouds about, and we made camp in the shelter of the great buttress roots of a cottonwood tree. We lit a tiny fire, and when Johnny found some wild yams we roasted them for supper. They tasted horribly bitter, but there was nothing else to eat. For the horses we found a few handfuls of grass.

Still neither of us could sleep, and we pushed on again as soon as it was light enough to see. The track petered out at the edge of a swamp, which we found impossible to cross. Going along the edge in search of a way around, we got lost, and it was only then that I discovered I had left my compass behind in the village.

During the day we sampled *Aframomum*, the gorilla food, and found it quite pleasant. The plant bears a red, elongated fruit, much like pomegranate inside. Natives call it monkey chop, for most of the monkeys and apes feed on it.

Johnny sprang a surprise on me in the evening. He went to his saddlebag and pulled out a strip of smoked elephant meat, which he had had for months. We cooked it in a tobacco tin, and ate it with wild yams. The taste was vile, but it was the best meal I had eaten since we crossed the Dja river. There was very little grass, and the horses were in a dreadful state. I managed to get Charley to eat a yam, but Corney would not touch them.

On the fourth night it began to rain heavily and we were soaked to the skin in a few minutes, but we got a smoky fire going. When the rain stopped I took off my socks and put them beside the fire to dry. In the morning I found that the fire had spread and they were burned to cinders.

Corney was obviously dying and was so tormented by the flies and mosquitoes that I took him aside and put him out of his misery. We, too, were plagued by insects, particularly at dawn and dusk, and it was worse than ever after the rain. Most of the time we traveled along well-worn elephant paths, but we were too weak to do more than a few hours a day. Sometimes we heard elephants trumpeting or crashing about in the forest, but we never saw them.

I still kept my eye open for signs of gorillas, though my only aim now was to save myself and Johnny. For the most part we were too ill and tired to talk, but one night I asked him what he knew about gorillas, and whether he had ever seen them. He hadn't; and what was more, he did not want to.

"All man savvy dis be bad beef. Some time, old Maka man turn into gorilla."

It is a common superstition that certain natives have the power of turning themselves into animals at will. A solitary bull elephant, gorilla or any other large animal is always credited with the possession of a human soul, very often the soul of one's father or grandfather. Johnny believed that gorillas walked upright and that they carried clubs which they used to beat down their victims.

Food was our constant problem. There were plenty of birds and an occasional duiker or bushbuck, but we dared not risk a shot, lest it should reveal our position to the Makas, whom we supposed to be hot on our trail. Johnny used to eat fat white beetle grubs, as thick as a man's finger, which he dug out of raffia palm stems. I shut my eyes and popped one in my mouth, closed my teeth on it and promptly spat it out again. I preferred to starve.

One morning Johnny cut the head off a gaboon viper, a fat, venomous, vividly colored creature which had joined us at the fireside during the night. There was plenty of meat on the snake, and we gulped down great lumps of it half cooked. In its stomach was a partly digested rat, but we threw that away. Another time we came upon a leopard's kill, a young bay duiker. Most of the flesh had been eaten, and what was left was putrid, but we scraped a little from the bones and it did not smell too badly after we had cooked it.

We were pushing westwards all the time, so far as the forest trails would permit, but we had only the sun as a guide and we were in fact hopelessly lost. On the tenth day we came to a river, flowing fast and clean over a rocky bed. It was about a hundred yards wide, too small to be the Dja, yet in desperation I forced myself to believe that it was, and we began to cross, hoping to find food and safety on the other side. A little way downstream were a series of flat, smooth rocks, lying an inch or two below the surface, and we walked over on these, coaxing the horse after us. Halfway across he lost his footing, plunged into the torrent and was swept away.

I thought he was lost, but he struggled furiously against the current and where the river turned out of sight he reached the shallows and got a foothold, standing up to his belly in water and trembling violently, without the strength or the will to climb up the bank. Johnny left me and scrambled after him, sometimes wading at the edge, sometimes chopping his way through vegetation on the bank. He reached the horse, took him by the bridle and helped and encouraged him to safety.

When I joined them I found a path leading down from the forest to the water, and it was a path that had been made by human feet. We followed it, still trying to convince ourselves that we had crossed the Dja. Before we had gone a quarter of a mile a crowd of young men armed with spears burst out of the trees and surrounded us and we saw at a glance that they were Makas.

They were as surprised as we were and they could not make up their minds what to do with us. With gestures and shouts that were anything but friendly, they forced us forward to their village, where they stood around us in a circle, discussing the problem and holding their spears ready. We both tried talking to them and making signs of friendship, but these were ignored altogether. Presently the chief joined them and they seemed to make up their minds. He gave a nod to the men behind me, and I sensed the intake of breath as they raised their spears to strike.

At that moment a parrot went flying high overhead. I was carrying my shotgun, which is more useful and deadly than a rifle for shooting quickly at short range. On an impulse I fired at the parrot, and it came plummeting down to earth. There was immediate confusion among the Makas and the young warriors withdrew from me. They had seen rifles used before, but they knew nothing of shotguns. I would indeed have been an outstanding marksman to bring down the parrot with the single bullet of a rifle, but with the spreading pellets from a shotgun it was easy enough. The Makas did not know that; to them I was a hunter with a positively magical aim.

After a hurried consultation the chief again stepped forward and spoke slowly and deliberately in his own language. Johnny translated.

"He say, 'No want whiteman for him village. Whiteman go quickly. Maka man show way.' "

That was good enough for me. We asked for food, but they would give us none, and we did not stop to argue about it. We willingly followed the men who led us off into the forest. They showed us a path which, they said, led directly to the Dja River and then they hastily let us.

Two or three hours later we reached the river and on the other side we could see women fetching water. They ran off when we called to them, but returned quickly with their menfolk. For a long time we could not get them to cross in their canoes and fetch us, for they were suspicious and afraid. Eventually a single canoe put off. Approaching us timidly, the men in it asked who we were and what we wanted. When at last they understood the situation they eagerly helped us in and took us across, explaining that they could not believe that strangers had come through the Maka territory alive.

Their village was called Aveba, and they all treated us with the warmest friendliness and sympathy. Some of the women began making a meal, and soon we were feasting on boiled fowl, plantains and groundnut soup. We were given a hut and a couple of native beds and an hour later we had fallen into a sleep that lasted for forty-eight hours. Meanwhile, Charley was also well looked after—fed, brushed down and given a thorough rest. He ate ravenously and filled out again in a few days.

When we had sufficiently recovered we walked to N'Yemjum, another village a day's march away, from where we intended to go to the Government station at Akoafim to make a report. We found the people of N'Yemjum busy tidying up their village and we were told that they expected the Governor—they meant the District Officer Adjutant Marcelin—with many soldiers the next day. We spent the night at this village and in the morning met the Adjutant on the Akoafim road. When he saw me he almost fell from his horse in surprise.

"Merfield!" he kept repeating. "My God, Merfield!"

I greeted him cheerfully and asked where he was going. He stared at me for a long time before replying.

"This is very difficult," he said at last. "As a matter of fact I am leading a punitive expedition to the Maka country to avenge your death." Then he brightened a little. "Well, anyway, if *you* haven't been eaten, *someone* certainly has."

He told me that the hand of a white man had turned up at Lomie Government station, brought by a native who had promptly disappeared. Since I was the only European known to be anywhere near the Maka country, and certainly the only man they knew of who would be crazy enough to go there, they had naturally supposed the hand to be mine, and the native to be one of my carriers who had run off lest he be implicated in my death. A cable had been sent to England informing my parents that I was dead. My house at Ebolowa had been sealed up, according to French law, and an inventory of my property had been made ready for auction.

Marcelin had only twenty native soldiers with him, and I was astonished to learn that with this tiny force he intended to subdue the Makas. But he saw his duty quite clearly and went off and did it, as I afterwards learned, with great thoroughness and success. Major Dominick could have done no better.

Who was the white man who had died in my place, and why did the Makas let me go when I was within their grasp? When Marcelin returned we learned a little of the truth, but most of it will always be a mystery. The victim was apparently one of the many European adventurers who roamed Central Africa doing a little trading, a little prospecting and perhaps a little of those things that are best kept from official eyes. Hence he had not informed the various Government stations of his movements, as I always did, and with no one to warn him he had entered the Maka country from the Congo without knowing the sort of people they were.

On our last, terrible night of imprisonment he had reached a village only a mile away from us. The Makas there had used different tactics, welcoming him and giving him food. Then, as he sat eating outside his hut, they speared him in the back. The Makas who were surrounding us had gone off to join in the feast, but why they should have left us entirely without a guard and apparently made no attempt to catch us again afterwards, I shall never know. I can only guess that they thought us too weak to need watching, and after eating the other man they had, like children, become suddenly afraid of retribution, in the form of another punitive expedition.

I was able to return to Ebolowa in time to save my effects from auction, and a successful elephant hunt produced enough ivory to pay for the replacement of everything I had lost to the Makas. Years later, after I married, I went with my wife to Lomie, where the District Officer showed her the official report of my supposed death.

Many of my old friends in the Cameroons will have been interested to read for the first time the details of how I escaped. Dr. LeBriese, who had made the inventory of my possessions at Ebolowa—and drank all my whisky while he was at it—now lives at Nice. Harry Francis, the Yaounde trader in whose back room I was sitting when the Rev. A. B. Patterson rushed into the store to tell him I was dead, will be returning to England and to retirement soon; and Mr. Patterson's widow, a dear friend of mine, now lives at Chelmsford, in Essex.

As for Johnny, I tried hard to get him to stay with me, but

soldiering was in his blood and he left me to join the French
Force de Police. I met him again ten or twelve years later
while hunting in the N'Gounderie district with Major Powell-
Cotton, the great hunter and collector. Johnny bought his
new wife, and when their first son was born they called him
Merfield.

the Mole Cannibals · 41

3. Chimps, Chogas and Gorillas

No one can live for long in the interior of West Africa without hearing the large families of chimpanzees which roam the forests, often quite near the towns. They are noisy and excitable animals and when they get really worked up they utter blood-curdling hoots and screams which can be heard for miles. In all zoos, young chimpanzees attract the greatest popular interest, for they are lively and amusing caricatures of ourselves. Intelligence and character vary just as much among them as among men. A clever little chimp will outstrip a human child in intelligence up to the age of three or four, but after that the chimp's development rapidly slows down to a standstill, while the human child catches up and overtakes it.

Though they are so beguiling when young, chimpanzees can rarely be trusted beyond the age of six or seven, as many a misguided animal lover has found to his cost. An adult chimpanzee is not as big as a man, but he is much stronger and is prone to fits of ungovernable fury. With his huge mouth and long, canine teeth he can be a dangerous antagonist.

Chimps can learn an amazing number of things. It is possible, for instance, not only to house-train an intelligent youngster, but to teach him to use the lavatory, toilet paper and all, as efficiently as a child. He can learn to ride a bicycle, switch the right lights on and off, answer the door and sit down to dinner with table manners that would put many a human child to shame. But as he grows older he wearies of these things. The novelty wears off, and it is not replaced by the consciousness that certain actions have good and useful results. The lavatory no longer amuses him, and since he can see no point in being clean, he no longer bothers about it—and is hurriedly offered to the local zoo.

I learned much about chimpanzees during the years following my trip to the Maka country, when I began exploring the more remote regions of the Yaounde forests in search of gorillas. How intelligent is a chimpanzee? How far is his learning derived from unreasoning imitation? There is a classic experiment in which a chimpanzee is left alone in a room where a bunch of bananas hangs out of reach above his head, and the only way of getting them down is with the aid of poles which must be fitted together, like a sweep's broom-handle, in order to reach that far. After a time the animal will discover the solution to the problem, and to do so requires the exercise of intelligence. Only once have I seen such intelligence put to good account by wild chimpanzees, and the incident is important enough to be worth recording.

In 1932 I was tracking the rare Bongo antelope through thick forest when my attention was attracted by the noise of chimpanzees. They appeared to be highly excited and I decided to stalk them and see what they were doing. With my gun-bearer N'Gombie I crept through the bush and found eight chimpanzees—six of them almost full-grown—sitting in a circle at the edge of a small clearing. Like gorillas, they have a poor sense of smell, and since we moved silently they did not detect us. They were making a lot of noise and kept beating and pushing each other aside, but for a time I could not see what they were up to. I sought the opinion of N'Gombie, who was a very experienced hunter.

"Massa," he said, "dey do chop honey."

A small black bee makes a nest in the ground and collects

a rather coarse kind of honey. Watching through my binoculars, I could see that the chimps were sitting round the entrance to one of these nests. Each ape held a long twig, poked it down the hole and withdrew it coated with honey. There was only one hole and, though for the most part they took turns at using their twigs, quarrels were constantly breaking out, and those who had licked off most of their honey tried to snatch the newly coated twigs. We watched them for over half an hour at a range of fifty yards before creeping away as silently as we had come, so as not to disturb the party. This is one of the few examples I have known of a wild animal's employing a tool.

N'Gombie was well qualified to instruct me in the behavior and habits of chimpanzees. I have already mentioned the African's inclination to romance, and it is true that gullible travelers will be told the wildest tales about animals and native customs in the hope of an extra "dash" in money or gifts. But it is another matter when long-established European residents of the country are concerned and there is a chance of the African's being caught out. I do not think I was lied to often, at least by those who knew me, and from time to time I was given information which is worth reporting. Naturalists are, of course, at liberty to reject these stories until such time as they are confirmed by trained observers.

Chimpanzees are difficult to follow up when wounded, N'Gombie told me, because they stuff the wound with grass and leaves, and are careful to wipe away all traces of blood from their coats. However, if the blood flow is copious they are not able to clean it all away and may then be tracked.

A year earlier, N'Gombie said, his brother found a young chimpanzee up a tree and threw sticks at it. When it came down he tried to catch it, but it was too strong, so he struck it on the head with his machete. The youngster's mother then arrived, jumped on the man's back and tried to poke his eyes out. He yelled loudly and, said N'Gombie, the old chimp left him, picked up the youngster, wiped the blood from its head and carried it off.

It will come as a surprise to learn that chimpanzees, gorillas and most monkeys, far from taking refuge in trees when attacked, will usually descend to the ground and try to make off through the undergrowth. Chimpanzees drop crazily from the branches, like ripe fruit, making a fearful hullabaloo, but gorillas, grunting and coughing with anger, come down slowly and carefully, as befits animals of their great weight.

At dusk, the chimpanzee family climbs into the branches of a big tree, where, with the exception of the very young, each makes for himself a rough bed or nest in which to spend the night. These nests are seldom used more than once, for the next morning the family moves off again, roving widely about the forest. Their food consists mostly of vegetable matter, but, unlike gorillas, they are not averse to insects and even young birds.

By far the most intelligent chimp, of the many that passed through my hands on their way to zoos, was Bo-Bo. She was a choga and was ten years old when her European owner decided that her temper no longer fitted her for life in a bungalow. She came to me armed with a detailed list of her requirements, which I found to my surprise included a daily ration of twenty cigarettes, a glass of red wine and an *apéritif*. She wore a collar to which a long, stout chain was attached, and having been warned that she was not always to be trusted, I did not think it wise to take it off.

At that time I had a concession at Yaounde and the prospect of Bo-Bo's running amok in the town was not an appealing one, particularly since her peculiar tastes might well have decided her on a pub-crawl.

During the six months she stayed with me, I therefore provided her with a paddock of her own, and the end of the chain was secured to a tree-stump. For shelter, she had a large packing crate, and for warmth a voluminous old sack. The latter was precious to her and she was most particular about keeping it clean. When she got up in the morning she carefully wrapped it round her shoulders or over her head, picking off invisible bits of dirt, and muttering with annoyance when she could not get it draped to her liking.

A cigarette was essential before breakfast could be thought of by so confirmed a slave to nicotine. English cigarettes were expensive out there, and she did not get her twenty a day, but she was an inveterate scrounger with a perfect technique, and sooner or later someone would succumb to her appeals. Having lit a cigarette, she would lie on her back with her legs crossed and one arm under her head, inhaling deeply and with the greatest relish. She was most particular about the ash, examining the end of the cigarette from time to time with the air of an expert. If she could get a second cigarette, she would light it at once from the stub of the first. When there was obviously no chance of a second in the foreseeable future, she was careful to make the first one last as long as possible, improvising a cigarette holder with a rolled-up leaf, as she had seen the natives doing.

One day Mr. Darwell, the British Vice-Consul in Douala, paid a visit to Yaounde, and since Bo-Bo's fame had spread widely, he came to see her.

After giving him an exhibition of her tricks, she stood up, beat her chest and held out her hand for a cigarette, which she regarded as the suitable fee for a performance. Darwell had a tin of fifty and he took one out and gave it to her. She smoked it as hurriedly as she could and then begged for a second.

"Oh no," said Darwell, "you don't get another; they're too expensive for chimps."

"Hoo, hoo, hoo," said Bo-Bo, looking very coy and appealing, and she flapped her hands in a desperate appeal. He continued to refuse, and she hoo-hooed again, this time stamping her foot with frustration. Then Darwell made a mistake.

To tease her he put the tin of cigarettes on the ground just out of her reach. Bo-Bo stretched as far as the chain would allow but there was still another six inches to go. She stood on all fours for a moment or two and regarded the problem. Then she solved it. She spun around, with her back to the tin, so that she added the length of her body to her reach, and got hold of it quite easily with her foot. Before the startled Darwell had time to snatch it away, she was back with it inside her box, hooting and jeering at him from under her sack.

"Well I'm damned!" said Darwell. "My last tin, too. Try and get them back, Merfield old chap."

"Not on your life! You teased her; get them back yourself."

Darwell walked towards Bo-Bo's box, but when he got within five yards she came tearing out at him with murder written all over her face. He took to his heels and as he ran a handful of black wet mud caught him squarely on the back of his previously white suit.

Monday, of course, was wash day, and Bo-Bo would be stamping with impatience to get on with the job of doing her smalls. She was given a bundle of dirty clothes—kept specially for the purpose—an old galvanized iron tub, a scrubbing board, soap, water and some pegs. A clothesline was strung up across the paddock, conveniently low. With this apparatus ready, Bo-Bo first examined the clothes, deciding apparently which should be washed first, in case of colors running and all that sort of thing. Her method was to alternate vigorous use of the scrubbing board with a technique of her own, consisting of holding the garment high in the air and bringing it down into the tub with a great thump and a splash, sending up clouds of soapy spray. The whole operation was repeated with great rapidity and enthusiasm. When she had finished washing the clothes, she rinsed them in a separate bucket, wrung them, and pegged them out to dry. She had done her best, and it was sad indeed to see that in the process the garments had become dirtier than before.

Bo-Bo herself, however, was plainly satisfied with the results of her industry, and she now set about the next chore of the day. With an old machete borrowed from one of my more indulgent men, she mowed the lawn, making great sweeps with this improvised scythe and flourishing it above her head before every new stroke. At the same time she stamped her left foot and muttered fiercely at the grass, as though she were wreaking vengeance on some long-hated enemy. Afterwards she swept up the cuttings, together with any other rubbish lying about, and paused now and then to examine the ground at her feet, in search of any microscopic scrap she might have overlooked.

She was always ready to help about the house or garden, and she could sift flour or dig up sweet potatoes as ably as my cook. During the afternoon she usually had a nap, but if she could not sleep she amused herself by throwing stones on the corrugated iron roof of the nearby bank, much to the annoyance of the busy folk beneath.

Six o'clock was the time for her *apéritif* and afterwards her glass of wine, which she poured herself and sipped like a connoisseur. She was discriminating as regards company and had few close friends. Candidates for her patronage were subjected to a close inspection and were more often than not rejected. Woe betide them if they refused to take no for an answer! My cook, who was normally one of the favored few, once somehow forfeited her affections and narrowly escaped decapitation by Bo-Bo's whirling machete.

It may be that only people with experience of chimpanzees will credit Bo-Bo's most remarkable and useful accomplishment, but it is true enough. One of the worst pests of tropical Africa are the tiny fleas called jiggers, which burrow unnoticed under the skin of one's toes and set up irritation and infection. Native children are often permanently crippled by

The author on the bank of the Sanaga River, in the French Cameroons

Courtesy, Powell-Cotton Museum

Young gorillas, unlike most other apes, are unhappy in captivity, likely to turn their faces to a corner and die within a few days.

These natives are building a fence (at right) to be used in a gorilla round-up. Their spears do not easily pierce the gorilla's tough hide.

Courtesy, Powell-Cotton Museum

Courtesy, Powell-Cotton Museum

Major Powell-Cotton also was able to shoot the rare giant forest hog—the largest and most dangerous of wild pigs.

A young gorilla bull shot by the late Major Powell-Cotton when on safari with the author

Courtesy, Zoological Society of London

Bo-bo, the author's pet chimpanzee, received a daily ration of cigarettes, a glass of red wine and an apéritif.

The court jester of the Sultan of Chamba, wrestling with his pet hyena

Courtesy, Powell-Cotton Museum

Hilda and baby Trudee beside a bull gorilla shot in the Mendjim Mey

Right: A truly magnificent bull gorilla. My gun-bearer, N'Denge, kneeling beside the great animal, was not a small man.

My wife Hilda was carried in a teepoy to the savage Mendjim Mey country.

these parasites, and at the end of each day it is always a wise precaution to have one's feet examined. The usual way of getting them out is with a fine splinter of bamboo, and this can be a painful operation unless performed by an expert. Bo-Bo was as good at it as anyone I knew. You had to sit down beside her, present your feet and a piece of bamboo, and leave the rest to her. With your toes just in front of her nose, so that she had to squint, she would winkle the beastly thing out in no time, and she was so skilful at it that natives would queue up for her attention. Dr. Bo-Bo's evening surgery was a sight to be remembered.

At length I had to part with her. She was suitably crated and shipped off to London, where she was the only choga ever exhibited by the Zoological Society. Her life there can best be described in the words of Mr. Laurie Smtih, Head Keeper of the Monkey House.

"Bo-Bo was a tremendous success in Regent's Park, and became widely known as the chain-smoking chimp. Because of the danger of setting fire to the straw, smoking in the monkey house is forbidden to visitors, let alone to the animals themselves, but somehow Bo-Bo often managed to cadge a cigarette. She quickly came to understand, however, that they were not so easily come by in the zoo as they had been in Africa, and she adjusted her economy accordingly. Instead of smoking the cigarette right through, she would stub it carefully when it was only half gone and place the remainder on a little ledge. She seemed to be well aware of the danger of fire, for she was careful to see that no sparks remained smouldering. Presently, when she fancied a smoke again, she would stick the cigarette on the edge of her lip and gesticulate wildly to passersby until she got a light. You could hand her a box of matches or a lighter, and she would not only use them properly but could always be trusted to hand them back when she had finished with them."

Not long after Bo-Bo's arrival at Regent's Park, she began

to lose weight and refuse her food. Tuberculosis was suspected, but when she failed to respond to treatment it was thought that decaying teeth might be the cause of her illness. The well-known dentist M. S. A. Kemp, a Fellow of the Zoological Society with long experience in the dental treatment of animals, was therefore asked to examine her, and I am indebted to Dr. Kemp for the following account of her treatment.

Bo-Bo's dangerous fits of temper were well known, and it was with some trepidation that Dr. Kemp and the keeper entered her cage. The possibility that pain might aggravate her temper made it too risky to attempt a thorough examination, but the keeper gently pulled down her lower lip and Dr. Kemp saw at once that she had a bad dental condition. Bo-Bo was coaxed into a suitable box, anaesthetized, and seven teeth were extracted. Professor Zuckerman, the authority on Primates who is now Secretary of the Zoological Society of London, still has those teeth in his possession.

For a week after the operation, Bo-Bo would eat no food, even though the choicest fruits and tidbits were offered her. When hope was almost given up, someone remembered her taste for wine and a bottle of Chianti was produced. A little of the wine was poured into a glass, but Bo-Bo brushed this aside, seized the bottle and emptied it in one draught. Soon afterwards, slightly tipsy, she began to eat, and she recovered her usual good health and spirits in no time.

During her postoperative treatment, Bo-Bo was a model patient. She not only allowed Dr. Kemp to swab out her gums and syringe the cavities every day, but was most anxious to learn how to do so herself. There was no doubt that she understood perfectly that Dr. Kemp was trying to help her. She managed to manipulate the cotton-wool swabs quite well, but the syringe had her beaten, for she could not get the hang of pressing the plunger.

While this treatment was going on, Bo-Bo became acutely

interested in Dr. Kemp's fingernails, and gave him a manicure every day, cleaning under his nails with a piece of straw. She and Dr. Kemp remained firm friends until her death nine years later in 1940. Dr. Kemp still has her skull, which was presented to him by the late Sir Peter Chalmers Mitchell, former Secretary of the Zoological Society, as a memento of a successful operation.

Bo-Bo was a black-faced chimpanzee, or choga, a rare variety about which from time to time I was given a great deal of intriguing but inaccurate information. Chogas were alleged to be extremely dangerous, since they had the strength of gorillas and the cunning of chimpanzees. In the Batouri district they are called N'Killingi, which means gorilla's brother.

After collecting and studying a large number of gorillas, chimpanzees and chogas I came to quite different conclusions. I once discovered a female choga that made repeated and unprovoked attacks on village children, but generally they are no more dangerous than common chimpanzees. On the other hand, they differ from all other chimpanzees and resemble gorillas in a number of interesting ways: like gorillas, they have prominent eyebrow ridges, and they are coal black all over. Male chogas have small, gorilla-like crests and the same smell as gorillas, though it is much less powerful. For anatomical reasons there can be no question of interbreeding between chogas and gorillas. Unlike gorillas, female chimpanzees and chogas have conspicuous menstrual swellings.

In some parts of the Batouri District chogas and common chimpanzees share the same habitat, so it is quite likely that they interbreed and that this might account for the considerable individual variation in color. Many chimpanzees have dark brown hands and feet and sometimes blotches of black on the face. In the adult choga, the ears are much smaller and more highly placed than in the chimpanzee.

One day, soon after my encounter with the honey-eating chimps, I found the tracks of a large family of gorillas and I decided to spend a fortnight watching them. The family consisted of four fully-grown females—three of them with babies and the other obviously pregnant—two half-grown males, and the "Old Man," a fine bull gorilla in the prime of life. Many authoritative books on natural history still give most romantic descriptions of the sleeping arrangements of gorillas. It is said that the females and young males sleep in nests high in the trees, like chimpanzees, while the Old Man sits guarding them all through the night on the ground below, with his arms folded and his back to the trunk.

What a pity that this attractive picture is entirely false! Gorillas never make their nests in trees: in fact, they seldom climb at all. As for the adult males, only the largest trees could support their weight, and even the lowest branches of such trees are well out of their reach. The gorilla always makes his bed at ground level, and he does so in a clever way.

He chooses an open glade where, among the secondary growth, there are plenty of canes and young saplings which he bends to the ground. Holding them down with his feet, he moves in a rotary fashion, interlacing them until he has a fine spring mattress capable of raising him above the damp earth. The leafy tops are then stripped off and laid under and about him until he is comfortably settled.

One typical nest I examined and measured was three feet six inches by two feet nine inches across, and was two feet six inches above the ground. A separate bed is made by each member of the family, except the very young, who cuddle up to mother.

Once he is comfortably settled, with his head pillowed on his arms in a bent-forward position, nothing will induce the gorilla to leave his bed until sunrise, when he begins foraging for food. On wet, cold mornings he is loath to get up, and fouls his bed. In the dry season he gets up early and the beds are then found clean. Gorilla beds are also made in virgin forest, but are then constructed of leafy vegetation on the ground, because sapling growth in the forest is scarce. Open glades or the secondary growth covering abandoned plantations are always preferred.

On fine days, my gorilla family got up just before dawn and set about finding its breakfast. They ate large quantities of *Aframomum* fruit and also the plant's juicy stalks, after stripping off the tough green skin. The young shoots of elephant grass were much sought after, and so were the rough leaves of the wild fig, sometimes called sandpaper leaves, since they are used by natives for scouring their pots. But their favorite food was the rich, oily fruit of the majap tree, which ripens towards the end of the rainy season in October, and from which the natives extract cooking oil. To get this fruit they had to climb trees, but this was left entirely to the smaller females. The Old Man made no attempt to climb, sitting forlornly on the ground and contenting himself with the fruit knocked down by his lighter and more agile ladies. During the majap season the whole family rapidly put on weight, becoming very fat, but they thinned down again when the fruit disappeared. This was a pattern I observed again and again with many other gorilla families.

I had no wish to shoot or capture any of my family, of whom I quickly became very fond, but I took the opportunity of testing their reaction to my presence. When I showed myself at close quarters the result was always the same. The Old Man stood erect and stared at me, screamed and beat his abdomen—not his chest—with his open hands in a rolling movement. When I showed signs of advancing, he dropped on all fours and charged, screaming and showing his teeth as he came. I know of no other animal more terrifying than an angry charging bull gorilla, and it is little wonder that hunters sometimes lose their nerve and run away.

I took care to face the Old Man in an open clearing, where I could see what he was up to, and I held my rifle ready, knowing that I could drop him with a brain shot if he came too close. I was sufficiently confident of this to resolve to let him approach within fifteen yards before firing, but to my surprise, although he must have charged me a dozen times, he never came nearer than twenty yards. At that distance, he wheeled round and returned to his family, scolding me as he went. Then if I moved forward he charged again, and the whole performance would be repeated two or three times. When this failed to scare me off, the family retreated at such speed that it was difficult to find them or catch up with them again.

I began to realize that the Old Man's threats and charges were pure bluff, and this was abundantly confirmed by later experiences. With the possible exception of a few bad-tempered or wounded individuals, gorillas will not attack a man who stands his ground. However, if the man's courage fails him and he turns to run away, the gorilla will chase him and wreak terrible wounds with his hands and nails. I have seen the flesh stripped from the back and buttocks of natives in this way, but I know of only two occasions on which a gorilla used his teeth to inflict injuries. In one case a native hunter who had tripped over a root was bitten through the ribs and died a few days later.

There is only one tribe in the Cameroons—the Mendjim Mey—who regularly hunt gorillas for food, and among them it is a disgrace to be injured by a gorilla. Should a hunter return with such injuries he is laughed at as a coward, for the people know that the gorilla would not have attacked if the man had not taken fright and run away. Of course, there are exceptions to this. If you happen to tread on a gorilla's toes in the forest, you can expect to be torn to pieces, but even then the gorilla will be more concerned with getting away than with killing you. His action will be to sweep you aside with his powerful arms and hands, which is what had happened to me with the Ambam gorilla.

As for the females, they are completely harmless. I have

seen native hunters, having dispatched the Old Man, surround females and beat them over the head with sticks. They don't even try to get away, and it is most pitiful to see them putting their arms over their heads to ward off the blows, making no attempt at retaliation. The bull gorilla's charges are certainly bluff, but it is not true to say that he is a coward, for he will protect his family at the cost of his own life. This contrasts strongly with the behavior of chimpanzees. When they are attacked the males make off at once, leaving the others to their fate.

Leopards abound in the West African forests, and they will sometimes include young chimpanzees or gorillas in their diet, but stories of bull gorillas engaged in mortal combat with leopards are imaginary. Gorillas, however, seem to have no fear of leopards, in spite of the danger from them to their young, as the following incident will show.

My gorilla family was feeding quietly at the edge of an abandoned plantation, with the babies tumbling about happily under the indulgent eye of their gigantic father, when I noticed the movement of a branch above and behind them. Using my binoculars, I saw a leopard crouching on the branch, watching the youngsters with shining, round eyes. None of the gorillas appeared to be aware of its presence. I did not want to lose any of "my" babies, but neither did I want to disturb the family by shooting, for I had had enough trouble keeping up with them as it was, so I asked N'Gombie to try and get the leopard with an arrow.

He was reluctant to do so, for there was a chance that if he hit but did not kill the leopard, it would spring on the babies and kill them all in retaliation. A breeze springing up behind us resolved the situation by carrying our scent across to the leopard. Alarmed, it jumped down into the open within a few yards of the gorillas, and then bounded off into the bush. It was astonishing that even then the gorillas were unperturbed. The Old Man just glanced at the leopard and went on eating; one of the young males got up and coughed a bit, and the others took no notice of it at all. Most animals would have stampeded at the sight of a leopard.

The relationship of gorillas with other animals is equally interesting. I have found that they are terrified of dogs, but have no fear of elephants. On several occasions I found them feeding within yards of an elephant herd, neither party seemingly concerned about the other's presence. Only once was this harmony disturbed. I am not sure what went wrong, but for some reason the Old Man, backed by his two hefty sons, suddenly turned screaming on the elephants and apparently stampeded them. It may be that the gorillas had heard and were threatening me, not the elephants, for I was moving about a lot, or perhaps I had been scented by the elephants and in some way their alarm was instantly communicated to the gorillas.

Gorillas breed at any time of the year, but no reliable observer has ever witnessed their mating and they have never bred in captivity. Consequently, the gestation period is unknown, though it may well be roughly the same as our own. The pregnant female of my family group had her baby at the beginning of my second week of observation. One morning I found her considerably thinner, but I stared for a long while before I could identify the wispy black creature, like a hairy spider, which she hugged with one arm to her breast. Against her own black skin and hair it was difficult to see the tiny thing at all. The older babies rode on their mothers' backs when traveling, and N'Gombie reported that he once saw a baby gorilla riding on its father's back. I never saw that happen, but I always had the impression that the Old Man, in his dim and brutish way, was fond enough of his offspring.

Except when disturbed, the family made very little noise. At night, the Old Man could be heard making a queer, gargling sound from his bed and N'Gombie believed that this was to warn off intruders. After feeding, they sometimes beat their bellies with the flat of their hands and I am convinced that this is done more usually in play or as an expression of well-being than to denote anger and offense. Other signs of good humor were clapping, patting their cheeks and slapping the ground. The females rarely made any vocal sounds, but all three males, and more especially the Old Man, puffed and grunted as they tore at the vegetation in search of food. When they sat down to enjoy a meal they heaved gusty, noisy sighs of satisfaction. The babies were to be heard only when they were upset, and then their resemblance to human children was most remarkable. Seated on their little black bottoms, with their legs stretched out and their faces screwed up, they bawled exactly as children do.

For hour after hour every day I stood watching the gorillas, often up to my neck or chest in thick undergrowth, and by the end of each day I was infested with ticks. The apes are apparently unattractive to these pests, for I never found external parasites of any kind on my specimens. Gorillas are by no means as clean as chimpanzees. They scratch themselves, but seldom trouble to look and see what is causing the irritation, while chimpanzees will promptly and most delicately remove any kind of fluff or seed sticking to their bodies. They also detest dirty or sticky hands, but gorillas are not so particular.

My family lived in perfect harmony most of the time, but towards the end of the fortnight the largest of the two half-grown males had begun to cheek his father. I was sorry, for the Old Man was an excellent parent and he did not deserve his inevitable fate of being challenged and finally driven out to a lonely old age by the younger and more vigorous males.

My notes contain abundant details of the titanic struggles for leadership that take place between bull gorillas. I have never seen such a fight, but many of my specimens bore several injuries which I believe were the result of them. One very large male had had his right arm torn off from above the elbow, but the wound healed perfectly and in this case he had won the battle, for he was still the head of his family when I met him. Old Males driven away from their families continue thereafter to lead solitary lives, but young males soon join with other groups, where they are apparently accepted by the Old Man. Females are never found alone.

Nothing would have made me happier than an indefinite stay near my adopted family, but five miles away was my camp, with a dozen carriers, gun-bearers and servants—a necessary but costly burden. I had to earn my living, so at the end of the fortnight I packed up and went about my business.

I shall not easily forget my last view of the family before I turned my back on them and stole away through the forest. The warm bright sunlight of early morning was filtering through the branches of a great cottonwood tree, and the gorillas, finishing their breakfast, were warming themselves after a damp and chilly night. The Old Man, sitting with his legs crossed, was chewing a majap fruit, and though there were lots more lying about, one of the babies, with the perversity of extreme youth, was trying to pluck it from his mouth. Several times he was pushed away, the Old Man twisting his head out of reach. Soon the fruit was gone and the baby trotted away towards his mother. He was helped on his way with an affectionate and gentle pat on the bottom from his gigantic parent's hand—a hand that could have crushed a human skull in a single blow.

What of the future of gorillas? Will they, too, join that long and melancholy line of animals driven to extinction by the greed and intolerance of man? The spread of cultivation in West Africa during the past thirty years has certainly reduced their range and their numbers, but I fancy that there are vast tracts of mountainous forest which are never likely to produce those things that men desire, and it may be that in those regions the gorillas will manage to survive.

We may be encouraged in this optimism by a decision made at the third International Conference for the Protection of

African Fauna and Flora, which was held at Bukavu, in the Belgian Congo, in October 1953. Under the 1933 Convention, certain of the rarer animals were placed in either Class A or Class B. Those in the A category were to be completely protected, while those under B were not to be hunted, killed or captured except by license, and such licenses were granted only under special circumstances. At the 1953 conference the French delegation reported that gorillas were increasing in numbers and becoming a nuisance, doing considerable damage to plantations. For this reason it was successfully contended that they should be relegated to Class B.

The situation, then, is promising, but even so one must not be complacent. The suggestion made by American authorities that every effort should be made to breed gorillas in captivity deserves serious attention. There are several animals, such as the European bison and Pere David's deer, which are extinct in the wild and now exist only in zoos. If the worst comes to the worst, it may be that we can save the greatest and most romantic of the Primates in this same fashion.

4. Big Game Hunters

One of the most profitable but at the same time most exasperating tasks of a professional hunter is to organize safaris for visiting sportsmen. These wealthy gentlemen are sometimes experienced hunters and naturalists, with whom it is a delight to work, but more often they are idle fatheads whose only wish is to acquire a spurious glory by the slaughter of some of Africa's finest animals. You take your client into the bush, coaxing, bullying, wheedling or threatening him into the correct behavior, show him an elephant, a rhino, a buffalo, or whatever it is he wants to shoot, and then you say: "Well, there's your trophy. Point your rifle at it and pull the trigger." Afterwards the big game hunter returns home and is applauded as a hero by admiring friends.

I always tried to avoid such commissions. Hunting and collecting brought me a modest income, which was usually enough for me to indulge my curiosity about gorillas and other rare creatures; and that was all I ever wanted. Unhappily, I acquired a reputation as a hunter and explorer which proved to be most inconvenient and troublesome. In the nineteen twenties and thirties all sorts of weird and wealthy characters from Europe and America, encumbered with elaborate and expensive equipment, were demanding my services on safaris. I dodged them whenever I could, preferring to remain in the deep forest away from the towns, but now and then I had to return to Yaounde to settle business matters or to get supplies.

On one such occasion I was approached by a gentleman who very badly wanted to shoot a gorilla. He was a European manufacturer, and though his name was not Vincent, for the purpose of this story we shall pretend that it was. M. Vincent, then, wished to prove himself a man by taking home a stuffed ape, and he was prepared to part with a surprisingly large sum of money to make this possible. During the previous two months I had been wandering about the Yaounde forests in pursuit of a very large frog—a story told elsewhere in this book—which was a most engrossing but, alas, quite a profitless occupation. Not to put too fine a point on it, I was flat broke. I was, therefore, able with some difficulty to subdue my distaste for Vincent's proposal, my resentment of his patronizing attitude, and my immediate dislike of him personally. After an hour or two of persuasion, in both liquid and verbal form, I agreed to take him into the forest.

Vincent was a middle-aged man, stoutly built and with a dark, florid complexion. He assured me that he had had considerable experience, hunting in India and South Africa, but I noticed that his guns were new. When a suitable opportunity occurred I examined them.

"Looks as though you'd better clean those rifles before you use them," I told him afterwards.

"Oh, you can do that," he said casually. "You'll find the brushes and things in one of my boxes."

I cleaned his rifles and saw to it that they were kept clean. A few days later we and our carriers were set down by lorry at a village thirty-five miles southeast of Yaounde, in a district I thought suitable for the hunt. Amugu, the village chief, was an old friend of mine and was delighted to see me. He put two of his best huts at our disposal, and after I had settled in mine he came along to discuss the hunt and ask what help

I would need. When these matters were attended to, he arranged a dance for our entertainment. This was of the usual pattern. The girls danced around in a circle, making undulating, muscular movements of wonderful skill and grace, punctuating the dance by clapping their bent arms against their sides, and chanting all the time. The music was provided by a dozen young drummers, who sat on the ground behind the girls, with long wooden, skin-covered drums, which they beat with the palms of their hands.

Vincent sat on one side of me and Amugu on the other. Vincent was drinking heavily from a bottle of whiskey, and when it was almost half gone he asked me to join him.

"No thanks, Vincent. I only drink in town, but it might be a good idea to offer the chief a drink."

"What? Waste good Scotch on that dirty nigger? Let him stick to his native rot-gut."

My own conversation with Amuga had taken place in his own language, but he knew enough English to understand that he was being abused. I told Vincent to be careful what he said, but I got cursed for my trouble. I was about to leave him in disgust, when he staggered to his feet and reeled among the girls, kicking up his legs and grinning in a drunken parody of their dance. After that he began to chase them, grabbing at their bare breasts, trying to tear away their little bunches of leaves, and yelling that he would give them wonderful presents if they came to his hut.

Native hospitality in West African villages is liberal and uninhibited. It is believed that no man can or should sleep without a woman, and accordingly every guest, whether black or white, is offered a suitable companion. The chief will be surprised but not insulted if she is refused. Vincent's behavior would have earned him at least six months in any European police court; here in Africa it was equally offensive, but since he was a white man, and supposedly a friend of mine, the chief's only action was to complain to me.

Vincent shouted and struck out at me when I tried to drag him to his hut, but finally he gave in and slunk off in a foul humor to his bed, cursing and belching as he went. I could hear him moving about for a long time afterwards, but I fell asleep before I could make up my mind to get up and see what he was about. I rose very early next morning to make preparations for the hunt, and surprised two young girls sneaking out of his hut wearing head-clothes and beads they had certainly lacked the night before. Vincent came out for breakfast an hour later and I asked when he wished to move into the forest after his gorillas.

"When I'm ready I shall tell you," he said, and turned to walk away.

"If you fool about with the girls like that," I told him, "you'll be in trouble. Do you realize that if the chief makes a complaint to the District Officer you'll go out of the Cameroons on your ear? Don't depend on me to back you up."

He flushed, told me that if I did not mind my own business he would have *me* run out of the country, and walked off. I had half a mind to go back to Yaounde and leave him to the mercy of Amugu, who would not be so forbearing in my absence, but I did not relish the thought of a client ending with a spear through his ribs. Anyway I had a duty to him, having accepted his commission.

Consequently I hung about the village for a few days waiting for him to tire of the girls, which he did quickly enough. One morning he came into my hut, wearing the sort of hunting kit that Hollywood might have dreamed up. It consisted of heavy leather boots, reaching to his knees; smart cord jodhpurs and khaki bushcoat; a brand new leather belt and bandolier, both crammed with cartridges; an enormous pair of field glasses; and a hunting knife about the size of a cutlass.

"We're leaving today," he announced. "Have you got the carriers ready?"

"Good heavens, no! How on earth could you expect me to, without knowing when you wanted to leave?"

His face burned bright. "If you knew your job," he shouted, "you'd have them ready to move at any time. What do you think I'm paying you for? If those rotten niggers aren't ready by ten, I'll use my boot on their backsides."

The Negroes weren't ready by ten, but I managed to get the safari moving by noon and exercised as much restraint as I could on Vincent's footwear.

He had a tepoy—a sort of hammock—and eight men were detailed to carry him. His feet hung out on either side, and he used them freely to prod the men in front. Consequently they moved well ahead of the rest of us, and it was difficult for the other carriers, with heavy loads on their heads, to maintain such a pace. I always stopped at intervals when on the march to let my carriers drink, wash themselves down in a convenient stream, and have a rest and a smoke. It was impossible to do this while Vincent moved so fast, but I had no intention of abusing the men. If they were treated like that they would give trouble, and with every justification. I therefore left them and caught up with Vincent myself. Before I could open my mouth he began raving at me for being so far behind. He said he had never known such a slow safari.

It was obviously time for a showdown, so I did not answer him directly. Instead, speaking in Pidgin, I ordered the carriers to put down his tepoy. Vincent countered by threatening to murder them if they did, and for a moment they were too confused and frightened to know which of us to obey. Then I repeated the order in their own language and with broad grins they promptly dropped Vincent none too gently on the ground. Down there he looked very foolish indeed.

I caught him by the lapels of his jacket and yanked him to his feet. I explained that he had obviously never been on any kind of safari before, and that if he was not prepared to accept my command of the present one I would go back to Yaounde, leaving him on his own. This frightened him, for he had good reason to lack confidence in his ability to handle the villagers, and he calmed down considerably. There was no need, he said, for me to lose my temper, and he had never for a moment wished to challenge my command. So long as he got his gorilla, he would be quite satisfied to leave all the arrangements in my hands. He got back into the tepoy and went black in the face when he saw that the men were laughing at him, but he said no more and we continued at a more reasonable pace.

Later in the day we found a good site and made camp. Soon afterwards, Vincent and I, with two gun-bearers, left to explore the forest. In his heavy boots, Vincent made as much noise as a rhino, and kept chattering in a loud voice. Thus every creature for miles around was warned of our approach and we saw nothing. When I suggested that it would be wiser to move with as little noise as possible, Vincent assured me that he knew what he was doing, for he had many times stalked impala in South Africa. Soon he was grumbling that I had shown him nothing to shoot, let alone a gorilla. The gun-bearers were disgusted.

"This white man fool too much," said one of them.

Vincent heard him and swung round with fist raised to strike the man. As he did so, he spotted a monkey sitting in a tree some way off, and with a wild shout he bounded off after it. He disappeared and presently three shots from his heavy rifle shook the forest. The two gun-bearers were sitting on the ground, rocking with laughter, while I tried hard to keep a straight face. Suddenly there came another shout from Vincent, this time of a different nature.

"Merfield! Merfield! God almighty man, come here quick! Merfield! MERFIELD!"

We ran after him and found him up to his waist in the deep, stinking mud of a small swamp, and sinking fast. To the uneducated eye, it looked firm enough on top, and only the nature of the vegetation it supported told of the deathtrap beneath. Vincent, hot in pursuit of his wretched monkey, had run straight into it.

Resisting the temptation to let him sink until the mud reached his chin, I cut some stout lianas, and using these as ropes we soon hauled him out. His lovely "bush-kit" was ruined, and the mud inside his boots had glued them firmly to his feet. All three of us took turns at tugging, but we could not move them. Finally I got him to lie on his back, with his legs vertically in the air, so that the mud would ooze out slowly. He looked, and must have felt, perfectly ridiculous, and as his fear evaporated, anger took its place. When we got back to camp he went straight to his tent and sulked there until next day.

Much to my relief, he then asked me to look for gorillas alone. Five miles from the camp I picked up the tracks of a fine young family, and watched them until I decided they were too precious for Vincent to destroy. Later, I found a solitary bull, and the moment I saw him I realized that a bullet from Vincent's rifle would be a mercy to him. He was very old, with a badly deformed left leg, and from the way he charged me at sight, I guessed that pain had given him a bad temper. I was not surprised to find, from teeth marks on vegetation he had chewed, that his teeth were in a terrible condition, as they often are with very old apes. He was probably in constant pain and what remained of his life would not be very pleasant for him.

Vincent was nowhere to be seen when I returned with my report, but my gun-bearer said that he had found a village nearby and had gone there in search of girls. When he returned he was towing a giggling mammy behind him. Without a word to me, he shooed her into his tent, let down the flap and stayed there until next morning. This went on for days and I could get no sense out of him at all. At last I went off again by myself and shot the old gorilla. The boys carried it back and laid it at Vincent's feet. At first he was furious, but later he asked me to take a photograph of him with the animal. For this he posed in full bush-kit, holding a gun across the hook of his arm, and with one foot on the gorilla. By now he had had quite enough of the forest and its discomforts, and it was not difficult to persuade him to return to Yaounde.

He gave a party in the bar a few nights after our return, but I was not invited. In Yaounde, as in any other town, an appreciative audience is always to be bought for the price of a few drinks. Vincent had the gorilla skin spread out on the floor beside him and was entertaining his guests with a graphic account of how he shot the animal.

At the other end of the room I sat with a group of old friends, including Sam Barton, a trader who had formerly been a Liverpool policeman. Sam was a veritable giant of a man; simple, forthright, and with a heart of gold. After expressing his disgust of Vincent, he asked me about my fees.

"That skunk paid you yet, Merfield?"

"Not a franc! He says I made a mess of his gorilla skin when I preserved it, and that it's rotten already. As a matter of fact it is. His boy tells me he's piddled over it half a dozen times when he's been drunk. I don't know of any preservative against that!"

"But haven't you taken any action against him?"

"No thanks! I'd rather . . . Now look here, Sam . . ." I broke off as he rose to his feet and strode across to Vincent.

Before I could stop him, he had cleared Vincent's table of glasses and bottles with one sweep of his arm, hoisted him to his feet by the shirt front, and placed before his face a fist as big as a gorilla's. Sam was always direct in his manner.

"Are you going to pay Merfield?" he demanded. Vincent gasped and tried to fight him off, but he was held like a baby. Sam repeated the question, shaking the unfortunate man until his teeth rattled, and that proved quite effective.

Ten minutes later, feeling rather dazed, I was buying Sam

a drink, my wallet stuffed with notes. Vincent hurried off at once, leaving the gorilla skin behind, and left for Bouala on the coast by first train next day. I never saw him again.

To Sam and the rest of them some sort of celebration was clearly called for. After Vincent left the bar we began a party of our own, and this was well under way when a most unexpected interruption occurred. A tall, broad-shouldered man, with a white, neatly trimmed beard, entered the room and after a few words with the bartender came across to our table.

"I believe one of you gentlemen is Fred Merfield," he said courteously; and when I had identified myself, he went on: "I'm here on a shooting trip after gorillas and I'm looking for a guide and hunter. Several people have mentioned your name. If you are interested, perhaps we could have dinner together and discuss it."

The idea of accepting another client after my experience with Vincent struck me as so amusing that I almost burst out laughing. For a moment I could think of nothing to say, and the man, perplexed, shifted uneasily and gave me a stern, puzzled look.

He began again: "My name is Powell-Cotton. . . ."

But I gave him no time to continue. I rose at once and shook him by the hand. Here was a man I had heard a great deal about, and never thought I would be fortunate enough to meet. Major P. H. G. Powell-Cotton was a world-renowned naturalist and big game hunter, perhaps the greatest of his day. He had already hunted in Tibet, Ladak, Kashmir, northern and central India, and in Abyssinia, the Congo, and many other parts of Africa. His museum at Quex Park, Birchington, Kent, contained one of the finest collections in the world and the largest collection of big game ever shot by one man. Now here he was in the Cameroons, and seeking *my* services. I could imagine no greater honor.

"When do you want to leave?" I asked him.

"Now wait a minute! Hadn't we better discuss it first?

Perhaps if your friends could excuse you for an hour we can have a chat."

We did; and in that hour a friendship was formed which was to prove of the greatest advantage to us both. It was from Powell-Cotton that I learned the difficult and delicate business of preserving skins and skeletons so that they could be of greatest value to science; he it was who brought order and system into my hitherto haphazard collecting, and who put me in touch with museums and other scientific institutions in many parts of the world. Whereas before I had sought only those animals whose rarity and mystery had attracted my attention, I now began to learn what scientists wanted, and, more important, *why* it was wanted.

Gorillas were the main object of Powell-Cotton's visit to the Cameroons, though he wanted many other animals as well, and he was anxious to set off after them as soon as possible, for his time was limited. I told him I knew of a promising area, and that I could be ready to leave early next morning. In the bar, at the other end of the hotel, we could hear my party in full swing. Powell-Cotton smiled, and cocked his head to one side, listening.

"But aren't you going back to your friends?" he asked.

"Yes, but don't let that worry you. I'll be here at six in the morning!"

"I doubt it," he said drily, with twinkling eyes, "but when you *are* fit to travel, I shall be waiting."

I returned to my friends in high spirits, and then the party really got going. It was not until three a.m. that I remembered my promise to Powell-Cotton. I went home at once, had a cold bath and swallowed three prairie oysters in rapid succession. I woke my cook, Atanaga, my houseboy, Sumba, and told them to be waiting for me outside the hotel with all my guns and camping kit by five thirty. Then I roused a friend in another part of the town and after a little persuasion, managed to borrow his lorry. At six a.m. precisely, I knocked at Major Powell-Cotton's door.

"What? You really are ready? You and your friends have kept me awake all night with the noise you've been making. I thought you were still with them. Anyway, give me an hour and I'll be with you."

And at seven thirty precisely we were bouncing up and down on the back of the lorry as we were driven along the dusty, bumpy Akonolinga road to the village where I had taken Vincent. Amugu, the chief, bore me no grudge because of Vincent's behavior and readily supplied us with carriers. This time I decided to try another district and we marched for a whole day through hilly forest to the village of Paramount Chief N'Vondo, whom I had known and respected for years. N'Vondo was a highly intelligent man, much loved and always obeyed by his people. He owned a big wooden house, with several bedrooms and deep, cool verandahs, and he at once put it at our disposal.

As I expected, there were many gorillas in that neighborhood, but N'Vondo had his own ideas about hunting them. He told us that a family of gorillas had been laying waste his plantations and arrangements had already been made to round them up.

I was most distressed to hear this, for native roundups are appalling affairs. The skin and flesh of a gorilla are very tough. If you poke a big one with your finger—which I do not recommend—you will find that he has the consistency of shoe leather. Against an animal like that, the natives' spears are feeble weapons, for they do not pierce deeply. Spearing a gorilla to death therefore takes a long time and many spears.

Moreover, the native is not interested in killing the animal cleanly and quickly. He is a savage, who desires the pleasure and satisfaction of revenge, and often mutilates the animal before killing it. Unhappily, little can be done to stop this cruelty. The tribes are fiercely independent and, if a white hunter's bullet were to rob them of their fun, a stray spear might easily come his way—an accident, of course. In this part of the Cameroon forests, roundups were fairly frequent. They also sometimes took place in the gorilla country of the Mendjim Mey, where I lived later, but there, by a little subterfuge, I was able to stop the mutilation of the animals altogether.

A gorilla's roundup requires the services of many men. During the day and night after our arrival, N'Vondo's drummers were constantly in action calling the people from miles around. Some of the replies came from villages so far away that their drums were scarcely audible, at least to us. The men were told to assemble at a prearranged spot and drum signals were sent to N'Vondo as each contingent was ready to start. Many parties of villagers passed our camp, the men armed with bows and arrows, spears and cutlasses, and their women carrying baskets of food. They were full of enthusiasm for the hunt, which meant not only a feast of gorilla meat, which is highly prized, but relief from animals which, in a couple of hours, were capable of destroying half an acre of bananas or plantains.

N'Vondo told us that a gorilla family had made their beds near a footpath, which was not a convenient situation for a roundup. Later, trackers came in and reported that a severe thunderstorm which raged during the night had made the animals restless, and they had twice moved their quarters, thus frustrating N'Vondo's plans.

He took us to see the damage the animals had done. No wonder the villagers were cross! The plantation we examined was barely a hundred yards from an inhabited hut, yet the gorillas had been bold enough to destroy it almost entirely. Plaintains in full bearing had been broken down and torn to pieces, but the fruit was untouched, for the gorillas preferred the pith of the stems. Nearby were the family's beds, made of elephant grass bent over to form a springy mattress about two feet six inches above the ground. Dried grass had been placed on top.

Powell-Cotton was anxious to preserve one of these beds for the gorilla group he wanted in his museum, and we chose the biggest, presumably that of the Old Man. It was first photographed from several angles, then bound together with lengths of liana, and finally removed bodily by cutting away the stems beneath. Swarms of black ants hampered this work and there were frequent yells as one or another of us fell victim to their strong, sharp nippers. The bed was crated and shipped to England, where it was in the Powell-Cotton Museum for several years.

I could not believe that one family of gorillas had done so much damage, and I soon discovered that there were, in fact, several families in the neighborhood. For twelve days they evaded N'Vondo's efforts to encircle them. Finally he split up his men into four groups, each deputed to follow a separate family and to signal when they were in a position convenient for the roundup. One of these parties came upon a solitary male, who attacked and was wounded by the men. The animal made off at once, but was followed and fired on by a tracker who owned an ancient rifle. Of the eight shots fired, two were said to have found their mark. This information was tapped out by drums, and Powell-Cotton and I went off to try to track the wounded animal. On our way, we met the hunters returning, and were told that the gorilla was traveling fast and making for the main forest, where there was no hope of overtaking it.

At three o'clock one morning, N'Vondo woke us and said that a gorilla family had been found in a suitable locality and that the roundup would take place that day. With the chief as our guide, we set off at once, traveling by lantern light for six or seven miles along a muddy forest path, as slippery as a greasy pole. After crossing a rickety wooden bridge, most of which was rotten, and going along a newly cut path through dense leafy undergrowth, we came upon the assembled hunters about six o'clock, just as it was getting light.

There was no sign of the gorillas, or for that matter of anything else—for the forest was too thick to see more than a few yards ahead—but we were assured that the animals were there, encircled by the waiting hunters and their attendant womenfolk. Everyone now began to work furiously, clearing a circular band five or six yards wide around the trapped animals. On the inner perimeter of this, a tall rough fence of five-foot stakes, stuck into the ground at two-foot intervals, was rapidly constructed. Lengths of creepers and bundles of palm-leaf ribs were brought to lash them together, and the fence was strengthened by ties attached to tree trunks. Finally, leaves and branches were piled against it to give it a more solid appearance.

While this work was going on, numbers of spearmen stood on guard in case the gorillas should break out and make a dash for freedom. The women marched around the cleared circle, singing and making an incredible din with drums, bells, rattles and empty kerosene tins. Some of them were still carrying their lanterns and their baskets of food. The most conspicuous figure of all was the witch doctor, who gravely stalked round inside the fence, tootling on a Situtunga horn which had a pad of "medicine" attached to it. With his left hand, he made gestures which would, he believed, keep the gorillas quiet until the fence was complete. Then, with the help of his small son, he dug a hole in the ground and buried various roots and oddments. These were charms to keep the gorillas from charging through at that spot, which was a much-used gorilla path. All the hunters were convinced that this would work, and the path remained entirely unprotected throughout the roundup. The gorillas, in fact, did try to break through the circle several times, but they never tried that route, which was the most obvious one for them to take.

N'Vondo, who always wore European clothes, was dressed

in a trench coat intended for a considerably larger man. Followed by his cup-bearer, who supplied him with palm wine, and his cook, whose responsibility was snacks, he supervised all these operations. By now Old Man gorilla was making his presence known by repeated, deep-throated growls, and every time he growled he was answered by renewed efforts from the drummers and the shrieking women.

Towards nine o'clock all preparations were completed, and within the fence the men began to widen the cleared ring. They were guarded by a line of spearmen and three or four "shootmen" who were armed with elderly firearms of various kinds. The area of bush hiding the gorillas slowly diminished, and several times we caught a glimpse of the Old Man, as he made halfhearted attempts to lead his family through to freedom. Each time he was beaten back by the spears and a crescendo of noise from the women.

We could not, of course, see what was happening on the other side of the ring, and it was there that the first real action began. A female gorilla, deserting her baby, had tried to break through and had been speared to death. The youngster was still alive and was brought to me, unharmed but extremely frightened. Powell-Cotton hurriedly bought it, and our own carriers took it back to the village with strict instructions to preserve it alive. Powell-Cotton had handed over his rifle to his gun-bearer and was using his motion picture camera when a young male broke out of the jungle on our right and stood for a moment between him and me. I was afraid to fire, for Powell-Cotton was directly in my line of sight, but one of the native shootmen had no such scruples. Fortunately he was a good shot, on that occasion at least, and it was the animal, not Powell-Cotton, who fell dead.

There were more shots and yells and everyone was pointing upwards. Climbing a big tree in the center of the bush was another female, with her baby clinging to her back. Two spears projected from her left side. In her fear she grew careless, transferred her weight to a branch not strong enough to support her, and came crashing to the ground. Spears, cutlasses and several shots from the old guns finished her off, but even when she was dead they could not resist the delight of stabbing and slashing at her body. Powell-Cotton, by dint of shouting and threatening, managed to rescue the baby unharmed, but at grave risk to himself, for the people were beside themselves with excitement and in no mood to be argued with.

The next gorilla to show itself was also a female. She came out of the bush like a rocket and charged straight through the line of spearmen. There were three spears sticking in her back by the time she reached the fence, but she got over all right and disappeared. Hunters were sent after her, but they came back later without having found the animal, and I have no doubt that she escaped and recovered from the spear wounds.

The death of the Old Man was one of the most terrible things I had ever seen. He had tried to get out on the opposite side and we were attracted there by the yelling of the spearmen. Running around, we found the poor beast sitting in the undergrowth, as I had seen gorillas do so often before in more happy circumstances, and there were at least a dozen spears projecting from his chest, back and sides. Making no attempt to retaliate, he was just sitting there, rocking to and fro as more spears were thrust home at close quarters; his mouth was wide open, crying shame on his tormentors.

The gorilla's anguish was too much for me and I put up my rifle to shoot, caring nothing for the consequences, but before I could fire a native stepped forward between me and the stricken beast. Three or four more spears hit the gorilla and then another man, armed with a heavy club, leaned forward and slowly, methodically, began clubbing him to death.

Altogether the family had numbered nine. There were three females—two of them mothers of the youngsters we had captured—the Old Man, and one young male which the natives had hacked to pieces, severing his arms and legs. Two others had climbed the fence and escaped.

Several natives were injured. The man with the club had a cut to the bone just below his knee, from his last encounter with the Old Man. Another hunter had a superficial wound on the thigh inflicted by a gorilla's sweeping fingernail, and a third had had his hand bitten. One of the spearmen had been wounded by his own comrade, who had accidentally thrust a spear through the flesh of his left thigh. In order to get out the barbed head, it had to be pushed all the way through and out the other side, like a fishhook, but although the pain must have been terrible, the man did not so much as wince while this was being done.

It was late afternoon before the dead gorillas were brought in. Last of all came the Old Man, whose great weight required relays of four men at a time. I managed to keep the excited people away from the animals for a time while Powell-Cotton took photographs and made measurements and notes of scientific value. Some of the skins were too badly damaged by spear cuts to be of any use to us, but we bought the others, and all the skeletons, from N'Vondo—at rather a stiff price—and shipped them home to England.

While the villagers made a feast of the gorilla meat, Powell-Cotton and I worked like slaves to preserve the skins and skeletons. The witch doctor, too, had his hands full, filling his magic horn with gorilla blood and busying himself with other obscure and curious activities to ensure the success of future hunts. None of the women joined in the feast, for gorilla meat is forbidden to them.

When we had the gorilla skins cleaned, laid on frames and left to dry slowly, Powell-Cotton and I settled down for a rest and a smoke, and we began swapping tales of our experiences with animals. He told me of the time when he was badly mauled by a lion. The beast had knocked him down and was tearing at his back, when, with tremendous courage, two natives attacked it with a whip and a stick. The Nubian askari took advantage of this distraction to shoot the lion at close quarters and Powell-Cotton was dragged free. This lion is still on exhibition in the Powell-Cotton Museum.

"And what about you?" Powell-Cotton asked me. "How did you get out here in the first place?"

"Well, my father apprenticed me to a wholesale draper's, and I worked all day long in a gloomy basement near St. Paul's. But I couldn't stand that. I'd always loved animals and the open air. One day I saw an advertisement for an assistant on a plantation in German West Africa and I applied for the job. There were twenty applicants, but I was the only one who knew any German, which I had learned at school, so I won out. I was on my way before my parents realized what was happening. That was in 1910."

"What was life like out here in those days?"

"Oh, pretty wild and primitive. The plantation was British-owned, but the manager was a German who was almost always drunk. Our laborers were recruited from the bush tribes. I remember one lot we had who were decimated by disease after they had been working with us for a few months. They thought there was an evil spirit about, so to propitiate it they tortured one of their men. They tied his arm horizontally over a slow fire, and when I found him there was only charred bone left up to the shoulder. I had no idea of surgery, but I knew I had to amputate somehow. The bone was so brittle, though, that it broke off when I touched it. There was nothing more I could do but make the poor chap comfortable until he died, which he did during the night."

"And hunting? How did you begin that?"

"Sometimes I went off shooting birds and small game with the manager. Funny thing about him—when he was drunk he was a crack shot, but when he was sober, which was only in the morning, he couldn't hit a haystack at twenty yards.

Anyway, I began to realize that the forests around the plantation were full of life, and I started to take an interest in the animals. One day I tried to shoot an elephant, but I made a mess of it and only wounded the poor thing. Then I met a professional hunter, a chap called Marcus, and he took me off on a hunting trip and taught me how to shoot big game.

"Gradually I did more and more hunting, and found that it could be made to pay. Marcus told me a lot about gorillas—most of it nonsense as I discovered later—but I was sufficiently intrigued to put in a bit of research on the subject when I went home on my first leave. I was surprised that so little was known about gorillas, and when I came back I decided to find out for myself. Before I could get very far, the 1914–19 war disrupted everything and I joined the West African Frontier Force until the Germans were driven out of the Cameroons. When it was over I took up hunting as a full-time occupation and, whenever possible, I went looking for gorillas. I've found some, as you know, but there's a great deal of territory where they might live which I haven't explored at all yet. Perhaps I will one day."

"What about the babies we rescued from the roundup? Do you think they'll live?"

"I doubt it. They're eating out of my hand already, but they've had a terrible shock and young gorillas seem to lose heart when they are caught and caged."

And so it was. That night the little gorillas cried for hours, though they quieted down whenever I got up to comfort them, which was frequently. I had a large cage made as soon as I could, but they hated this so much that I let them run loose whenever I was there to watch them, and confined them by a long high net when I was not.

Baby chimpanzees, caught in much the same way, show the very greatest interest in their surroundings and their captors; in fact, they find life so interesting and amusing that they forget the tragedy of their capture in no time, and consequently thrive. But gorillas are different; newly caught, they are suspicious, sullen and morose. When I put our two babies in the cage, they simply turned their backs on the world, making no attempt to get out, and I could see that if they were left like that they would die in a day or two. Romping about in the compound, however, they seemed much happier, and while we stayed with N'Vondo they got on very well. Powell-Cotton made a motion film of them at play and it is now at the Powell-Cotton Museum. Unfortunately, we still had the long trek back to Yaounde before us, and for this there was no alternative to caging the young animals. Before we reached Yaounde they had both died.

Our return, however, did not take place immediately, for Powell-Cotton wished to get gorillas and other animals on his own. I suggested that he take with him Abong Lube, one of N'Vondo's most gifted hunters, whom I had employed several times myself. One of Lube's many accomplishments was to call up duiker by making a nasal sound which may be transcribed as "Nnnyo"—the "N" being long and drawn out and the last syllable short and sharp. Duiker would come for miles through the bush in answer to this call.

A few days after the gorilla roundup, our safari moved off into the main forest, with Powell-Cotton, myself, Lube and another tracker called Imbie keeping slightly ahead and casting about for gorilla tracks. For several days we found only monkeys, duiker and pigs. Most of the latter were Red River pigs, but then we came upon an abandoned plantation and we noticed that pigs had been feeding on the leaves of *Dioscorea*, a kind of yam. We knew that only one kind of pig ate those leaves—the giant forest hog.

We were both really excited, and with good reason, for this was a rare and lucky find. The giant forest hog is the biggest wild pig in the world, reaching a weight of 500 pounds. It was first heard of about the time that the okapi—that strange relative of the giraffe—was discovered, but it was not until 1904 that the reported existence of a huge black pig was finally confirmed. The animal can be readily distinguished from bush pigs and wart hogs by the pair of gigantic, warty excrescences below the eyes which look like the fungus growth one sometimes sees on the trunks of decaying trees. The muzzle has a large terminal disc, and the whole body is covered with long black hair. All wild pigs are dangerous, but the giant forest hog is probably the worst, and is feared even more than the buffalo. Native women gathering wood have been attacked without provocation, and the animal has no hesitation in charging a hunter. Its long, upward-curved tusks are deadly weapons.

There were three of the pigs, and their tracks led us along a tunnel through the thick foliage of a plant resembling a giant arum lily, twelve feet high. Pushing our rifles before us we went forward on hands and knees, stopping to listen at intervals, for hearing was more reliable than sight in vegetation of that density. Powell-Cotton was leading, followed by the tracker Imbie, and when we suddenly heard a chorus of grunts and a great deal of scuffling, threw himself into a sitting position with his rifle ready. The pigs crashed away from us, and we began to despair of coming up with them at all. Giant forest hogs are certainly the most difficult forest animals to stalk, for they can travel great distances at an astonishing speed and are capable of hiding in bush so thick that it is impossible to approach them.

We had half an hour's rest and went off again, creeping along still more warily. Then I saw Imbie tap Powell-Cotton on the ankle and point behind him to the left. Leaning forward, I could see what looked like an enormous black barrel bulging above the leaves. Slowly and with infinite caution, Powell-Cotton leaned back on his heels and sat down, bringing his Paradox to bear on the pig at the same time. Then he fired. There was a loud squeal and the animal spun around, rolled on its back, kicked convulsively for a second and then was still. The pig undoubtedly had heard us coming, doubled back on its tracks, and was preparing to charge us when Imbie spotted him.

Afterwards, Powell-Cotton, with Lube as tracker and gun-bearer, went off by himself in search of gorillas, while I followed with the main safari, shooting duiker occasionally to provide meat for the carriers, and looking after the skins. They found a solitary bull gorilla, and the three of them played a sort of follow-my-leader game for nearly a week, until the gorilla dropped with a bullet from the Major's .256 Mannlicher in his skull. The animal was a young bull turned out of the family by his father, and not an Old Man turned out by his more vigorous son, but Powell-Cotton's disappointment over this was quickly dispelled. He found yet another lone gorilla, and this time it was the full-grown bull he wanted. When I came up with him later in the day, he already had it half skinned.

This marked the end of our safari, and Powell-Cotton returned home. I was still smarting over the insults I had received from Vincent, and Powell-Cotton's warm appreciation of my management of the safari was therefore doubly welcome. For my part, I had enjoyed every minute spent in the company of this cultured and courteous gentleman, for whose skill and knowledge my admiration had daily increased. While he was in England we kept up a continuous correspondence of mutual benefit and satisfaction. A few years later he came back to the Cameroons, and together we penetrated into the remote, independent sultanate of Rei Bouba, in the far north of the country. The story of our journey there, of the animals and the strange, medieval people we found, is told in another part of this book.

5. L'Inspecteur de Chasse

There are usually so many village children watching what goes on in a "shootman's" camp, and always anxious to help, that at first I did not notice Coppers. Gradually, I became aware that I was being followed about by a boy of twelve, a sturdy, healthy-looking lad, with bright, intelligent eyes and a smile that never left his face. He seemed to anticipate my every want. If I stooped to pick up something, he darted from behind me, snatched it from the ground and presented it to me with a shy, delighted grin. If my hand went to my pocket for a match to light my pipe, before I had a chance to get one out he was offering a burning stick from the fire. Wherever I went he was there, either trotting behind me like a little dog, or watching from a distance, his strong white teeth gleaming in an everlasting smile.

"Who and what," I asked at length, "is this boy?"

Atanaga, my cook, did not know. Neither did N'Denge, my gun-bearer, or any of the carriers. The boy had simply appeared one day and followed our safari. Sometimes he did odd jobs for Atanaga, and received scraps of food in return, but apparently he had no other means of support. No one knew his name, for he could not speak Pidgin or any of the local languages, but it was believed that he had somehow drifted up from the Congo.

And that was all I ever found out about him. He listened anxiously while I made these inquiries and for once the smile had left his face. He looked forlorn and wretched standing there in his pathetic little scrap of a loincloth—his sole possession—and was obviously terrified that I was going to send him away.

I told Atanaga to feed him up and give him work to do, and when the boy understood my intentions, I was rewarded with a dazzling smile.

He soon picked up a little Pidgin and was sublimely happy in camp. Now and then I gave him centime pieces, which have holes in the center. He never spent them, but threaded them on a string and hung them around his neck. Because of this and because he lacked a better name, I called him Coppers.

One day I found him at the fireside busily engaged in fashioning a crude bow and some arrows.

"I make t'ing for kill beef for Massa," he said, and a few days later turned up with four large rats impaled on his arrows. I was impressed, for the rats were of an uncommon variety and their skins were valuable. I paid him for them, and afterwards began to reduce his domestic duties, much to the annoyance and jealousy of Atanaga, so that he could have much more time for hunting. He quickly developed into one of the most skilful hunters of small game I ever knew in all the years I spent in the Cameroons. Every day he returned with something new, either alive or dead. From rats, mice and small birds of infinite variety, he graduated to bush-babies, pottos, monkeys and, on one occasion, a porcupine.

Some of these he had shot with arrows, but many were caught alive either with his hands or with original and cleverly designed traps. One day he found a pangolin, that scaly, toothless, miniature dragon that feeds only on ants. I had no time for the difficult business of weaning it from ants to minced meat, the usual substitute diet for these animals in captivity, so it was released again into the bush, none the worse for its adventure. Some of the bush-babies and pottos were kept as pets; others were sold to a collector who wanted them for zoos in Europe and America.

Coppers' most astounding capture was a live and very large crowned eagle, a monkey-eating bird with a wing span of nearly four feet. Covered with blood, the boy came limping into camp hugging the bird in his arms, and at first I assumed it was dead, for it was incredible that a small boy should be carrying so wild and dangerous a creature if it were alive. But it was alive, and N'Denge hurriedly stuffed it into a box while I attended to Coppers' wounds.

The boy had been hiding in the undergrowth watching a rat hole and waiting for its occupant to appear. On the low branch of a neighboring tree the eagle was watching the same hole with much the same ideas in mind as Coppers. When the eagle pounced on the rat, Coppers pounced on the eagle, and in spite of being fearfully torn and lacerated by its sharp hooked bill and talons, he held on until it had exhausted itself, and then carried it off, to appear before me in bloody triumph.

I did not want the eagle, for at that time I knew of no way of disposing of it, but I could not break Coppers' heart by letting it go immediately. So together we made it a fine roomy cage and presently it was taking meat from our hands. Coppers was delighted, and after a few days he tied a string to its leg and let it fly about outside. Not satisfied with that, he soon became convinced that the bird was sufficiently tame to be released altogether with no danger of its escaping. I must confess that I did not try to dissuade him from this, for I rather hoped it would fly away. It did; and I shall never forget the look of dismay on that little boy's face as he watched his fierce friend circle higher and higher, and then soar away over the trees to be lost forever.

But sorrow never lodged for long in Coppers' cheerful heart. He was off again that evening, seeking new conquests in the jungle he knew and understood so well. Already his boyish pleasure in killing had begun to yield to a nobler love and interest in the creatures he sought for, and he spent many hours watching birds, animals and insects for no other reason than his delight in living things. I gave him all the encouragement I could, for I imagined him in manhood as my ideal companion in the forest.

Then one day Coppers went out into the bush and never came back. I sent everyone out looking for him, fearing that he might have stumbled upon a python, a leopard or a buffalo, and been killed or badly hurt. We searched the bush for miles around, but we could find no sign of him or of any such encounter. I came to the conclusion that he had wandered off a long way and would rejoin the safari sooner or later. It would have been easy for him to find me, although I was now once more on the move, for the progress of a white hunter is always widely known among the people, either by word of mouth or by "bush telegraph"—the big drums that are constantly tapping out news across the forests. But Coppers never returned. He disappeared as suddenly and mysteriously as he came, and none of us ever saw him again.

In any case I could not wait for him at that time, for I was going into the gorilla country again, this time for the French Government, the most important commission I had so far received. Soon after Powell-Cotton's departure, I received a note asking me to call on the *Inspecteur de Chasse*, the Government official in charge of game conservation, who had arrived in Yaounde and was staying at the rest house reserved for traveling officials. Up to then, game regulations in the Cameroons had been hazy and were seldom observed, but I had heard that new ones were to be introduced and more rigorously enforced. This had my full approval, but I knew I was suspected of ignoring the game laws, and I supposed that M. Bruno de Labourie, the *Inspecteur*, wished to lecture me on the subject. This was not so. In the following year, a big colonial exhibition was to be held in Paris and the *Inspec-*

teur had been asked to provide a gorilla group for the *Pavillon de Chasse.*

Since he was supposed to be the chief game warden of the country, I was surprised when he asked me where gorillas could be found and how I preserved my skins. The time was 11 A.M., when all Europeans in the Cameroons have an *apéritif;* yet no welcome clink of glasses greeted my ears, and it is a grave discourtesy for an official not to offer refreshment to his guest. I was thirsty and I was hot; therefore I could not help but notice the omission.

"Do you know, Monsieur, how skins are preserved?" I asked him.

"But, of course! Brine is by far the best preservative. Er . . . what do you use?"

As a matter of fact I always use "Atlas," a patent preservative, proof against insects, molds or bacteria, which retains the full bloom and beauty of a fur for all time. But I wasn't going to tell him that, not without an *apéritif!*

"What are you going to put your gorilla skins in?" I countered.

"I have some cans," he said, pointing to the corner.

There were two of them, small galvanized cans about the size of small milk churns.

"I see. So you are interested only in baby gorillas, M. *L'Inspecteur?*"

"I don't understand you."

"You will, when you try to get the skin of a full-grown gorilla into one of those little things."

I left the *Inspecteur* and strolled along to the hotel, where I made up for his deficient hospitality. For two or three months I heard no more of him. Then I was summoned to Government House by M. Marchand, the Governor of the Cameroons.

"M. Merfield, I understand that some time ago *L'Inspecteur de Chasse* approached you and asked your advice on the collection of gorilla skins."

"That is so, your Excellency."

"Unfortunately, the advice you gave him, whatever it was, has proved ineffective, for the gorilla skins he obtained were rotten by the time they reached Paris."

"But I gave him no advice."

"Never mind. I believe you have yourself successfully preserved many skins for museums and other scientific institutions. Would you, then, be prepared to accept a commission from my Government to procure suitable skins for the Colonial Exhibition next year?"

"I would certainly consider it."

"Three gorillas are needed—a big male, a female and a youngster. The commission would not, however, be confined to gorillas. We shall also require numerous other animals—buffalo, antelope, leopards—in fact, any and everything you can get."

"How much time can you give me?"

"Three months."

"That's not much. May I have until tomorrow to think it over?"

"By all means. And if you decide to accept, as I hope you will, may I wish you the very best of luck."

We shook hands and I left him. Though I did not wish to seem over-enthusiastic, I had, in fact, already decided to accept, for I was delighted to have the opportunity of serving the Government. Once I had done so, my status would ever afterwards be high among the European officials and paramount chiefs throughout the country, and my future activities would therefore be made much easier.

So, after a discreet interval, I accepted the commission and signed an agreement with the Governor. My preparations were complete in a few days, and when I left Yaounde my safari was accompanied by an official escort in the form of two native policemen. Each was armed with a long-barreled French rifle of the type called *La Belle*, which have magazines holding only three cartridges, and a heavy machete called a *Coup Coup*. These two men were of great value to me: not only did they lend my safari an unaccustomed prestige and authority, but they did most of the work of engaging and handing the carriers.

Village chiefs are expected to provide carriers for European travelers, and to feed carriers who come with them from other villages. They are paid, of course, but the negotiations are sometimes protracted, and it was a pleasant change to have all this done for me by the policemen.

We went first to the village of Zembani, thirty-five miles down the Akonolinga road from Yaounde, and I stayed the night in the official rest house. The policemen engaged ten carriers and we started in the morning at six o'clock. During the night there had been a violent storm with torrential rain, and the forest path was deep in a greasy mud, so slippery that the carriers, with heavy loads on their heads, had great difficulty in keeping to their feet. The forest was saturated, every leaf dripping like a leaky tap. At several points the path was blocked by great trees, torn from their roots by the storm, and it took hours of hard work to cut a way around them.

Towards midday, N'Denge, my gun-bearer, who knew this district better than I did and was acting as a guide, led us off onto a new path. I saw no reason why we should change our direction, so I stopped him and asked what was wrong with the other path.

"No go that way, Massa. There be bad bush."

This was inexplicable to me, so I left the safari and went back to see what "bad bush" looked like. No wonder N'Denge wanted to avoid it! There was an area of perhaps two or three acres where the forest was quite dead. The giant trees stood gaunt and leafless against the sky, their vast trunks blackened as though by fire. Creepers still clung to them, but they were dead and withered, too, and so was the thick undergrowth below. Nothing lived in this vast sepulchre; there were no birds, monkeys or insects, nor anything green and growing. It was a silent, eerie place. Superficially, at least, it looked as though the forest had been scorched to death. Yet how could this be in the rain forests of West Africa which are too wet for forest fires? When I got back I asked N'Denge for his opinion, and this was what he told me:

Many years ago, he said, when his great-great-grandfather was a suckling child, a great animal roamed this country, terrifying the people. It was like a giant lizard, with scales and a long, pointed tail. Out of its mouth came fire and smoke, and when it roared the forest was burned and blackened by its breath. After a time it went away, and this is one of several places where the forest still bears the scars of its anger!

Africans have a limited sense of time and when a man speaks of the days of his great-great-grandfather, he might mean anything from three to thirty generations ago. As for N'Denge's giant lizard, what could this be but our old friend the Dragon again, popping up in the heart of Africa?

Many scholars have tried to explain why such myths are universal. It has been suggested that the Dragon is our racial memory of the dinosaur, but when those huge reptiles flourished in the primeval swamps there were few mammals of any kind, and the world had many millions of years to wait before the earliest man made his first feeble appearance on the stage of life. Perhaps we are wrong about the disappearance of the dinosaurs; perhaps a few of them lingered on in the warm, damp forests of the tropics and were seen by early man. They did not breathe fire, of course, and in any case could not have been responsible for N'Denge's "bad bush."

I could not stop to make a thorough investigation, but I think that the death of the forest was due to a simple, natural cause. The ground there was very wet—not like the wetness caused by rain, but soggy, like a marsh. I believed that a stream had changed its course, waterlogging the land and forcing up salts from the subsoil in such quantity that the forest died.

A year after this I discovered the work of another dragon, hundreds of miles away on the Sanaga River, among a tribe who had no contact with N'Denge and his people. This time I was shown a rock, rising from the bed of the river. The rock was deeply and widely fissured, like a piece of cake with a slice cut out, quite unlike anything I had seen before. When I made inquiries, I was told that long ago a giant lizard had lived in the river. One day the rock had impeded its progress, and it had brought fire from its mouth to blast a way through.

Other tales of legendary animals that I heard from time to time in the Cameroons are worth recording. In the lakes of Tibati, in the Northern Territories, I was told of a water stallion, called Poutchou N'Dien. This was a horse that lived under the water. It was white, with black spots, and had red lips and a long flowing mane and tail. The nomadic Fulani tribes were said to tether their brood mares beside the water at night, to be served by the stallion. This curious tale has an identical counterpart in the *Thousand and One Nights,* where Es-Sindibad (Sinbad the Sailor) meets the grooms of King El-Mihraj, who "bring the swift mares, and tether them in this island, every mare that hath not foaled . . . that they may attract the sea horses."

In the N'Velle district of Yaounde I heard of another strange beast called the Zemendim, or water leopard, and in this case I spent a great deal of time looking for it.

Zemendims were said to be leopards that lived in small rivers and frequently took women and children. I was shown tracks in the mud at the edge of a stream. They did not look like leopard spoor to me, but the mud was thin and fluid and it was difficult to tell. I tried tracking the animal, but failed, so I decided to sit up for it, and had a platform built in a nearby tree.

I sat there night after night and saw and heard all sorts of creatures. Lemurs with glowing green eyes came and visited me in the branches, while below there were elephants, crocodiles, bush pigs, porcupines and once a civet cat. I also saw a leopard, but it was young and ordinary and went nowhere near the water, so I could not believe it was a Zemendim.

One morning, just as it was getting light, an animal swam rapidly upstream and landed on the opposite bank. The light was still poor and all I could see was something furry, spotted and four-legged. I fired. When the sun rose and my men turned up, we found the animal dead and washed ashore a few hundred yards downstream. It was a big dog-otter, a very old fellow whose fur had gone gray and blotchy, giving the appearance of spots. The natives would not admit that this was their Zemendim, and having no more time to spare I gave up and went home.

Owing to N'Denge's detour away from the dead forest and the repeated halts to hack our way past fallen trees, we did not reach our destination—the village of N'Vonde Manga—until well after dark, but we were received most hospitably and in a short time I was enjoying an excellent meal of groundnut soup and chicken. As was the custom, the chief asked me how many men I had, and then ordered the women to prepare a meal for them. Village food usually consists of cassava, groundnuts, sweet potatoes or plantains, spinach and fish or meat if it is available. Portions are placed on plantain leaves and laid in front of the traveler's tent, hut or rest house for his inspection before being handed to the carriers. On this occasion the policemen attended to the food, and I was able to have my dinner and a palaver with the chief without interruption.

The people here were of the N'Velle tribe, closely related to the Yaounde. There were only about twenty-five huts in all, and I noticed that they were all placed on one side of the village street, while on the other side were plantations—an unusual arrangement. When I asked the reason for this I was told that, with the huts on one side and the plantations on the other, a close watch could be kept against marauding gorillas and Red River pigs, of which there were many in the surrounding forest.

The villagers had little skill as hunters and lived mainly by agriculture. The chief, however, possessed a gun and a "shoot-man" who knew how to use it. In this he was favored by the Government. Chiefs who were lazy, corrupt and without control over their people were not permitted to have firearms, but those who kept their people well behaved and their plantations productive were allowed to purchase one 12- or 16-bore shotgun.

I had had a long and tiring day, so I slept without a break until seven next morning—very late for me. At that time I was awakened by the sound of two rifle shots, and, still dazed with sleep, rushed out of the hut to see what had happened. Men were running down to the other end of the village, shouting, "N'gi! N'gi!" Atanaga was lazily making my breakfast.

"What's happened, Atanaga?"

"Soldier done kill beef," he answered shortly.

I pulled on my shirt and trousers and went to have a look. Halfway down the little street I met one of my policemen.

"I kill you one big N'gi," he told me smiling. "*Il est très grand.*"

And "*très grand*" the gorilla was. In fact he was one of the finest specimens I ever saw. I found him lying at the edge of the plantation no more than twenty yards from a native hut, with two bullet holes in his chest. The policeman told me that he had got up early and had gone down to the plantation, where, he had been told, gorillas frequently appeared. Climbing to the top of an ant hill, he saw the gorilla only twenty-five yards away, standing upright and watching him. He fired twice and the animal fell dead.

I had never heard of such an easy kill. This was obviously

going to save me a great deal of trouble, for the gorilla was a young male in the prime of life—just what we needed for the exhibition—but I thought ruefully of the long and difficult hunts I had undertaken to get what the policeman had stumbled on by sheer luck. I was to become even more disgruntled during the three frustrating weeks I spent searching for the other gorillas to make up the required number.

Much to Atanaga's annoyance—for he had my breakfast ready—I began skinning the animal at once. Even with the help of my two trained "skinmen" this took three hours, and another three or four hours were spent thinning the skin. Then we set it up to dry slowly in the shade, a process taking two or three days. The popular idea that skins should be dried in direct sunlight is entirely wrong; many fine skins have been ruined by too-rapid drying and consequent shrinkage in the hot sun. One of my policemen cut the gorilla's flesh into strips. Most of it he dried and afterwards took back to Yaounde, but with great condescension he distributed a few pieces to the meat-hungry villagers.

One of the recipients of this bounty was a young lad who seemed to take more interest in hunting than his elders. Instead of eating it, he set up a trap and used it as bait. He told me that with this he hoped to catch duiker, of which there were several kinds in the forest.

Now the idea of an antelope eating meat sounds as crazy as a cow chewing beef, but it is a fact that these herbivorous animals often eat meat—and rotten meat at that—if they get a chance. Yellow-backed duiker, the biggest of the group, are particularly susceptible to this perverse taste, and I have even found them chewing bones. For this reason, natives often set duiker traps where game has been killed, and if they kill an elephant they leave a few bones about as bait.

There is another curious thing about duiker: in each groin is an opening, a sort of pocket of skin, which is of unknown function. I believe, however, that the whistling sound uttered by duiker when alarmed is made by expelling air from these openings.

Bay duiker and Red River pigs will also eat meat, but I have never known giant forest hogs to do so. In the London Zoo many species of antelope have been known to eat meat, sometimes rats and occasionally sparrows, which have been pinned to the ground by a quick movement of the hoof.

To find the next gorillas, I sent several N'Velle scouts into the jungle. One of them came back before dark with the news that he had located a suitable family, and I decided to try for them early next morning. I set my alarm clock to go off at three A.M. and told Atanaga to have some sandwiches and a thermos of hot coffee ready. It was pitch dark when the alarm woke me, with heavy storm clouds obscuring the moon, and very chilly.

N'Denge was already awake and we roused the guide, one of the policemen and my two skinmen. Carrying hurricane lamps, we left the village and plunged into the forest. For over an hour we stumbled along after the guide and then he decided he had lost his way, so there was nothing to do but sit down and wait for dawn.

At six o'clock we moved off again, and after a while the guide, with great delight, showed us eight gorilla beds and many *Aframomum* husks. The man was obviously inexperienced, for the beds were at least four days old, and the gorillas who made them could have been miles away by then.

N'Denge was disgusted. He at once volunteered to find gorillas himself, and refused to allow me to come with him. While he was gone, I sat on a tree trunk and suffered the attentions of clouds of sandflies and mosquitoes. Presently he returned, looking more cross than before. He could find no fresh trace of gorillas and was of the opinion that there weren't any for miles. I squashed what promised to be a lively quarrel between him and the guide, and we trudged back to camp.

Though there were no gorillas in that forest, the place was

alive with monkeys of all kinds: blue-faced, putty-nosed, Diana, Mona and mangabeys. I was sorely tempted to catch a few of the youngsters and take them home, for they were always in demand by the zoo collectors from Europe and America who seldom hunted for themselves but depended for their livestock on white or native hunters. Unfortunately I had no time for diversions of that kind; I had hardly begun my work for the Government. Moreover, I already had quite a collection of pets and looking after them took up enough of my time.

Back in camp, I had two fox terriers, a cat, a parrot, a white-collared mangabey called Red Top and a black and white hornbill called Horace. Most of these animals had been with me for years, and accompanied me wherever I went, even on safari. The cat, the parrot and the hornbill shared the same traveling box, perched on the head of a carrier, while the monkey sat on top. They were all allowed to run about loose in camp and they always shared the same plate of food in perfect harmony. How strange that such oddly assorted animals should become so fond of each other! Every zoo keeper will tell you stories of friendships that spring up between animals of different species, friendships so strong that the animals are heartbroken if they are parted.

The undisputed leader and mentor of my gang was Horace the hornbill, who was almost as well known in Yaounde as my horse Charley. He was a wise and wily old bird, very friendly towards people who were as respectful as he thought they should be, but the devil incarnate with people who were not. Even the monkey thought twice before pulling Horace's tail feathers, though now and then he could not resist the temptation. Loud squawks from Horace and shrieks from Red Top made it known that this had happened and that Red Top was being put in his place.

Horace flew with slow, dignified wing-flaps, his absurdly large beak turning inquiringly this way and that, and the sound he uttered was rather like the puffing of a locomotive. His long, sweeping eyelashes were the envy of every lady who met him. He loved to sit on the back of a chair and catch tidbits, which he did with marvelous dexterity. One day I threw him a nut, and to my surprise he tossed it from the tip of his beak into the back of his mouth and swallowed it without bothering to crack the shell. Birds have incredibly fast digestions and a few minutes later there was a tiny thud as the nut, still in the shell, left Horace's other end and dropped to the floor. This gave me an idea. I fashioned a piece of wood into the shape of a tiny egg and threw it across to him. The same thing happened, and Horace promptly laid a wooden egg. Horace and I played that trick hundreds of time afterwards, much to the astonishment of my friends, and I believe he enjoyed the joke as much as I did.

Red Top, the monkey, was called after a brand of champagne which was popular in those days, and after his magnificent head of reddish hair. He always slept on top of my mosquito net, which made a wonderful hammock for him. It is not generally known that monkeys, like geese, make excellent watchdogs, for they hear and comment on the slightest unusual sound. Red Top always warned me of the approach of any man or animal, even the servants he knew well. Sometimes, at my instigation, N'Denge or Atanaga would pretend to attack me, and then Red Top would fly at them, scratching and biting furiously until I called him off.

When I left the forest for the savannah lands in pursuit of other animals for my Government commission, I decided that Red Top might find it too hot on the plains and would suffer from the lack of shade. I handed him over to N'Denge with instructions that he should be taken two or three miles into the forest and released among his own people. N'Denge performed his part of the task faithfully, but Red Top followed him back and refused to be shooed away. We tried to lose him several times, but he always came back, so at last I took him with me. Luckily he did not seem to feel the heat as much as I had feared, and he not only survived the trip but lived with me for many years afterwards and at last died, much lamented, of old age.

Though I kept many pets in those days, this was nothing to the number I had after I married. Friends who visited our house in Dja Posten soon learned that it was wise to examine any chair they wished to sit on, for its cushions might well conceal some small escapee from the row of cages along the verandah. Most of the animals we had were orphans of one kind or another. Some of them we found ourselves after they had lost their parents; others were brought in by natives, who knew we would never turn away a helpless young creature. The animals must have known they were on to a good thing. Just you try taking in a stray cat, and in a day or two you will find two or three more begging for admittance. I believe they tell each other ("Try the Merfields, old chap, they're always good for a saucer of milk!")

Several animals, most of them young monkeys, came my way when I was with the N'Velle people, but I could not keep them, so I had them sent back to my house in Yaounde to be looked after until my return. Meanwhile, I had to find more gorillas, and N'Denge and I set off again into the forest. This time we stumbled on the worst patch of bush I had ever known. The trail was very narrow and on both sides there were trees with three-inch spikes that stuck out and tore at our clothes and flesh. Before we had gone far our hands were badly scratched. There seemed to be streams every few hundred yards, and we had to wade across, up to our waists in raging flood water. After an hour of this we were thoroughly fed up, but our tempers sweetened a bit when we found a shallow stream with a sandy bed, along which we were able to walk with comparative ease.

Half a mile upstream we heard a family of gorillas. There was a low growl, followed by the sound of several animals pushing away from us through the bush. We left the stream and found a system of gorilla tunnels where the smell of the male animals was strong. Soon we came to more open forest, and three or four hundred yards away we saw the bush being agitated by the movement of large animals. They were gorillas all right, and the tap-a-tap-tap of them slapping their bellies came to us clearly through the bush. Now and then we got a glimpse of their black hides as they ambled about under the trees, but there was no chance of a certain shot.

I decided to try an experiment, and told N'Denge to slap the ground with his open hand, just as I had seen gorillas doing. To my astonishment one of the gorillas—probably the Old Man—immediately came forward in answer to this sound, but he caught sight of us and wheeled round and went back before I could get a good look at him. I tried this ground-slapping trick many times afterwards on gorilla hunts, and it always worked. The animals seem to be deceived into thinking that the sound is made by other gorillas and come forward to investigate.

We waited for fifteen minutes, hoping that the gorilla's curiosity would get the better of him and that he would come back, but nothing happened. N'Denge tried slapping the ground again, and sure enough this brought him forward, though this time more cautiously. We could not see him, but we could follow his progress by watching the movement of the bush above his head.

In order to encourage him, I thought I would do a bit of slapping myself, but instead of hitting the ground, my hand touched something alive. Three movements then took place almost simultaneously: I withdrew my hand as though I had touched a live coal; the green mamba whose tail I had slapped whipped round and struck at me with his jaws gaping and glistening pink; and N'Denge, moving faster than either the snake or myself, brought down his machete with a great thump that almost chopped the deadly serpent in two.

That was the end of the day's hunt for us all. The gorillas heard the sound of N'Denge's machete and my own gasp of horror and surprise, and they made off as fast as they could. N'Denge decided it was time to go back to camp for a meal. All I could think of was my need for a rest and for a smoke; I had never been so close to certain and unexpected death.

Following this incident, I went out day after day, and though I always found gorillas, I could not get near them. It appeared that the village had once been much larger than it was at that time, for there were many abandoned plantations in the surrounding forests. Cultivation had been given up years before, and they were covered with low but dense secondary growth, which I found it impossible to penetrate without making a great deal of noise. The gorillas seemed extraordinarily shy, making off at the slightest sound, and I guessed that the village shootman had been using his gun freely and none too accurately. Though the African is expert with spears, bows and crossbows, he finds it difficult to learn how to sight a gun. That is why native trackers are usually given shotguns to carry, for these, with their spreading pellets, do not require accurate aiming when used at close range.

Time was getting short, so reluctantly I decided to give up tracking the gorillas and to drive them from their hiding place. After consulting N'Denge and the policemen, I called on the village chief and asked him to provide me with "plenty man" for this task. The idea of a gorilla drive was new to the chief, but he was overawed by the presence of the policemen, and the promise of a big "dash" for his cooperation presently decided him to give it a trial.

The plantation I had chosen lay just below a range of low hills and was bounded on the east by a wide stream. This could be left unguarded, since gorillas will never cross water. On the north and west sides I intended to put my beaters, while on the south we could clear a ten-foot strip of jungle, where N'Denge and I would be waiting for anything that came out.

At four o'clock on the appointed morning I led the entire village out into the forest—men, women and every child large enough to be capable of making a loud noise on demand. The forest was pitch dark, so the villagers kept chattering and singing to keep up their spirits, but there was no fear that they would frighten away the gorillas prematurely, for gorillas never move about before dawn. It took me a long time to get the excited crowd ranged in their appointed positions, and to get them to understand that when they heard my whistle they were to make as much noise as possible by shouting, beating drums and rattling tin cans.

Other men soon had the strip cleared on the south side, and were then sent back to join the noisemakers. Dawn was just breaking when our preparations were complete. I blew my whistle, and at once, from across the plantation, came a noise that would have brought down the walls of Jericho in half the time it took Joshua and the Israelites. The women shouted, the children shrieked, the men howled and beat their cans and drums. They were not able to move forward into the plantation because the bush was too dense, but I was banking on the row to make the gorillas decide to leave—and the only way they could go was past N'Denge and myself.

N'Denge stood ten yards away from me on my left, armed with my 12-bore shotgun, while I had my Mauser loaded and the safety catch off, ready for anything that came out. For a long time nothing happened. I began to think I had failed again, and that the gorillas had left the plantation on the previous day. After an hour, the villagers began to lose enthusiasm and their voices grew so hoarse that I feared the noise would die away altogether. I heard my policemen yelling encouragement and threats. This had the desired effect, and the noise grew louder again.

I fully expected the gorillas to show their uneasiness by

screaming and beating their bellies, but the first sign that they were there at all came as a most unpleasant surprise. N'Denge was holding his gun loosely, pointing downwards, and was looking towards me, when a big male gorilla suddenly crashed out of the bush and swept him aside with a terrible blow full in the face.

N'Denge was knocked flat on his back with blood streaming from his mouth and nose. It happened without warning and so quickly that I had no time to shoot and save N'Denge from the attack, but I got the gorilla with a clean shot through the side of the head as he tried to push through the bush on the other side of the clearing. N'Denge was sitting on the ground, nursing his face and groaning quietly, but even then his only thought was for me.

"Massa, look out; udder one go come out."

In fact, a veritable procession of gorillas followed the Old Man. I shot a full-grown female and then a youngster two or three years old. The others—three young males and six or seven females, some with babies—I let go, for I had already exceeded my quota.

N'Denge was badly shaken, but though he had lost two front teeth and his face was badly bruised and swollen, no bones had been broken or serious damage caused. He made very little fuss about the injury—in fact, I think he was rather proud of himself—and in a day or two he was as cheerful and effiicent as ever. By the time we got back to Yaounde he had learned a trick of spitting out of the hole between his front teeth that was to stay with him for the rest of his life.

6. The Ghost of the Sanaga Grasslands

The Sanaga grasslands may be haunted, as the Yaounde people say, but at least I can claim to have laid one of its phantoms. And I never killed more gladly nor with so great a feeling of pity.

Now that I had gorillas for the Paris exhibition, the next task was to get leopard, buffalo, waterbuck and other antelope, and I decided to take a trip into the savannah country north of the Sanaga River, where these animals were plentiful.

I wasn't at all sure that my carriers would be keen on this trip, for although they were good men, the best I had ever had, they were forest dwellers who were unfamiliar with the grasslands, where they would miss the protection of the trees. They would be ill at ease among the ten-foot elephant grass, which blankets and distorts sound as fog or a snowstorm does, and they feared, too, the floating, downy seedcases of the elephant grass, each carrying a tiny, wicked hook which scratches and poisons the flesh. Moreover, I had heard them telling tales about the Baboutu tribe, who lived on the grasslands, and who, they said, had a predilection for putting ju-jus on unwelcome visitors.

Some ill feeling between the Yaounde people and the Baboutus was understandable, for the Baboutus were of different stock and customs. It seems that many years earlier the Baboutous lived far away to the north, and were driven south by Arab, Haussa and Fulani slavers. Eventually they took refuge south of the Sanaga River, which the mounted slavers could not easily cross to reach them. They still wear long, flowing robes and retain many customs peculiar to North Africa.

In spite of these considerations, my boys were delighted to hear of the proposed trip and begged to come with me. The attraction of the unlimited supply of meat my gun would bring them was, for the moment at least, irresistible. Game was scarce and difficult to hunt in the forest, and consequently they rarely had meat.

Off we went to the town of Yaounde to pick up sugar, salt, tobacco, ammunition and other supplies I would need. There the trouble began. Some of the local boys, jealous of my carriers and hoping to get the jobs themselves, began playing on their fear of the Baboutu people and of the grasslands, in an attempt to scare them off. N'Denge came to me complaining that the carriers had lost their earlier enthusiasm for the trip and were now reluctant to go.

I reminded him of the meat they would get—some to eat and a lot left over to sell—and asked him whether men of their caliber were to be frightened out of their wits by the idle chatter of foolish townsfolk. This did the trick. When we started out a few days later, my boys, though grown as timid as maiden ladies, were all with me.

After three days' march we got to the village of Nartindati, which lies on the main road between Yaounde and N'anga Eboko, some two miles from the banks of the Sanaga. The dry season was well advanced, and when we reached the river we found that the water was low so that we were able to cross easily, taking advantage of projecting rocks and small sandy islands. From these, great crocodiles slithered noiselessly off into the water, disturbed by our approach. The carriers were dismayed to see them, for they were considerably larger than the crocodiles they were accustomed to in the smaller rivers of the forest.

On the northern bank of the river was a wide belt of elephant grass, which we would either have to skirt or pass through before reaching the open grasslands. I had no idea how far along the river it extended, and so decided to push straight through it. The going was as tough as it could be. There was a narrow track, winding tortuously through, but it was only wide enough for a single file and here and there great clumps of the grass, grown brittle and top-heavy through lack of rain, had fallen across, blocking our way and costing us much in temper and energy as we broke through. It was so bad that after a while I decided to turn back to the river and find a way around the grass.

For the most part, the river banks were free of scrub and grass, easy going for my carriers. To them, however, it was soon a case of out of the frying pan into the fire. From around the bend of the river came a roaring and bellowing as though all hell had been let loose. The noise stopped suddenly just before we reached the scene, but a small sandy beach on the opposite bank was much trampled and soaked with blood, while the water near the shore boiled and seethed as though Satan himself were about to emerge. I guessed at once that under the water a hippo fight was going on.

Hippopotami are normally placid, peaceful vegetarians, but terrible fights sometimes take place between bulls for the possession of females or for the leadership of the school, fights that often go on for hours before the contest is decided.

Suddenly, and with another outburst of noise, the hippos made a dramatic appearance. They reared out of the water, their great jaws locked together, the tusks embedded deeply in each other's hide. Heads and shoulders of both animals were scarred with long, deep gashes, streaming with blood. Locked together in this way they wrestled in the shallows, shaking their heads like dogs in their efforts to throw each other down.

At intervals they broke away, backed a little and stood panting and gasping. Their roars shook the air and sent my boys, who had seen nothing like this before, into renewed shivers of terror.

After a time it became clear that one of the animals was tiring. During the wrestling bouts he seemed more and more concerned with preventing himself from being thrown than with throwing the other, and this defensive attitude became more marked every minute. Then at last he turned and ran. The other was after him like a flash, and we saw how fast and agile these bulky, clumsy-looking beasts can really be. The loser found himself cornered against the steep bank on one side of the little beach, knew that he had lost, and with a despairing effort flung himself past the other and plunged into the river. The victor came to the water's edge and began to drink, slowly and painfully, but with the knowledge of victory to support him.

I had settled myself on a boulder near the water's edge, captivated by this leviathan struggle. My boys squatted some way off, hoping, I suppose, that I would soon have done with this dangerous business and take them off to safety. Hidden entirely from view was Atanaga, my good and faithful cook.

Faithful? Well, yes, except when there was any danger about. While on the march he always stuck as close to me as he could, and in an emergency he could find the deepest hole, the biggest boulder or the highest tree quicker than any other man I knew. But the instant danger was past he would be in the forefront again, cursing the boys for their cowardice and explaining loudly how his own fortitude and presence of mind had averted disaster. The man had a genius for improvising pure fiction on the spur of the moment. He also had a genius for cooking and could be trusted to carry a loaded shotgun behind me without blowing off the back of my head.

I was about to get up, thinking that the hippo incident was over, when suddenly N'Denge yelled, "Look out, Massa!" and from the water almost at my feet, with bloody foam and water running from its gaping jaws, rose the vanquished hippo, which had swum across deep below the surface to our side of the river in search of peace and safety.

I reached for my gun, but almost before I touched it I saw that there was no danger. The poor beast, dazed and weak with the loss of blood, staggered past within a yard of me, oblivious of my presence. A weak and wounded hippo will keep away from water, for in that condition he may be attacked by crocodiles, though the two creatures normally share the same pools in reasonable harmony. The animal certainly meant no harm, and was concerned only with its search for a place to recover or to die, depending on the severity of its wounds, but my boys, seeing this drooling, gory monster stagger towards them with jaws agape, expected to be swallowed whole and ran for their lives, scattering their loads. The hippo crashed off through the grass, taking no notice of them whatsoever, and after a few moments of silence Atanaga popped up from behind a sturdy shrub and began to yell at the departed carriers.

We gathered the boys and the scattered equipment together again and I tried to explain that the hippo had had no intention of attacking them.

N'Denge spat sorrowfully through the gap in his front teeth. "Dis no be we country, sah. We no savvy kis kin' beef."

I knew the boys were thinking of ju-jus already, and probably had been since we saw the big crocodiles. We had not gone far, yet we had already encountered crocodiles that were abnormally large and hippos that were clearly hostile. What doubt could there be that the Baboutu people and their ju-jus were responsible for all this? And what further horrors lay in wait for us? The boys consulted together for a few minutes in low voices and then N'Denge stepped forward again.

"All man say better go back for grass," he announced.

The prospect of pushing through that elephant grass again did not appeal to me, but I thought it wiser to concede the point just then.

"Other time I go shoot beef," I told them bitterly over my shoulder as I led the way back into the grass, "I take woman for carry my cargo."

We pressed on again with the sun scorching our backs. Occasionally a kob, alarmed by our progress, went crashing away to the right or left, and then these disturbances too ceased and there was silence save for the incessant chirping of cicadas. Far too much silence, I thought, after a while, for the boys had stopped their usual chatter and I noticed that they were traveling much faster than before and were bunched closely together. I asked N'Denge what the trouble was.

He dropped his eyes and muttered that there was nothing the matter, nothing at all. I began to get cross, but no jibes of mine could stir their courage, and I was certain that something strange was troubling them for I had never seen them like this before. When we reached a small stream I called a halt, for carriers usually welcome a wash and a drink while on the march. This time they just dropped their loads and huddled on the ground beside them. There was none of their usual gossip; no one started to smoke.

To cheer them up I took out one of the heads of American tobacco I always carried for use as gifts or currency in the bush and tossed it over to them. They let it fall to the ground and made no attempt to pick it up. Neither N'Denge nor Atanaga would tell me what was wrong or even meet my eyes. They just sat about, miserable, twiddling their toes in the dust. I grew more and more angry and finally seized N'Denge by the shoulders and shook him. Only then did he mutter, "Massa, somet'ing follow we."

I told him again, in short simple terms, what I thought of him and his perishing ju-jus, but he insisted that for the last half an hour something had been following us through the grass and that it was, in all probability, a ju-ju of the Baboutu people, who, as every one knew, could turn themselves into animals at will.

I got the carriers on their feet again and hurried them off, saying that if there was something following us the wisest plan would be to get on as fast as we could. Hardly had we started, however, than N'Denge came to me and whispered, "Massa, you no hear somet'ing now?"

I listened intently, but no sound reached my ears save the rasping cicadas and the slight wind rustling the tall, dry grass. Nevertheless I began to get uneasy myself, for N'Denge's ears were twice as sharp as mine, and I could not believe his imagination would play tricks on him to that extent.

Wearily we walked on, for perhaps another mile, with no sign that we were nearing the end of the elephant grass. Then, quite suddenly, I caught a sound from behind us. N'Denge spotted the look on my face, knew what it meant and nodded gravely, without saying a word. Not far behind us came the sound of the footsteps of some creature moving steadily through the grass. What alarmed me was that in all the years I had hunted in Africa I had never heard anything like it before. I ran through the names of every large animal I knew to exist in the Cameroons, but this was not the sound any of them would have made. There was something decidedly unpleasant about those slow, muffled footsteps, and, as N'Denge had said, they were indeed horribly ghostlike.

A little shiver ran down my spine. The boys were terror-stricken and crowded around me, almost knocking the loads from one another's heads in their fright. Atanaga dropped his hat which he had bought only a few days before, and did not even trouble to pick it up. I took the shotgun he carried and unloaded it. This was an affront to him of course, but in his present state of agitation he was no longer safe with a loaded gun. There was nothing much else I could do immediately except to go on, and after checking to see that my rifle was in order, I led the way again.

The noise became clearer as we pushed along the winding trail. I could see now why the boys had become so frightened, for what made it really uncanny was that sometimes it seemed to come from behind us, sometimes from in front and sometimes from either side.

This, N'Denge told me, had been going on from the first. It was not until afterwards that I understood how it had come about, and cursed myself for my stupidity.

Not far ahead of us, and to the right where the footsteps could now be heard, I noticed a small hillock standing out above the grass. Our ghost, or whatever it was, appeared to be moving toward this, and I decided that the open sides of the little hill would make a suitable arena in which to face whatever danger there might be. Leaving the boys where they were, I took N'Denge, who carried my spare rifle, and hurried off as fast as I could, circling through the grass towards the hill, in an attempt to head the thing off. When we arrived, N'Denge climbed a small tree, while I faced the direction of the sound and loosed the safety catch of my rifle.

The footsteps were certainly getting nearer, though their progress seemed agonizingly slow. I stood below N'Denge, while his trembling foot rested on my shoulder to nudge me if he should see anything. I gripped my rifle more fiercely than there was any need and the sweat trickled down into the corners of my mouth. N'Denge prodded me with his toe and when I glanced up he touched his eye and pointed towards the grass.

"Grass he move," he whispered.

Still those dreadful footsteps drew nearer, slowly and ponderously through the whispering grass. And then, when I had begun to think I could stand it no longer, the tall stems before me parted, and I stood face to face with the ghost of the Sanaga grasslands. For a moment or two I stared at it in horror, and then, raising my rifle, I brought it crashing to the ground with a single shot.

The ghost that had haunted us for the best part of that afternoon was an elephant, but such an elephant as I had never seen before and never want to see again. The bulging, elephantine belly had become an empty, withered, wrinkled bag, hanging like a dewlap from the spine. Every bone of the massive frame stood out clearly under the hide; the ribs were like deep, rolling corrugations along the sides. The head drooped and the trunk dragged uselessly on the ground between the forefeet. The neck, shoulders and flanks were a suppurating mass of stinking sores, covered with black sheets of flies and alive with filthy, wriggling maggots, eating into what little was left of the living flesh. One of the tusks had fallen from its rotten socket and where the eyes had been was only pus.

This poor, suffering creature, I realized now, had been slowly wandering through the grass, waiting for death to end its misery. It had been pushing along in a straight line, oblivious to everything around it, and must have crossed and recrossed our track a score of times, which was why the sound had kept changing direction so mysteriously.

I tied a handkerchief over my mouth and nostrils and went forward to examine the carcass. With the point of a long knife I pried from the sores on the neck and behind the ears bits of lead and iron pots, such as natives use. The animal had been shot—about two weeks earlier, I judged—at close range, with a muzzle-loading gun charged with these scraps of metal, a common practice among the tribes. The wounds were superficial, but they had become infected and the flies had done the rest.

Atanaga now came running up at the head of the boys, waving the shotgun joyfully. He took a good look at the dead elephant.

"I no been tell you he be only beef?" he asked them all triumphantly.

The solitary tusk of the elephant stuck up grotesquely from the fallen body—fifty pounds of valuable ivory. I saw no reason why this should be left for the Baboutu people who must have been responsible for shooting the poor beast and causing it so much suffering. We carried it off. An hour later we stood in the open savannah, with the elephant grass behind us.

7.   The Woman Chieftain of Cheke

None of the men had visited savannah land before, and its effect upon them was remarkable. Never had they been able to see so far, and they kept pointing and straining their eyes in their efforts to distinguish objects many miles away. They were pleased and excited, like children on their first visit to the seaside, and their good humor was an agreeable contrast to the gloom that had hung over us since we left Yaounde. The ju-ju of the grasslands had been quite forgotten.

We found a small but beautifully clean stream, where I decided to camp. My tent was erected in a twinkling, and for themselves the men built tiny shelters of grass and saplings. While Atanaga cooked my dinner—it was corned beef stew —the carriers bathed in the stream, playing and splashing each other with the abandon of schoolboys. Then they cooked their own meal of rice and stockfish, which is dried, imported cod, a nourishing, popular and most convenient food for carriers.

After four days of hard marching, I thought a day or two at rest would do us no harm, and the camp did not stir next morning until gone eight, when the sun had already half-completed its welcomed task of banishing the cold and mists. By ten, it was hotter than we ever knew it in the shady forest.

Taking N'Denge and one of the carriers, a man called Esomba, I went for a scout around. N'Denge found a good deal to puzzle him: there were the tracks of lions, an animal he had never seen, and of herds of kob and buffalo. Over the latter he spent many minutes, shaking his head and muttering with astonishment. In the forest, antelopes seldom occur in groups of more than two or three, and to N'Denge it was little short of miraculous to find herds consisting of twenty or thirty. His only worry was that we should get lost, for he missed the narrow game trails of the forest and could not understand how anyone could find a way through this vast, featureless plain. He recommended that we should employ a local guide, and I agreed with him, though in view of the men's attitude to the Baboutu people I doubted that they would get on together.

The problem had already been solved when we returned to camp, having bagged half a dozen plump young partridges on the way. My carriers were gathered round two Baboutu spearmen, talking to them happily and plying them with food. Atanaga said that the men came from a village a few miles away and wanted us to go and stay there with them while we hunted. I could not speak Baboutu, but one of the carriers knew a little and when I asked how far away their village was he answered:

"Three waters." This meant that three streams or rivers had to be crossed before one reached the village.

Lest the reader laugh at such a primitive way of reckoning distance, let him consider how much more valuable it is than mere mileage in a land where a ten-mile journey might take hours, days or weeks, according to the nature of the terrain.

The relationship between my carriers and the Baboutu could not have been better; in some queer way the ju-ju incident had quite purged them of their fears and prejudices. I told the strangers, through the interpreter, that we would come to their village next day and I was assured that their chieftain would welcome me. For chieftain they used the words *Ku-kuma Mininga*, which surprised and intrigued me, for *Ku-kuma* means "chief" and *Mininga* means "a woman," a curious phenomenon where women are kept in gross subjection. I had heard of *Kukuma Miningas*, but they were very rare and I had not met one before.

Finding and crossing the "three waters" took about four hours, but presented no great difficulty. The village was small —about fifty huts placed neatly and symmetrically in two lines—but it was clean and well-kept, a tribute to the stern but warmhearted *Kukuma* who now came forward to greet me.

She was an elderly lady wearing a bright "mother hubbard" and a green silk headscarf. To my surprise, she welcomed me in excellent German and invited me inside. Native huts are often dirty and seldom contain any sort of furniture. Hers was spotlessly clean, with a mat of Haussa origin on the hard mud floor, a table spread with a large, colored cloth, and two comfortable armchairs. On the walls were pages cut from European magazines and faded photographs of native German troops and of German officers in uniform. A simple hole in the wall acted as a window, and there were doors leading to two smaller rooms at the back. The *Kukuma* made me a cup of coffee, chattering away cheerfully all the time, and presently I heard her story.

"In the days when my breasts were no bigger than hen's eggs," she told me in German, "my father, who was the chief of this village, took me to Yaounde with him to carry his food. In Yaounde we met another Baboutu man who was the servant of a German officer. The German was looking for a native mistress—'some fine small girl'—and was prepared to pay a good price for one who was really comely. My father decided that I should be offered to him at once, and I was taken along to be looked at. The German liked me and saw that I was nice and clean, so he gave my father money, salt and tobacco and made me his mistress.

"He named me Anna and that is what I am still called. He was very kind to me and I stayed with him for several years and bore him two children. I was sorry when the war came and he had to run away. My father put the children in a mission school and I don't know where they are now.

"When my father died I came back here and made the people keep the village clean and tidy. Thus I became the *Kukuma* and now I look after the seventy people who live here. They are happy and we always pay our taxes regularly."

I liked Anna. She ran her village efficiently but kindly, and was most hospitable to me. She told me that the surrounding country was rich in game and was seldom hunted, so it appeared that I need go no further for the animals I needed. In the morning I went off with N'Denge and stalked a herd of kob, a dark, rufous-colored antelope, about three feet high, with gracefully curved horns. "Stalking" was hardly the word, for these animals showed little fear, and when I brought down a buck, the others ran off only a few yards and then stopped and stared first at me and then at the fallen buck in blank astonishment, not understanding what had happened.

One writer on the West African forests has said that "the semi-darkness of the dense forest defeats the white man's skill, and only natives can hunt in it." I had done no savannah hunting for years, and the contrast between this and the forest was so striking that at first I felt bewildered. At the same time I had to make the most of this good fortune, and before the day ended I had added bushbuck, wart hog and reedbuck to my list.

Soon after I fell asleep that night I was awakened by the shouting of men and the terrified bleating of goats. N'Denge came in to tell me that a tiger (he meant a leopard) had broken into the goat enclosure and seized a kid, but the goats had raised such a hullabaloo and the villagers were so promptly on the scene that it had dropped its prey and made off. The little goat was terribly mauled but still alive, so I killed it at once. The leopard spoor I examined next morning showed that the animal was a big male. I wanted leopards, and since this one had been troubling the villagers for some time, the opportunity was ideal.

Building a suitable platform was difficult. The only trees in the savannah are short and stunted, giving the land the alternative name of "orchard" country. On the other side of the village, however, was a wild date palm, the tallest tree I could find, so I had it chopped down and used the stem as the main support for my platform. Branches from smaller trees, piled with leaves and finally covered with my tent canvas, completed this rickety structure, which stood only six feet high, a very modest jump for a leopard.

For bait I chose a dog, since, as N'Denge said, "Tigers like dog too much." A morose-looking young pup was purchased from Anna, tethered below my platform and provided with food and water for the night. No sooner had darkness fallen than the wretched creature set up a dismal wailing, which was maintained, without interruption from the leopard or from any other quarter, until next morning. I was frozen stiff during the long, sleepless watch, and the dog's howling gave me a splitting headache which lasted for hours.

Anna suggested that, in view of the leopard's taste for goats, a kid might be more suitable than a dog, and when I took up my watch on the platform the following evening a half-grown kid had taken the place of the puppy below me. From the start, the kid behaved in a most curious fashion, shaking its head repeatedly as though trying to rid itself of some irritation, and bleating piteously all the time. I could not remember a more vocal goat, but this was exactly the kind of advertisement I needed to attract the leopard, and I thought no more about it until next day.

Nothing happened until nearly one o'clock, when my legs were beginning to lose all sense of feeling. Suddenly the kid stopped bleating and turned about, facing up-wind. With my finger on the button of a powerful torch which I had strapped to the barrel of the rifle, I turned my head slightly and looked in the same direction. At first I could see nothing but blurred shadows and patches of moonlight, but then my attention was held by one particular shadow. Superficially it looked like all the others—just a vague, ill-defined patch of darkness—yet there was something about it that struck me as suspicious. It moved, but there was nothing alarming in that, for all the shapes and shadows of the night appear to be in a constant and sinister state of flux. Then the kid jerked backwards, straining at its tether, and began bleating again, much louder than before. Now the shadow seemed to have gone, but another had appeared ten yards nearer the kid, and on this I shone my torch.

It was the leopard all right, and as the light struck his lovely rosetted coat, he spun round, staring straight at the beam. His eyes were glowing with a fire of their own, and his forelegs were splayed out ready for a spring, but before he could make another move a heavy, soft-nosed bullet struck him deep in the throat, and he rolled over and lay still.

N'Denge, followed by a crowd of villagers, arrived within a few seconds and helped me down. From a distance of perhaps twenty yards we began throwing pebbles at the leopard. Several of them struck him, but he did not move, and I approached cautiously, holding my rifle ready. The leopard gave no sign of life until I prodded him in the tummy with the tip of the barrel. Then he lashed out with his right paw, narrowly missing my leg as I jumped back, firing at the same time. The second bullet took him full in the chest and killed him at once.

I suppose more hunters have been killed by animals they wrongly presume were dead than by any other means. I remember a French postmaster who lived at Garoua and once went shooting rhino. He brought down a fine bull rhino, sat beside the carcass quenching his thirst from a bottle of *vin rouge*, and then climbed on top of it, rifle in hand, to have his photograph taken. An instant after the camera clicked, old man rhino suddenly got to his feet, throwing the postmaster in a graceless heap on the ground, and ambled away without so much as a glance at his would-be executioner. Later in the day the rhino was shot again, properly this time, by another hunter, and an examination showed that it had been only stunned by the postmaster's bullet, which had clipped a chunk of bone from its thick skull.

A similar incident—though on a smaller scale—happened to me while I was hunting hyraxes, those funny little animals, about the size of rabbits, which are the "coneys" of the Bible. Hyraxes are of great zoological interest, for, although they are small, they are the nearest relatives of the elephant. I shot one of them and put it in my haversack, along with a few partridges. A little later I felt something wriggling inside the bag, and I foolishly put in my hand to see what it was. The hyrax, which presumably had been only stunned, gave me a severe bite on the finger, and when I dropped the bag in pain, it popped out and disappeared in the grass.

It occurred to me, as I walked back to bed after killing the leopard, that the long-suffering goat was still bleating for all it was worth, and I remarked on this to N'Denge.

N'Denge giggled. "Massa, man put small stone inside ear for make him holler all night," he told me.

I discovered that this was an old dodge of village hunters. A tiny pebble, pushed far into a goat's ear, causes sufficient irritation to make it bleast continuously. I went back and got N'Denge to hold the kid down while I tried to get the stone out again, but it had gone in too far, and there was nothing I could do but have the animal slaughtered to save it from further suffering.

In the morning we skinned the leopard, which was a fine male, about four years old and in prime condition. I gave N'Denge strict instructions to guard the skin while it was drying, and when this long process had been completed, I put it in a padlocked box to preserve the whiskers from the villagers, who were already eyeing them nervously.

I wonder how many leopard skins in museums and private collections have false whiskers. Like giraffe tails, which are used as fly-whisks, and rhino horn, which fetches a fantastic price from senile Orientals with young wives, leopard whiskers are highly prized by Africans. No leopard skin sold by a native has its whiskers intact, and if you keep a leopard skin in a house where there are native servants, the whiskers will mysteriously disappear. This is because the long stiff hairs of the leopard's moustache are believed to be a potent poison. It is said that they are unnoticeable when chopped up and mixed with food, and that by piercing the intestines they cause agonizing death. Few Africans are potential murderers, but they all think of themselves as potential victims, and consequently they cut off and burn any leopard whiskers they find, lest they be used by an enemy. I have seen houseboys shake with terror at the sight of a leopard skin with the whiskers intact. Leopard claws are also valuable, but they are used as charms and not for evil purposes.

There are many other ways of poisoning. Some of them involve magic—to the African there is no clear division between the natural and the supernatural—and others are more practical and extremely cunning. Powdered glass—called "tear belly" in Pidgin—is popularly regarded as an efficient poison. A tiny, poisoned thorn planted in the hard earth outside the doorway of a victim's hut is also supposed to be effective. There is always a foot-high strip of wood or bark across the lower part of the doorway, so that its occupant treads more heavily than usual when he comes out. This forces the thorn into the foot, but the skin is too thick and insensitive for it to be noticed. Gradually it works its way in, carrying the poison with it. I believe that this system is often used and sometimes works, though it is obviously indiscriminate and likely to kill the wrong person.

Murder is not always done out of personal animosity; it may involve one or another of the numerous secret societies that exist everywhere in West Africa. Some of these societies are harmless, with widely varying functions and many degrees of secrecy. They may be concerned only with initiation into manhood or womanhood, involving the circumcision of boys and excision of the clitoris in women, though, as far as I know, the latter practice is not followed in the French Cameroons. The vast majority are mutual benefit clubs of a useful character, but there are a few whose functions seem to be wholly malignant. Of these, the most troublesome, notorious and puzzling is the Leopard Society, which at various times has caused great anxiety to more than one Government in West Africa.

When I first came to the Cameroons I worked on a plantation called Bai Farm, in what is now the British Cameroons. Our native laborers were terrified to go out after dark because the leopard men were about. One of my duties was to visit the cocoa-drying fires at intervals during the night, to ensure that they were burning well. I used to take a boy with me on this patrol, but had to leave him behind eventually because he became literally sick and later very ill with fear of the leopard men.

I talked this over with a German colleague and we determined to get to the bottom of the business. Armed with shotguns, we lay in wait night after night, while the fear of the laborers neared the point of panic and our own tempers began to fray. So that when we saw what looked like a leopard moving among the trees we both fired at it, and were rewarded with a terrible, but human, scream. We shone a lamp into the leopard man's face just as he died, and found that he was one of our own laborers. Tied about his head and shoulders was a leopard skin; on each finger he wore a long, curved claw, made of iron sharpened to a fine point and attached to his fingers by tight iron rings. His chest and abdomen had been painted with white spots to complete the illusion.

A few years later leopard men caused panic among the native people of Kribi, on the coast. A woman was pulled from her hut one night and mauled to death. Her heart was cut out and carried off. Two days later another woman died in the same way, and again the heart was missing. The Government set up a patrol, but a few nights later a third woman fell victim to the leopard men and once more the heart was cut out. In each case the claw marks looked as though they had been inflicted by a leopard, but no leopard would have made off with only the heart.

The murders took place around Christmas time and they stopped as suddenly as they had begun. No explanation was ever forthcoming, no culprit ever brought to book.

I have known a great many Leopard Society murders. They all took place around Christmas time; the victims were always women, and their hearts were always excised. I suppose the hearts are used for some ritual which takes place only at that time of year. Perhaps this has some faint link with the druidical rites that took place at Stonehenge and other temples at the winter solstice. Whatever the truth, no one has lifted so much as a corner of the veil that shrouds this dreadful organization in secrecy.

There were two occasions when I thought I was going to learn something about the Leopard Society. When I was hunting elephant in the Akoafim mountain region, I saw a most curious dance performed by a man wearing a leopard skin. I think he might have belonged to the Society, for the villagers regarded him with great fear and awe. I arrived, unheralded, after the dance had started and left before it ended, and I do not think he knew I was there. His dance was unlike anything else I have ever seen. He writhed and jerked his body in a fantastic way which it is impossible to describe, and he stamped his feet and made great leaps into the air. Several young girls stood watching, and he seized them each in turn, embracing them closely and continuing his dance with the girl lying limp and apparently helpless in his arms. Then he threw her down, and for a long time she lay still, as though in a trance.

The villagers told me that the dancer was a hermit who lived in a cave far up the mountain, but when I returned to the village next day and asked more questions, they shook their heads and denied any further knowledge of him or his activities. I spent a long time trying to discover the significance of the dance, but with no success.

The second occasion was equally frustrating. I was staying with Adjutant Marcelin, the District Officer of Akoafim, where there had recently been several Leopard Society murders. The Adjutant's Senegalese policemen caught a man in possession of a leopard skin, which he could not account for, and though this was pretty slender evidence, he was brought to trial in the hope that something concrete would emerge. Marcelin knew of my interest in the Society and thought I might be able to help, so he asked me to attend the trial. The prisoner, however, refused to say a word, and none of the witnesses, including the woman who was supposed to be his mother, would admit ever having seen him before. Marcelin and I tried every trick we knew to overcome their fear and stubbornness, but for once neither of us could get the natives to talk. The man was acquitted through lack of evidence, but the silence of the witnesses confirmed our belief that he belonged to the Society.

I took a great deal of care preserving my leopard skin, for it was one of the finest I had seen. When it was finished a few days later, I went in search of buffalo with N'Denge and a Baboutu who could speak Pidgin. We walked for miles in the early morning through grass heavy with dew, until I was soaked to the knees. Then we crossed a stream, climbed a short incline on the other side, and came upon country that recently had been burned. The savannah tribes periodically set fire to the grass to drive game into their lines of waiting spearmen. The surviving game benefits from licking up the ash and feeding on the fresh green grass that soon comes sprouting through. While the fires are burning, scores of black kites sweep about through the smoke, taking a heavy toll of smaller animals, such as rodents and lizards.

On the far side of the burned country was a shallow valley, and in it a swamp surrounded by elephant grass, in which our guide believed we would find buffalo. We walked across the charred ground towards the valley, and after a few yards my soaking boots and trousers were black with ash.

There were no buffalo to be seen, but by separating and casting around we came upon the tracks of a herd numbering about a dozen. I climbed a small tree and studied the vegetation of the swamp through my binoculars, trying to locate the animals, but soon my attention was arrested by a curious movement in the short savannah grass at a spot about thirty yards from the tree. With the glasses I could see individual blades of grass toppling and then falling from sight. I called to the Baboutu man in a whisper and asked him what he thought it might be.

"Cutgrass, Massa," he replied.

And since that was all the information I could get from him, I decided to find out for myself. I took my .22 rifle from N'Denge and told him to drive the hidden animals towards me when I had taken up a position on the far side of a patch of bare ground which stood down-wind of them. I got there with as little noise as possible, and at my signal N'Denge came walking through the grass towards me, shooing the still invisible animals in my direction. Two of them broke cover barely twenty yards from me. They were large ratlike animals, which I had never seen before, but which I identified as giant cane rats. They moved so fast and were out of sight again so quickly that I could not get a shot, but later I trapped several of them alive and sold them to a collector.

Giant cane rats are not rats at all, and the Pidgin name "cutgrass" suits them better, for they live on grass and roots. They are, in fact, relatives of the porcupines and are covered with spiny, dark brown bristles. From the nose to the tip of the tail they measure about twenty-seven inches, of which a third is tail. The natives have a taste for their flesh and frequently hunt them.

It was just as well that I had not fired, for a few minutes later the buffalo came drifting out of the elephant grass like great black shadows. These were comparatively small West African buffalo, not the big Northern variety, but leading them was a truly magnificent jet black bull. The cows were much lighter in color and there were three calves of a distinctly reddish hue. They came out of the grass ahead of us, but there was no cover in between and a direct approach was impossible, so I made my way around to the right, following a slight ridge, and appeared again on their flank.

They must have got wind of me as I was moving, for when I looked again they had turned and were still facing me, the bull tossing his head and trying the air suspiciously. Between me and the herd there was a thin belt of trees and I was well out of sight. Taking advantage of every scrap of cover, I worked my way to the far edge of the trees. Beyond them was an enormous ant hill, and I slithered along flat on the ground until I reached it. Then I stood up and cautiously peered around, but the herd had vanished. N'Denge and the Baboutu came up and said that the animals had gone back into the elephant grass while I was moving from the trees to the ant hill. It was terribly hot and I envied the buffalo the shade they were finding in the elephant grass. The Baboutu thought they would come out to graze again when it was cooler, and suggested that meanwhile it would be a good idea for us to find a bit of shade ourselves, and have a rest.

When the bull led his family out of the elephant grass later in the afternoon he was still uneasy, but the animals were hungry and they badly wanted to graze again. From my position behind the ant hill I watched while they waited for the bull to decide whether it was safe to go further, but though I was down-wind of him and he could not get my scent, he still kept staring in my direction.

On the backs of the buffalo were upwards of a dozen tickbirds, which perform the dual function of removing parasites and warning their big friends of the approach of enemies. If they see anything that moves, or anything strange, they fly up into the air uttering squeaky warning chirps. I kept well out of sight, without moving a muscle, but when I thought the bull was in a suitable position I began, infinitely slowly, to raise my rifle. This movement was instantly spotted by the tickbirds, which fluttered upwards squeaking like mad. The herd withdrew backwards, for the elephant grass was only a few paces behind them, but the bull, who was further out, swung round to enter the grass head first. As he came side on to me I sent a bullet straight into his heart, and he dropped like a log. Once again I had been lucky, for he was a fine specimen, with horns measuring nineteen inches from tip to tip, and with a breadth of twenty-five inches between the extremities of the curves.

Waterbuck were the only other animals I was anxious to get on the savannah, and my hunt for these a few days later produced another leopard under the most surprising circumstances. Waterbuck are among the largest African antelopes, weighing as much as three hundred and sixty pounds. Unlike the others, they are not found in herds, and I have never seen more than two together. Except during the rutting season, these pairs are always of the same sex. As their name implies, waterbuck are found in the vicinity of water, and since the nearest locality was the Nyie river valley, which lay to the north of Anna's village, I set off there as soon as I could.

I had gone only half a mile when a bushbuck came bounding through the shrubs straight towards me. It sometimes happens that frightened animals will run towards a man, and though various sentimental theories have been suggested to account for this, the truth is probably that in its panic the animal mistakes the man for a tree stump or other natural obstacle which might afford some shelter. In this case I was astonished not because the bushbuck was making for me, but because it was being chased by a leopard, which was bounding along at its heels like a wolf. I stood quite still until the animals were within fifty yards, and then took a heart shot at the cat, which cartwheeled over and over until it came to a stop in a crumpled heap. The bushbuck careered away at the sound of the shot and that was the last I saw of it.

Leopards normally hunt at night, and, like other cats, they do so by stalking and not by running down their prey. Yet here was one that hunted like a dog—and at high noon! I never heard of them hunting in that way before, though I have found them at work in broad daylight several times. In Yaounde a leopard took a lamb from my stockade, right under my nose, at nine o'clock in the morning; and on the banks of the Kom river in the Akoafim district I once saw a leopard kill a blue duiker just about noon. Some years later, when I was with my wife, we surprised a leopard on its kill—a civet cat—about ten in the morning.

In the present case the leopard was a female, and her dugs were distended with milk. It was clear that she had cubs not far off, and I was sorry to have killed her. Perhaps she had been hunting all night without success and had adopted this unorthodox method in desperation. Since she was dead, it was important that we should find the cubs as soon as possible so that they would not starve. I went back to the village at once and with Anna's cooperation borrowed all the men and boys to hunt for them.

Anna thought it most likely that the leopard had come from

an extensive outcrop of rocks that lay a mile or two from the village, and that she was probably the mate of the one I had shot several nights earlier. We went there, found likely-looking leopard spoor among the boulders and, when we followed them up, came across a few bones and the skulls of two young antelopes, probably kob. It seemed that we were on the cubs' track, but from birth the leopard is an expert at concealing himself, and we spent the best part of the morning hacking down thorn trees, pushing aside stones and boulders, peeking and poking into crevices and getting ourselves scratched and filthy before a yell went up from N'Denge. "Massa, Massa, come quick."

His cries of pain were accompanied by a great hissing and spitting, and when I ran up I found him holding at arm's length a scrap of spotted fur that scratched, snarled and spat and had already torn three bright red furrows from his wrist to his elbow. We popped the little fellow into a sack and after a minute or two he lay still in its comfortable darkness. Then we found his sister playing possum under a thorn bush. If anything, she was rather more belligerent than her brother, and she too was hurriedly provided with a sack and marched off to the village.

I think the cubs must have been without food for a long time. The leopard is one of Nature's most efficient killers, yet even Nature sometimes fails. The cubs' hunger, coupled with their mother's strange behavior, convinced me that she had not killed for two or three days. I gave them a dish of warm milk, diluted with water, and almost at once they started to lap it up. Then I went out and shot a young bushbuck, cutting out the liver and presenting it to them still warm. They pounced on it and tore it to bits, swallowing great lumps of it as fast as they could. Afterwards, with distended tummies and satisfied expressions, they made themselves comfortable on my bed and began to lick their paws.

In a day or two they became fairly tame, and could be

handled at the risk of a few mild scratches. I made soft, comfortable collars for them out of a kob's skin, and though it took quite a struggle to get them on and several days before they got used to them, eventually it was possible to take the cubs about on leads.

When I got back to Yaounde I made a present of them to a lady friend, who kept them as pets until they were nearly full-grown. By that time she could handle them only when wearing thick leather gloves and breeches, for in their rough, though not unfriendly, play they scratched dangerously. I saw them not long before they were sold to an animal dealer and sent to Europe, and I could not wonder at her anxiety to be rid of them. It was something of a shock to me, entering her living room, to see two big leopards jumping about all over her furniture.

I got two good waterbuck in the Nyie river valley and that completed my savannah hunt. Taking my leave of Anna, I turned back to the elephant grass of the Sanaga river, using the same trail that I had come by. It was a curiosity of this district that there were no hyenas or vultures, and therefore the carcass of the elephant still lay where I had shot it, advertised from an appreciable distance by thick clouds of flies and a most powerful smell. I found that every scrap of the elephant's huge toenails had been gnawed away by porcupines or cane rats.

The river had no terrors for my carriers this time, and though Atanaga and the others looked warily up and down stream before crossing, there was not a hippo or a crocodile in sight.

8. The Silent City of Rei Bouba

M. Carras, the District Officer of Garoua, raised his hand for silence.

"Listen," he said.

We listened.

"Hear those hoofbeats?"

"Well?"

"My friends," said Carras, "less than five minutes ago you told me that you are going to Rei Bouba, and the city is seventy-five miles from here, without radio or telegraph, but I'll wager that the Sultan will know of your intentions before we finish breakfast tomorrow. He has a most concentrated and efficient intelligence service and, if I know anything about it, the news will be carried by relays of fast horsemen throughout the night."

"How will he receive us?"

"That depends on you and on what kind of mood he happens to be in. He has a healthy respect for my Government, so a letter from me and a couple of policemen as your escort will help a lot. I also happen to know that the Sultan, or Lamido as they call him, has a weakness for sparkling wines, so I suggest that you send him a few cases of muscatel with my letter, which can go off tomorrow. Mind you, he'll do you no actual harm whatever mood he's in, but unless you can get him to cooperate you'll be wasting your time. If he doesn't approve of you, his people will follow your safari and scare off all the game."

With me at Carras's was Major Powell-Cotton, who had returned for his second hunting trip in the French Cameroons. During his absence I had been making inquiries about a number of animals he wished to add to his collection. One of these was the Derby eland, a rare variety of the largest of all antelopes, and I had discovered that they existed on the sandy, hilly country of Rei Bouba, a mysterious, medieval sultanate in the Northern Territories. The country was rich in many other kinds of animals—reedbuck, gazelle, oribi, giraffe, northern elephant, hartebeest, lion and rhino—many of which we hoped to study and hunt.

Carras did his best to help us. His message, accompanied by the wine, was dispatched next morning. What we heard about Rei Bouba made it as interesting to us as the animals we hoped to find. The people of the land were the Fulani, who had swept down as conquerors from the north a century earlier, and were now settled pastoralists. They came to Africa—probably from Western Asia—over a thousand years ago, and though their skins had darkened through miscegenation, their features, hair and slender build bore witness to their non-Negroid origin.

Unlike the primitive tribes they conquered and enslaved, the Fulani were a sophisticated though brutal race, with a flair for feudal administration. For a long time their Lamidos owed allegiance to the Emir of Yola in Nigeria, who was in turn the vassal of the Sultan of Sokoto. When the Germans ruled the Cameroons they disliked the Lamidos' being subordinate to native princes in British territory, but they were unable to destroy the Fulani administration.

Four days after dispatching Carras's letter and the wine, our safari set out from Garoua, with Powell-Cotton and myself traveling on horseback. Following the River Rei, a tributary of the great Benue, we soon entered pleasant undulating grassland, and late in the afternoon came upon a large Fulani village. We were surprised to find the headman waiting for us. He greeted us gravely but courteously, and told us that food for ourselves and for our carriers had already been prepared. This was a most agreeable start, for it meant that the Lamido had decided to receive us and had given instructions that we were to be well treated.

Nature, however, was not so kindly disposed, and on our second day's march we ran into a storm which lasted only half an hour but which was the most violent I can remember. First came a great wind which struck us with such force and so unexpectedly that we were almost bowled over. Our horses reared with fright at the impact, and refused to move on, turning their backs to the wind and lowering their heads. The carriers dropped their loads and crouched behind boxes of stores and bundles of bedding, where we quickly joined them. Then came the rain, swamping us and everything we had into a sodden mess.

The storm ended as suddenly as it had begun, and we rode on again with our clothes clinging to our skins. In the afternoon we came to another village, where Powell-Cotton and I were provided with a small hut. Our bedding was soaked and we spent a most uncomfortable night sleeping on the hard mud floor. The sun deserted us, and we stayed there for three days trying to dry our equipment.

Powell-Cotton went down with dysentery after that, I think because he drank too much milk, of which there was a plentiful supply from the cattle-owning Fulanis. But later the weather improved and the sun came out to warm us up. While my companion was recuperating, I took my .22 rifle and went off in search of birds for the pot.

Not far from camp was a stretch of dense scrub interspersed with a few taller trees which I thought were likely roosting places for guinea fowl. I found a hole in the bushes, went down on hands and knees and crawled inside, pushing my rifle before me. I moved slowly and quietly, heading for the taller trees, and I did not look upwards or forwards until I had gone twenty yards. Then I heard a low growl. I stopped and peered around. I could see nothing on my left and nothing ahead, but when I turned to the right I found myself looking straight into the eyes of a full-grown lion.

The great beast was barely ten feet away and must have been lying up away from the heat of the sun. I don't know which of us was the more surprised. Neither of us could get up, for the thorns were low over our backs, and for a moment or two we just stared at each other. I believe my mouth was wide open. The lion goggled at me a bit, stretched his head forward, sniffed and growled again, rather more loudly. Then he wriggled backwards an inch or two. I did the same, and the next moment we were both scrambling backwards as fast as we could. The lion and I left that patch of scrub about the same time, but luckily by different routes, and I just had a glimpse of his yellow back from over the bushes as he went bounding away across the plain. I had no further ambitions with regard to guinea fowl; lions usually live in family groups, and for all I knew there might be half a dozen more of them in there. I returned to camp and gasped out my story to Powell-Cotton, who was resting on his bed.

"Why didn't you shoot the beast?" he asked comfortably.

I waved the small rifle wildly above my head. "What, shoot a full-grown lion with a pea shooter like this?"

"I should have thought that a hunter of your skill," he answered dryly, "could have shot him through the eye. Even a .22 bullet would have been fatal at that range if it were properly placed."

And that was all the comfort I could get from this extraordinary man.

Vultures were a great nuisance to our safari. They sat about everywhere and were very bold, often entering tents or huts to steal scraps of meat. I shot one of them, thinking it might interest Latimer Bates, my ornithologist friend, but it was in a filthy condition, having fed on and soiled itself with human faeces, and it was impossible to skin it. Then I decided to trap one or two of them alive. There were no vultures in the Yaounde district, and I wondered whether it would be a good thing if I took a few back and liberated them there, for vultures are most valuable scavengers in tropical countries. The headman of the village heard of this plan and came to see me, looking distressed. Did I not know that vultures were sacred, and that if I caught one of them all the wild beasts would come and set it free?

I tried to reassure him, but he did not like it, and our carriers were really scared. However, I pointed out that it would be most convenient if wild animals came into or near our camp, for then we could shoot them without the trouble of hunting them. This rather took the wind out of their sails, and they watched me in silence as I made and baited a trap.

Catching the vulture was the easiest thing in the world. As soon as I walked away from the trap, one of the birds waddled forward and went straight in, snapping the door shut behind him by tugging at the bait. Next morning I hurriedly let the beastly thing go again, for the carriers were on the point of panic and threatened to desert us. All through the night there had been lions roaming around the camp and about two o'clock in the morning I had to get up and fire half a dozen rounds to scare them off, for they stampeded our horses. This was exactly what the headman had prophesied.

And really there was not much I could say, for the lions had certainly not troubled us before. Several years later this story came back to me in an amusing way. A forestry officer of the French Government, who had just returned to Yaounde from the Rei Bouba district, was telling me about the superstitions of the people there. He, too, had wanted to trap some vultures and had met with the same opposition. He was told that once another white man (that was I) had caught a vulture, and that during the night lions, leopards and all sorts of other animals had invaded his camp and liberated the sacred bird! Superstition is not always an evil thing and here was a good one, for in the tropics vultures must be preserved until they are replaced by modern sanitation.

When we were two days' march from Rei Bouba, we received further confirmation of the Lamido's friendly disposition towards us. A few miles from the village of Djurum we were met by three horsemen, who told us that they brought the first of six salutes from their master the Lamido, and that food awaited us at Djurum. The Lamido had also decided that we must be tired after our long journey, and he suggested—it was more in the nature of a command—that we should now rest for two days.

Having delivered this message, one of the horsemen galloped off. The two others escorted us to Djurum, where we were presented with a couple of fowls, some doubtful-looking eggs, and a plump young goat. We soon had a splendid meal, and afterwards made camp near the river, in pleasant surroundings.

While we were at Djurum we had no difficulty in finding food. The water was positively choked with fish, and a random rifle shot could always be depended on to bring one or two floating to the surface. I do not know what kind they were, but Atanaga did wonders with them in his field kitchen. Honey cakes were another agreeable change of diet. The Fulani people hang long baskets of plaited straw in the trees and collect honey of a delicious flavor from the wild bees that nest in them.

We were by no means in need of a rest, but we thought it prudent to accept the Lamido's suggestion that we should stay at Djurum for two days, and we spent the time exploring the river Rei. Near the river there was a chain of lakes and though it was the dry season and they were barely six feet deep, they were full of hippo and crocodiles. We shot a bull hippo to provide meat for our carriers, and were disconcerted when the men nonchalantly waded out to the carcass and beat away the crocodiles that were already tearing at it. They said that crocodiles never attack men, but if that were so, then they were remarkable crocodiles: in the rivers of the southern Cameroons, dozens of natives are lost to these reptiles every year.

The two horsemen followed us about wherever we went and paid the closest attention to everything we did. I found out later that they were constantly sending runners to the Lamido, presumably with reports on our behavior. Our two days at Djurum seemed to be intended as a sort of probationary period. When it ended and we moved on again, the horsemen took charge of the safari, riding one on either side of us.

We crossed a range of low, grassy hills and entered a great plain. Far away on high ground, we could see the gloomy walls of the citadel, and galloping towards us in a cloud of dust was a single horseman, looking like a medieval knight about to enter a joust. When he was fifty yards from us he suddenly reined in his horse, so that it reared up and pawed the air, and at the same time he flung a spear towards us. Not knowing what to expect, we stopped and stared at the thing as it whistled through the air, and our horses shied violently when it struck the ground almost at our feet. The rider dismounted, walked up to us and salaamed. That was the Lamido's second salute.

Four more of these dramatic gestures remained, and they followed one another in rapid succession. First came twenty infantrymen, carrying spears and heavy, rhinoceros-hide shields. They were followed by a group of musicians, who beat drums and blew loudly on an astonishing variety of wind instruments. A third company of infantrymen, fifty strong, made up the fifth salute, and the sixth was the most impressive and startling of all.

Thundering towards us out of the dust came a squadron of the famous Rei Bouba cavalrymen. These men were of Sudanese origin, vassals of their aristocratic Fulani masters, and their resemblance to the Crusaders was remarkable. Their horses were canopied with cloth of crude designs and brilliant colors, covering the animals to their ears and reaching down almost to their fetlocks. Some of the riders wore mail, others were swathed in heavy robes, with colorful, plumed head-gear, and they all carried spears with blades two feet long. We watched with growing nervousness as they charged straight at us, and for a moment we began to think that their intentions were anything but peaceful; but when they were almost upon us they pulled up—a superb demonstration of horsemanship—and then the whole company fell in behind our safari.

I turned in my saddle to look back on this long, gaudy pro-cession, and my eye fell on Atanaga and N'Denge. They were both looking bewildered and frightened, and to tell the truth I was not particularly happy myself. This extravagant escort was all very well, but the soldiers showed no real inter-est in us. Their manner was dull and wooden, quite without enthusiasm, as though they greeted us only because they had been ordered to. Our entry into the city did not serve to encourage me.

Rei Bouba was probably one of the last completely walled cities in the world. The wall was of sun-baked mud, twenty feet high and twelve feet thick. There were massive wooden gates, thrown open for us by a crowd of soldiers and guards, who were armed with swords, axes, spears and knobkerries. They looked a rough and formidable crowd indeed and their attitude was sinister because they were utterly silent. When we passed through the gates they were slammed behind us at once, cutting us off from the rest of our safari, and at the other end of the wall was another gate, so that we felt as though we were at the bottom of a dry dock. The soldiers milled around, waving their swords and spears, but still they were silent. Powell-Cotton surveyed them pensively and then turned to me.

"Bit of a queer show, this," he remarked.

I fumbled for my revolver—not that it would have helped us much with that crowd—but before I could decide what to do the second gate swung open and we were led into the city. The narrow streets through which we passed were deserted and there were thick mats of plaited grass screening the houses, so that even from our horses we could only see the roofs. There were millions and millions of flies; everything was blanketed with them, and they rose up in clouds around our horses' hooves as we moved along.

We were taken to a rest house, which consisted of two round huts connected by a verandah. Leopard skins covered the floor, and in the corner of the verandah were large earthenware jugs containing water. We learned that water was a problem during the dry season, but when the rains started there was an excess of it, and the country surrounding the citadel became an impassable swamp.

The soldiers led away our horses and came back with some sickly-looking goat stew and honey cakes. I knew a little of their language, but they took no notice of me when I tried it out on them. Atanaga, N'Denge, the two policemen and our carriers turned up half an hour later, looking flushed and uncomfortable, but they reported that they had not been molested in any way. Smaller huts near our own were allotted to them and a number of silent women served them with food. The flies were as bad here as in the streets. We had to devise a sort of tent made of mosquito netting to protect us from them while we ate our meals.

In other parts of Africa, particularly where Europeans are seldom seen, the native people are intensely interested in everything about you. Men, women and children crowd around peering into your tent or hut and asking all sorts of questions. Your carriers and servants are also required to reveal everything they know of your way of life, which they do with great gusto and, it is to be feared, a certain amount of dramatic embellishment. Here in Rei Bouba no one came to look at us, and the women who served our carriers with food said never a word. Rei Bouba was always as silent as the grave; the only sound we ever heard came from the muezzins calling people to prayer. Apart from that there was nothing: no children laughing and singing, no shouts and cries from the streets and market places, no neighbors gossiping or quarreling. Throughout our stay in the city we were haunted and depressed by this terrible and inexplicable silence.

At the back of the rest house was a small yard, with a high wall, and in front there was an open space with a big baobab tree growing in the center. Here the cavalry squadron appeared again, this time to perform an exhibition ride. If they intended to impress and entertain us they were eminently successful, for they rode magnificently and had an uncanny command of their horses. When they left, six soldiers came and sat down under the tree, and from then on we were never without a guard.

Nothing at all happened the next day until I approached one of the guards and asked him when we were to see the Lamido. Without replying he got up and walked off. Half an hour later he returned and spoke for the first time.

"Soon. Perhaps tomorrow," was all he said, and I could not get another word out of him.

The same thing happened the following day, and again the day after that, and we began to get restless. On the fourth day I decided to see what would happen if I just walked out. Two of the guards sprang to their feet when they understood my intention, but they made no attempt to stop me. Instead they ran ahead, waving their heavy cavalry swords and shouting, "Out of the way! Out of the way! Behold the white man approaches! Out of the way, people of Rei Bouba!"

The people had evidently been warned to keep out of sight if we walked about, and though I strolled along the streets of the city for the best part of the morning, I did not see one of the three thousand people who lived there. I went back to the rest house and reported to Powell-Cotton.

"Don't worry," he said. "Mohammedans don't like strangers wandering about near their homes. As for the Lamido, he's just keeping us waiting to show how important he is, and how insignificant we are. He'll see us soon."

But another three dreary days of confinement went by before the guards told us that the Lamido was ready to grant us an audience. Dressed in the neat clothes we always carried for such occasions, and escorted by our policemen, we followed the guards to the palace. This was a huge building of whitewashed mud, surrounded by two high walls and a maze of stables, outhouses and courtyards. We were taken through a heavily guarded gate into the main outer courtyard, and there we began to learn a little of the Lamido's system of justice.

Ambling about the courtyard was a magnificent black-maned lion, wearing a peculiarly benign and self-satisfied expression. He also wore a stout leather collar to which a long silver chain was attached, and at the other end of this was a young man who looked most unhappy. Our guards had grown more talkative during the walk to the palace, and they laughed loudly when they saw the young man with the lion. I ventured to ask what there was amusing about the sight.

"The young man," explained the guard, "is a slave who has offended the Lamido. As a punishment he has been put in charge of his master's pet lion. The animal is of uncertain temper, and sooner or later it will kill him."

This, we learned, was a fairly common occurrence, and made a change from the orthodox executions which were performed by the unsavory character we encountered in the second courtyard. The public executioner of Rei Bouba was a strong, elderly man encumbered with charms, amulets, and leopard skins. In his right hand he bore an axe, and in his left a sort of iron hammer. Once more the guard was willing to explain:

"When a man is condemned to death," he told us, "he is handed over to the executioner, who places a chain around his neck and leads him about the street and public places collecting money from the charitable. After a few days the people grow tired of giving alms, and then the executioner fells his victim with a blow of the hammer on the back of his head and decapitates him with his axe."

We were allowed to photograph the executioner and also the pet lion—which we did from a safe distance—and then a naked slave took over from the guards and led us into the palace. Crawling on his hands and knees, never daring to look up, the slave presented us to the Lamido. His Highness was reclining on a sort of divan, clothed in a white and indigo gown, with a blue turban, ending in folds wound around and hiding the lower part of his face. Only his eyes were visible, and they betrayed no sign of interest in us. Standing beside him was his Chamberlain or Vizier, who silently indicated that we might make use of the chairs placed near the Lamido. Neither of them said a word as we sat down, and the slave remained crouching, with his head touching the sandy floor. We waited to be addressed, but five minutes passed in dead silence.

Powell-Cotton nudged me. "For goodness' sake, say something." I cleared my throat, and began the little speech I had prepared.

"Your Highness," I said, "we are pleased and honored to make your ... er ... exalted acquaintance."

There was no reply. I began again.

"We would like to tell you that our trip through your

lovely country was most enjoyable and that we are deeply indebted to you for your hospitality and . . . er . . . cordial reception."

There was still no answer, but I was beginning to enjoy myself now, and I went on with a swing.

"May we hope, your Highness, that you and your wives are well, and that your family and herds will multiply . . . ah . . . like the sands of the desert?"

This last bit pleased me no end, and Powell-Cotton glanced at me with a curious glint in his eye. But there was no response from the Lamido.

"As you know, your Highness," I went on, "we are hunters and we seek certain animals that are to be found only in these happy and blessed domains. . . ."

Here the Vizier rudely interrupted, speaking for the first time. "He is a Lamido, not a hunter," he said crossly.

I did not know what to say to that, so I decided to ignore it and went on. "We would be deeply indebted to your Highness if you would supply us with guides who know the country and who will show us where to find the animals we want."

Again it was the Vizier who spoke. "In two days' time you will be given guides, fresh horses, provisions and carriers. The guides will show you everything."

There did not seem to be much more to say, so we got to our feet. To our surprise, the Lamido took each one of us by the hand as we left and uttered the word "Bourdom," which means "It is well." I met him again on two occasions before we left Rei Bouba and that was the only word he spoke, though at my third meeting he took the covering from the lower part of his face, revealing a countenance that was petty and arrogant. This impression was confirmed by an incident which occurred when a senior French officer presented the Lamido with a decoration of honor. The officer pinned the medal to the Lamido's robes, and then, thinking to please him further, offered a lesser decoration to his cavalry commander. The Lamido was so overcome with jealousy at this that he tore off his own medal and threw it to the ground. But in spite of these shortcomings, he was liked and respected by his own people and was a brilliant administrator of his feudal state.

The guides and additional carriers provided for us at Rei Bouba belonged to the Kerdie tribe, a primitive people who had been enslaved by the Fulanis. They were sturdy, almost naked men who were reliable and hard workers, but their taste in food was revolting. Once they extracted the stomach of a hartebeest I had just shot and squeezed the liquid contents of it into their mouths, assuring me that it was a most nourishing and appetizing dish. The intestines were also eaten raw, after their contents had been squeezed out.

The headman of the Kerdies brought his wife along and one evening he announced that she was going to have a baby. Would I mind postponing our march for one day? In the circumstances I was quite prepared to wait as long as he wished, but the woman had her baby that night and twenty-four hours later she slung it on her hip, hoisted her calabash of food on her head, and was ready to move on.

For two months we explored the Rei Bouba district searching for the giant Derby eland, but it appeared that most of them had been almost wiped out by an epidemic of rinderpest. We found a few skulls, also the spoor of a few lone eland, but since they had been decimated by disease we left them strictly alone. Other game abounded, and we obtained giraffe, wart hog, gazelles, reedbuck, hartebeest, oribi, waterbuck, lion, buffalo, roan, and a funny little beast called the ratel or honey badger, which is a relative of the skunk and has the same noisome faculties.

Back in Garoua we reported to Carras on our reception by the Lamido and our failure to get giant eland. He suggested that we should try the Kone district, further southwest, and there at last we found those magnificent animals. Stalking them was difficult, for they moved like wraiths among the bush, and their striped hides blended so well with the vegetation that it was difficult to see where the leaves ended and where the animals began.

Eland do not graze, but browse on leaves, and I have never seen a herd at rest. They are constantly moving at a fairly fast walk, snatching a mouthful here and there as they pass the bushes, and their camouflage makes it almost impossible to tell how many animals there are in the herd, let alone to select a suitable bull. Their great bulk, their long twisted horns laid back along the length of their bodies, and their lovely golden skins, with white, vertical stripes, place them among the finest animals in Africa.

We followed our herd for over a week before shooting the single bull we wanted. Selecting him was a problem that took two or three days; at times it seemed impossible to get into position for a shot, for the animals were extremely suspicious and made off at the slightest disturbance; and then when everything seemed perfect and Powell-Cotton's finger tightened on his trigger, a cow eland or a smaller bull would move across the line of sight and the opportunity was lost again. But it was well worthwhile, for the animal we eventually secured was a prince of his kind. He stood five feet eight inches at the shoulder, and his horns were nearly three feet long.

After this we went to Chamba at the foot of the Atlantica Mountains, in search of smaller game, and at the court of the Sultan we met the strange person who was his court jester. He was a tall, excessively ugly man with a partly shaven head. Charms hung from his topknot and around his neck. He was naked above the waist, and his physique would have made many a "Mr. Universe" green with envy. We were invited to a display of his unusual talents, and he astonished us both with his skill as a conjurer. There, in the bright African sunlight, with no trick mirrors or black curtains, he went through his repertoire of magic.

We were asked to examine a calabash, and when we had satisfied ourselves that it was empty and contained no hidden compartments, he took it from us, swept up a few handfuls of sand from the ground, and after swinging it around a few times, poured out a pound or two of groundnuts. Afterwards he brought a live hyena and wrestled with it, putting his arm between jaws that were capable of crushing a cow's thigh-bone. Towards the end of this exhibition his little daughter joined him, and she too played with the dangerous animal with perfect trust and confidence. Several times he pushed the hyena's nose into his armpit, where it licked up the perspiration, and I wondered whether this had some sort of soporific effect on the animal. It certainly has on domestic cats.

I was not surprised that the hyena man's friends regarded him with superstitious awe. Harry Francis, the trader who kept a store at Edea in the southern Cameroons, once employed a European manager who made a hobby of conjuring and demonstrated a few of his sleight-of-hand tricks to the native customers, thinking it would intrigue them. It did more than that: the natives thought the man was bewitched and they hurriedly transferred their custom elsewhere. Harry had to get rid of the man, and even then it was months before he got back his trade.

From Chamba we went south to a little town called N'Gaoundere, where we added baboons, rock hyraxes and rabbits to our list. While Powell-Cotton rested, I went off alone to the wild M'Boum country east of N'Gaoundere, looking for buffalo and elephant, but here I met with decided opposition from the people. Long afterwards I learned that I had been trespassing near some sacred caves, which the people did not wish a European to see. They followed me about everywhere, and whenever I got near a herd of buffalo or elephant, they deliberately frightened them away.

Back in N'Gaoundere I reported to Powell-Cotton that it would be a waste of time trying the M'Boum country for elephant, and we went south again to Lelo, in the Batouri district, where I was much more at home. Powell-Cotton was pleased when I told him that there was a chance of obtaining Bongo in the forests round Lelo, for the Bongo is a very rare and elusive antelope confined to the densest forest, and consequently seldom hunted by Europeans. Moreover, it is a courageous animal which, if wounded or brought to bay, will not hesitate to charge, and since all hunting in the forest is done at close quarters, such a situation can be dangerous. I knew two native hunters who were killed by Bongo.

I already had some experience in hunting this animal, but even with N'Denge's help it was more than three weeks before I eventually found spoor which was indisputably Bongo. Then followed a chase lasting ten days, while we caught only tantalizing glimpses of the red, white-striped skins of cow Bongo and sought in vain for the darker bulls. Like most forest animals, Bongo depend more on hearing than on sight or smell, and they have a trick of doubling back on their tracks to investigate suspicious sounds. While you are cautiously following the spoor, the animal that made it might already have turned back and be watching you from behind.

The luck of the game fell to Powell-Cotton. N'Denge and I went off quartering the forest, leaving him resting on a tree stump. He had been sitting there in complete silence when there was a rustle in the leaves behind him. Not ten yards away, partly screened by the creepers, stood a bull Bongo, staring in the direction taken by N'Denge and me. He was dead with a bullet from the Major's rifle before he even knew he was in danger.

Our last hunt was to be for manatee and for a race of small elephants which we expected to find on the coast. There was ample time for this, and on our way westwards from Batouri my companion expressed a wish to see the Sanaga River, and in particular a stretch just above the Nightingale Falls, which was famed for its beauty. The river was low, for it was the dry season, and it was divided into a series of deep pools by high rocky walls cutting across its bed. Over each of these natural dams the water thundered in cascades some six feet high.

A year earlier, on my last visit to this part of the Sanaga, I had noticed a bull hippopotamus with an abnormal tusk growing sideways, projecting out of his mouth and upwards to his nostrils. Abnormalities of any kind are instructive and of particular interest to zoologists, and Powell-Cotton thought that this animal would be a valuable acquisition for the museum. Hippo were numerous there, but after some trouble we identified the animal we wanted in the second pool above the Nightingale Falls. We crossed by canoe to a small island standing about a hundred yards from the bank, and settled there waiting for the hippo to appear.

There is nothing clever about shooting a hippopotamus. They are easy to find, easy to see and seldom dangerous. The only difficulties are that they may disappear below the surface for long periods if disturbed and their carcasses are sometimes inaccessible in deep water. Hippos have never been considered as "game," and normally they are shot only for meat or for causing serious damage to plantations.

Our hippo was easily spotted, for his crooked tusk gleamed brightly in the sun, and Powell-Cotton shot him as soon as he surfaced. He sank immediately, but swam a considerable way upstream below the surface before he died and floated to the top. The current conveniently brought him drifting down to us, and he came ashore on a sandy spit of the island.

It was intensely hot, and I decided to get the carcass over to the bank as soon as possible, so that we could skin it before it began to decompose. We had only one canoe, and Powell-Cotton was left alone on the island while I, with N'Denge and my two skinmen, began towing the carcass across. This, I quickly discovered, was a mistake. The channel between the island and the bank was narrow enough, but the water was deep and the current strong. Before we had gone far, the hippo, dragged by the current, was solidly towing us downstream towards the falls formed by the dam. N'Denge and the skinmen paddled away like mad, but the hippo was posthumously getting his own back and he had us firmly under control. Before we went over the falls I had a glimpse of Powell-Cotton sitting on the island with his head in his hands. I'll swear he was laughing.

Over we went: canoe, hippo and all. The canoe was smashed to bits and the hippo floated away lazily in the direction of the Nightingale Falls. Luckily we were all at home in the water and our only fear as we struck out was of crocodiles, but we reached the bank unmolested.

Now the tables were turned on Powell-Cotton, for there were no other canoes for miles, and he was marooned there in the hot sun as securely as Robinson Crusoe. I sent off N'Denge to look for another canoe and relaxed comfortably under the shade of a big tree until he returned later in the afternoon. We got the Major off just before sunset.

I suppose that the manatee is one of the strangest animals in the world. The scientific name for the order to which it belongs is "Sirenia," yet nothing could be more inappropriate, for this ugly, ungainly creature is far removed from my conception of the lovely beings that lured sailors to destruction. "Sirenia" is, in fact, derived from the belief that manatees, and their cousins the dugongs of Indian and Australian waters, gave rise to the legend of mermaids. This is understandable, for the female manatee has large, human-like breasts. Rising from the water at twilight, with perhaps a strand or two of weed on her head to suggest tresses, she might well seem partly human to credulous eye. Once conceived, this idea would be supported by the female's practice of holding the single, helpless young to her breast with her foreflipper. The

Cameroon natives call the manatee "Mammy Water," and believe that some men fall under the spell of these animals and are compelled to spend the night with them—presumably above water.

Manatees are found in the rivers of both Africa and tropical America, and in their adaption to aquatic life they are surpassed among mammals only by the whales and dolphins, which they resemble in shape, having a horizontal tail fin, flipper-like forelimbs, and no external ears. The muzzle, however, is rounded and blunt, with a cleft, muscular upper lip, bearing a heavy moustache. They are about eight feet long and are pure vegetarians, feeding on river weeds.

We failed to find any of these queer creatures ourselves, though we spent weeks canoeing up and down the estuary and creeks of the Nyong River. One day a party of fishermen caught a male manatee in their nets and we were able to purchase the skin and skeleton. The natives have a great liking for the flesh and invited us to taste it. We gingerly accepted a morsel or two, and found that it resembled pork.

Only the elephants remained. There is really only one species of African elephant, though several races are distinguished by some authorities, and we were interested in a small race which lived in the coastal forest between the mouth of the Nyong River and the village of Malimba.

Apart from the smaller size, the differences between this and other races are perhaps of interest only to the specialist. There are some structural differences in the skull; the tusks seldom weigh more than eight pounds each and are considerably shorter and more curved. Because they are smaller, these elephants are more agile and therefore more difficult to hunt than other races, and they are also more aggressive, being apt to charge with little or no provocation. The natives call the common elephant "N'Jock" and the smaller one, which they fear much more, "Lokopak." The two races share the same territories, and distinguishing between them in dense bush is often difficult. Consequently we made some mistakes, and the first one nearly cost us our lives.

Powell-Cotton had not been feeling well, and was finding the hard tracking in heavy forest day after day rather too much for him. Nevertheless he persisted, and when we found the spoor of what we believed was a herd of the small race, we followed it up. Crossing a stream, we climbed a steep hill on the other side and, looking down, saw the trunk tips of several elephants waving at us as they tried to get our scent. My companion moved a few paces to my left and fired, wounding but not killing one of the beasts. He then came back and stood in front of me, getting a better view, but before he could shoot again we heard an angry squeal from our right, and a bull elephant came out of the bush towards us, bent on revenge. I fired and brought him down, and then, to my horror, Powell-Cotton suddenly collapsed at my feet.

I knelt beside him, but looked up again instantly to see that the bull I had fired at was back on his feet and was coming at us, all set to kill. The rest of the herd had panicked and were stampeding around us, trumpeting furiously. I just had time for one shot, with the bull's great gray bulk towering over us, and I fired from my kneeling position at an angle of forty-five degrees. The shock of the situation had ruined my aim, even at that close range, but my bullet raked across his shoulder, making him turn aside before he reached us. I loosed off more shots at the rest of the herd to frighten them off, and to my intense relief this succeeded and they charged away down the hill towards the stream.

N'Denge and the skinmen had been following us at a discreet distance, but not surprisingly they had made themselves scarce when the elephants charged, and there was no reply when I called out to them. Near us was one of those huge cottonwood trees with a heavily buttressed base, and I dragged my friend into the shelter of it. The elephant he had wounded was still struggling in the undergrowth and I went down and finished it off. It was not one of the small race after all, but a cow with only one tusk. Powell-Cotton had only fainted, probably through exhaustion and heat, for when I carried water up from the stream in my hat and dashed it in his face, he came round at once and without a word shook my hand.

Powell-Cotton was one of the coolest men and finest shots I ever knew. When eventually we found a herd of the small race, he shot two bulls, which were standing about thirty yards apart, with a right and a left barrel. The two shots sounded, and both animals must have died almost simultaneously. Another time, after we had parted to cast about for fresh elephant spoor, I heard him fire and rushed back. He was standing calmly surveying the undergrowth, with his rifle butt resting on the ground.

"I've just shot one," he said, "and there's another that might charge at any moment."

Among the trees just in front of him stood a fine tusker working himself up for a charge, but he changed his mind and made off. At such close range Powell-Cotton would have had time for only one shot, yet he was as undisturbed as though his target had been a clay pigeon.

Though I had hunted elephant many times before, I had never attempted the colossal task of skinning and preserving them. Under Powell-Cotton's supervision, and with the assistance of some thirty natives, I made a deep cut around the exposed side of the dead bull's neck, a second down the spine and a third down the chest and abdomen. Other cuts were made on the inside of each leg, across the soles of the feet and down the underside of the trunk. Half the skin was then removed, and with stout saplings and lianas tied to the legs, the huge beast was rolled over on the other side, where work was continued. The skin was so tough that our knives were quickly blunted and three men occupied the whole of their time sharpening them with files.

When the skins had been removed, they were stretched on

racks and laid out to dry. Meanwhile, scores of villagers had arrived, frantic to get at the meat. I had great difficulty in restraining them until I had the skeleton intact, for in the scramble I was afraid of losing some of the small bones. African villagers go crazy for meat when they find a dead elephant or hippo. Opening up the carcass, they crawl right inside, indifferent to the blood and mess, in search of the choicest pieces. Once I had to stop a fight over some tasty morsel between two women who were actually inside an elephant's stomach.

Another problem was that we had two elephants and the greatest care had to be taken to make sure that the two sets of bones did not get mixed up. I also had to guard the skeleton from the villagers, for though the huge bones of an elephant are solid and have no marrow, they produce an excellent cooking oil when broken and boiled down.

Back in camp, deep pits were dug and the bones buried in them, so that all traces of flesh and fat would decay without the nuisance of smell. The skins were treated with Atlas preservative, and while they dried they were cleaned and thinned down. A carpenter from the village of Dehane was set to work building large wooden cases, and when both skeletons and skins were ready they were packed up and dispatched to Douala, where the rest of the collection was already waiting, and Powell-Cotton accompanied them home to England.

9. The Mendjim Mey

The trip with Powell-Cotton lasted eighteen months and took us through many parts of the Cameroons, but wherever I was and whatever I was hunting, gorillas were never far from my thoughts. When we were at Lelo after the Bongo, I made friends with the old village chief, M'Boor, who knew a great deal about gorillas and asked me whether I had ever looked for them in the Mendjim Mey country. I had only heard of the place, and no one had been able to tell me much about it. All I knew was that the Mendjim Mey was a vast, almost unexplored forest region lying south of the Doume River, inhabited by Pygmies and by the primitive Mendjims, who hated strangers and were suspected of occasional cannibalism.

M'Boor knew the Mendjims well. He disliked them, for they were the traditional enemies of his own people, and said that they were a lazy crowd who never worked. At the same time, he believed them to be the finest gorilla hunters in Africa. Unlike other tribes, they had no fear of gorillas, regarding them with contempt as unarmed bushmen. No Europeans had gone far into the Mendjim Mey for many years, and M'Boor could not see why anyone should want to. But because I, too, was a hunter, he thought it possible that the Mendjims would not be hostile to me.

Naturally I could not rest after hearing that, and I had already made plans before I left Powell-Cotton at Douala. When N'Denge, Atanaga and the rest of my men saw the last of the cases loaded on his ship, they heaved gusty sighs of relief, for they were expecting me to go home to Yaounde, where they looked forward to a quiet and peaceful rest. There was consternation when they found me ordering stores for another safari, and panic when they knew where we were going. They knew about my escape from the Maka people and expected no better treatment from the Mendjims, but they had been with me for years, and I do not think that the idea of deserting me ever crossed their minds. When they had got over the initial shock they accepted the situation with their usual fatalism.

When we got back to Lelo I found that M'Boor's men had caught a young male gorilla—about four years old, I judged—and the old chief made a present of him to me. As usual, I had all my pets with me, and only the day before my fox terrier bitch had added to their number by producing four pups, so that a quarter-grown gorilla was something of an embarrassment at that time. However, M'Boor said that his men wanted to kill the animal in revenge for the damage it had done to their crops, and that they would certainly do so if I did not take it away. I asked N'Denge and Atanaga what they thought about it.

"Take dem N'gi for Mendjim Mey," they advised. "We go make box."

That settled it, and while the "box" was under construction I tried to find out how tractable the animal might be. The villagers had named him Lumbindon, a private joke of theirs, for that was the name of the particularly ugly chief of an adjoining village, but they could not tell me whether or not he was tame and no one had gone into his cage to see.

The cage was a huge affair made of saplings lashed together with lianas and hinged on one side. I filled my pockets with bananas and slipped in through the door. The gorilla made no move, but sat hunched up at the other side of the cage watching me out of the corner of his eyes in the suspicious, cunning way gorillas have. I made no attempt to go up to him, but sat quietly where I was, holding out a banana.

Presently he came over and snatched the banana from my hand, gobbling it down skin and all. After he had eaten half a dozen in this way I ventured to put out my hand to stroke him, but he bared his teeth and grabbed savagely at my arm, scratching me badly. That was enough for one day, so I left him to think things over. Afterwards I made repeated attempts to gain his confidence, always feeding him by hand, but he was too old to be tamed and could never be trusted. We took him with us on that safari and kept him nearly a year. Then, because there was no improvement in his behavior, I passed him on to my agent at Batouri, who eventually sold him to a collector.

It was not easy to get carriers from among M'Boor's men who were prepared to go into the Mendjim Mey, but several of the skinmen and gun-bearers who had been with Powell-Cotton and me came to Lelo and rejoined me. These included Collonel, who had been a skinman of mine for many years; Dinga, a Kaka tribesman, reputedly a member of the dreaded Labe Secret Society; and N'Gombe, a member of the Byar tribe near the Congo border, who were at that time in revolt. A new motor road had been made through the Byar territory, and it was a common sight to see lorries arriving at Yaounde from Byar with spears still protruding from their wooden sides.

Another old faithful was Wo-Wo Foot, so called from his deformed feet. Many were the jokes made, and good-naturedly accepted by Wo-Wo, about his deformity. If ever I wanted someone to do an errand hurriedly, the carriers always sent Wo-Wo Foot, and of course he took ten times longer over it than anyone else would have done.

In addition to these men I needed a large number of temporary carriers, for I had a lot of heavy equipment. Through Powell-Cotton, Professor Ian Hill of the University College, London, had asked me to send him anthropoid and other embryological material, and the late Sir Frank Colyer, of the Royal College of Surgeons, had asked for any skulls that showed signs of dental decay. This meant that I had to take several heavy cases containing jars of formalin and other preservatives, as well as my usual equipment. I needed about twenty carriers, and it was, surprisingly, Atanaga who solved this problem. I was arguing with M'Boor's men, trying to convince them that it was perfectly safe to go into the Mendjim Mey, when Atanaga suddenly chimed in.

"Look at me," he shouted angrily. "I be Yaounde man, and me, I no do fear."

This so stung the men that in a few minutes they were clamoring to come with me and I had to begin a process of elimination to reduce the number of volunteers. My final preparations were soon completed and a few days later we entered the Mendjim Mey.

The Mendjims, I discovered, were administered—after a fashion—through a Paramount Chief who lived at Beselebot on the northern fringe of the territory. This man spoke French, but he received me suspiciously and though he gave me a hut and provided my men with food, my first few days at the village were uncomfortable. Thereafter our relationship rapidly improved.

The Mendjims were a desperately poor people. During the rubber boom of the twenties they had earned a little money to pay their taxes and to buy knives and cloth by selling meat to the native rubber tappers who entered their country. When the boom ended they had nothing to fall back on. They produced only enough for food for themselves and their men knew no other art than hunting. Suddenly, a new and wonderful source of income had appeared in their midst. Here

was a European—slightly mad no doubt—who was prepared
to pay for useless bones and skins, while he gave them back
the only part of an animal that had any real value—its meat!

The whole village went off hunting and I accepted almost
everything they caught, alive or dead. Unfortunately, there
were only a few gorillas and chimpanzees in their area, so I
did not stay with them long. N'Denge learned that the Mendjim village of Arteck was the center of the gorilla country
and I resolved to go there. At first the Paramount Chief was
reluctant to let me go, and he warned me that the hunters
of the interior were not likely to be friendly, for they were
jealous of their hunting grounds. But he consented to lend
me a guide when I told him that I would leave two of my
skinmen behind to purchase and preserve the animals his people brought in.

No wonder few white men ever bothered the Mendjims!
The forest was exceptionally dense and difficult to penetrate.
There were the usual game trails, but they were blocked by
monstrous fallen trees, heavily shrouded with lianas and woody
creepers, so that it took hours to hack a way around them.
The country was laced with wide, deep streams with exceptionally strong currents, which made fording them extremely
dangerous. The occasional bridges were in various stages of
disrepair, and crossing them was a hair-raising adventure. The
going was so tough that I had to let the carriers rest every
hour or two. Birds and monkeys of many kinds abounded and
we saw much elephant and buffalo spoor, but the carriers were
not used to hunting and their constant chatter prevented us
from seeing any game.

The next village we came to was Kenyol, and waiting for
us at its approaches was a figure who looked from a distance
like a small boy dressed in the clothes of an adult. He was a
tiny man, not much bigger than a Pygmy, wearing an ancient
and enormous greatcoat reaching almost to the ground. His
hands were concealed far up the voluminous sleeves and his

head bobbed about inside the vast, gaping collar as though it belonged to an animated puppet. His color, too, was odd, for he was a partial albino, with a yellow skin and pale eyes. His antics were well in accord with this bizarre appearance; he couldn't keep still for a minute and was forever capering about chattering nineteen to the dozen. He soon had us all roaring with laughter, to his own intense gratification.

We were understandably amused and surprised to find that this born clown was the chief of Kenyol. His name was Mendjoum—"Little Chief Mendjoum," as we came to call him— and his authority rested entirely on his ability to keep everyone laughing. Mendjoum spoke good Pidgin and invited me to stay at Kenyol in what he called a "fine house too much," which turned out to be a five-room hut so small that when I slept in it that night my feet were in one room and my head in another. Before I turned in he came to see me, announcing that he had something important to say.

He had heard, he said, that I was a good man and a great hunter, and that I paid good money for animals. Moreover, I always gave back the meat. Therefore I was their father and their mother. What other man would do this thing? Who ever heard of a white man leaving his home to buy old bones? Did I know that he, Mendjoum, should by rights be Paramount Chief of the Mendjims, and that the other man at Beslebot had got the job by bribing native officials with gifts of girls? Did I know that this man was cruel to his people, whom he flogged and robbed, and was I aware that he had already taken away the money I had paid them for the bones? Mendjoum ended this recital with an assurance of his own veracity.

During the years that followed, Mendjoum was to become a great friend of mine and later also of my wife, but I stayed with him then for only a few days before going on to Arteck. Mendjoum, like the Paramount Chief, was reluctant to let me go, but I could not decide whether his motives stemmed from hope of personal gain or from genuine concern for my safety.

Yes, he said, the Mendjims of the interior were magnificent hunters and their country was full of gorillas and other animals, but they would certainly resent my intrusion, for they knew little of white men and their ways.

As it turned out, the situation was very much in the balance. Leaving Mendjoum, we plunged again into the forest and struggled on for three hard days until we were ready to drop from exhaustion. The forest was cool and dark, with the trees supporting a great canopy of vegetation which shut out all direct sunlight, and through this vast green cathedral of everlasting twilight the village drums were constantly resounding. What were they saying, I wondered. What were the people of Arteck being told about me, and what was their reaction to the news that a white man was coming?

When at last we reached Arteck and found it apparently deserted, memories of my nightmare stay among the Maka cannibals flooded over me in a wave of despair. There seemed to be three alternative lines of action: I could turn back, but that was unthinkable; I could arm N'Denge, Collonel and the others and hope that this show of force would frighten the Mendjims into cooperation; or I could go alone and unarmed into the village and hope for the best. It was the third course that I decided on, but I made two modifications in it. Under my shirt I concealed a revolver, and I took Dinga with me to carry my chair, for this was a native custom symbolizing a person of rank and consequence.

Crossing a small stream, I walked through a patch of grassy bush and entered the village, which consisted of two rows of huts facing each other. As I passed along the lines of huts I saw out of the corner of my eye that the villagers were inside, staring at me through cracks in the walls and doorways. I took no notice of them, but marched straight on to the guard hut of the village, which stood in the center on a small artificial mound. I sat down on my chair, with Dinga standing beside me, pulled out a packet of cigarettes and began to smoke.

I still remember those cigarettes—a full pack of ten Gold Flake. An hour passed without a sound or a movement in the village. Then the door of one of the huts cautiously opened; four men came out and walked slowly up to me.

Three of them wore only strips of bark cloth, supported by belts of gorilla skin. The fourth wore in addition a headdress of monkey skins and several large bangles of ivory. Each of them carried three heavy spears.

When they were six paces from me they stopped, undecided what to do. I spoke to them in the Yaounde language, hoping that one of them would understand.

"Where is your chief?" I asked.

They just stared at me, making no answer, so I put my hand in my jacket pocket and brought out another packet of cigarettes, which I offered to them. At this sudden movement they sprang back, raising their spears, but they relaxed again when they saw the cigarettes. One of them stretched forward, took the whole packet and surprised me by speaking in Pidgin.

"Massa, we t'ank you," he said.

"You savvy English?" I asked.

The man nodded, still looking uncertain. I repeated my original question in Pidgin.

"Which side be you' king?"

He pointed to the man wearing the monkey skin headdress. "Dis be him," he said. "Him name be Oballa."

I offered Oballa my hand, but he just nodded and waved. I thought he was refusing to shake hands, but when I looked around I found that a crowd of spearmen had crept up behind me and that Oballa was waving them back. At this sign, the tension disappeared like magic. Oballa shook hands with me, and grinned, revealing that he had only two teeth in his upper jaw. They had been filed to points, like those of all the Mendjims, and they so much resembled the canines of a cat that my men afterwards nicknamed him tiger-mouth.

Meanwhile the villagers came pouring out of their huts,

chattering and pointing to my clothes, which seemed to amuse them vastly. My waiting carriers on the other side of the stream, seeing that all was well, crossed over, bringing my pets and equipment. The Mendjim who spoke Pidgin said that his name was Besalla and that I might live in the guard hut while I stayed with them. This was the first indication that I was to be allowed to stay at all.

My things were unpacked under the curious eyes of all the villagers, who excitedly commented on each article as it came to light. A hundred black fingers pointed in astonishment at my cat, an animal that few had seen before. Then Percy, my parrot, fluttered up on to the eaves of the hut, stretched his wings and remarked, "Good morning, Massa."

There was dead silence. Everyone stopped talking and looked about for the source of these words. Percy regarded the assembly with a benevolent eye. "Morning, Massa," he said again.

This time the villagers spotted the bird and they crowded around, pointing to him in great excitement. With so appreciative an audience, what could Percy do? Cackling a bit to clear his throat, he launched off into a long speech.

"Morning, Massa. Morning, Massa. You well, Massa? Cook, bring Massa coffee!" he croaked, but by then his audience was convulsed with laughter. Never had they heard anything so funny as a parrot that talked! When they subsided a bit, I explained through Besalla that I had taught the bird to say these words, and they goggled in admiration at the mighty hunter to whom even the birds spoke when he commanded them. If there had been any doubt of my welcome before, Percy had cleared it up, and afterwards the friendliness and hospitality towards me knew no bounds.

That night I heard gorillas making their queer gurgling noise near the village. In the morning I had a long talk with Besalla and went off with him to explore the surrounding forest. Within an hour I had found twenty gorilla beds in three sets, all of them recently vacated, and there were abundant gorilla tracks and signs of their feeding. Besalla did not consider this remarkable. In the village there were many gorilla bones and skulls to be seen, and most of the men wore belts of gorilla skin. There was no doubt in my mind that here was the country I had sought for so long. Gorillas were my neighbors at last.

A day or two later I paid off the carriers and sent them back to Lelo. I kept with me Dinga, Collonel, N'Denge, Wo-Wo Foot, and Atanaga, telling them to prepare for a long stay. In that case, they said, they would need their women; could they send a messenger off for them? Of course I agreed, and amid much laughter, ribaldry and backslapping, they chose Wo-Wo for this important mission. I imagined it to be their usual joke on him, and expected them to send someone more fleet-footed at the last minute, for though Wo-Wo could keep up with our slow forest safaris, especially when he had only to follow the paths we cut, the trip to Lelo would have taken an able-bodied man five hard days, and Wo-Wo could not have done it in twice that time. But Wo-Wo went off grinning like mad; no one else was sent after him and he did not come back that night. I was much taken aback next morning when he returned with all the women, but it was considered the very cream of the joke that poor crippled Wo-Wo should have done a ten-day journey in ten hours. The truth was that the women had been following our safari all the time, and were hiding nearby in the bush, waiting for my approval of their presence.

The huts of Arteck had walls of bark and roofs of palm leaves, and were partitioned into three or four rooms. Later on I was able to make a complete census of the population. There were fifty-seven men, eighty-two women, seventy-one boys and fifty-one girls. These people were so poor that the Government had reduced their taxes to a minimum, and I believe that they were the lowest in the Cameroons. Taxes were collected by native soldiers who toured the forest for that purpose once a year, under a native officer, for no European official ever entered the Mendjim Mey. Even medical missionaries and Government doctors never went beyond Meyoss on the very fringe of the territory.

Almost all agricultural work was done by the women. Each had her own plantation, cleared of bush by the men, and in this she planted groundnuts, sweet potatoes, cassava and maize. Sometimes the women also grew bananas or plantains, but these were usually grown behind the huts by the men. Kitchen refuse—the only manure they ever used—was thrown round the base of the stems.

The men spent most of their time hunting or making weapons. They never hunted in groups of more than two or three, and it is a tribute to their courage that they fearlessly attacked big male gorillas with spears at close range. They were often injured, but I never heard of one being killed. It is important to remember that they hunted gorillas only for food or to protect their crops.

Religion, so far as I could gather, played no part in their lives, but they conformed to a strict and complex system of tribal laws. Taboos relating to the food eaten by pregnant women were of particular importance. Here is a table of the proscribed animals and the effects attributed to eating their flesh:

Bongo: Baby will have bad sores on its legs.

Water Chevrotain: Slight scratches on the newly born infant will increase in size and never heal.

Red or Yellow-backed Duiker: Stillbirth; or excessive menstruation in women who are not pregnant.

Giant Forest Hog: Child will be born hairy.

Elephant: Child with abnormally large feet. (This might be an attempt to account for the disease known as elephantiasis.)

Red River Pig: Flesh from the head of this animal produces children with warts.

Fish: Child will be born covered with a red rash and will die.

White-bellied Duiker: Newly born child might lose consciousness, but will recover again if a sitaunga skin is spread over it.

Fowls: Not to be killed during wife's pregnancy or child will die.

If the flesh of the yellow-tipped ear monkey is eaten by a woman, it will prevent her husband from shooting straight. The flesh of goats, gorillas and chimpanzees is entirely forbidden to women.

Polygamy is general. Besalla had four wives and the chief Oballa had six. Girls are considered nubile when they are between twelve and fourteen, and for the most part they get on well with their fellow wives. Each spends two consecutive nights with her husband, though the senior wife, who has authority over the others, may spend longer. The woman thus honored also has to cook for her husband during the period she is with him and to supply the food from her own plantation, so that the more wives a man has, the less work they have to do.

Intercourse is forbidden during pregnancy and during the two-year suckling period, and if this law is broken it is believed that the child will die. On the death of a man his women, along with his other property, are inherited by his sons, who may marry them or sell them again. Thus a woman is always some man's property, and may be sold and resold two or three times. It would never occur to these women that they could lead any other kind of life, and they are as happy as women anywhere else. If their owner-husband happens to be old or frigid, they soon find more vigorous love elsewhere, usually with the husband's consent.

I once asked Besalla why he needed more than one wife. "Man no want chop (eat) Jamba Jamba every day," he chuckled. Jamba Jamba is a kind of spinach which upsets your stomach if you eat it too often.

Boys are circumcised at puberty, usually in June, but there is no special ceremony. The operation is performed without anaesthetic by the village witch doctor, using a sharp iron knife, and is watched with great interest by the young girls. A boy who cries out or shows any sign of pain is teased for weeks afterwards and has great difficulty in finding a wife. As soon as possible the boy is given over for instruction in love-making to his father's eldest wife, usually a woman past child-bearing, and remains with her until he is old enough to buy a wife of his own. This, as I had learned before, was a custom practiced by several tribes in the Cameroons.

The Mendjim men file their teeth to points, without any ill effect, yet if a European breaks a tooth or even cracks the enamel, decay soon sets in.

In the Mendjim Mey, girls are bought with goats, sheep and dogs—which are kept principally for that purpose—and with "bride money" called N'Jouice, flat, oblong pieces of native-smelted iron with long, tapering handles. A virgin, of less value than an experienced woman, costs five or six pieces of bride money, and a woman who has had one child by another man may fetch eight or nine. Bride money pieces are made by the men, who believe that if they have relations with a woman on the day of smelting, the ore will produce little iron.

Witchcraft plays an all-important part in the tribesmen's lives. Once, when the men had no luck in hunting, Oballa decided to "make medicine" to see if their luck was going to change, or whether someone among them "had witch." The men lined up in the village street, laying their spears, cross-bows and arrows beside them on the ground. The women and girls formed up in another line facing the men. Oballa then took a fowl, slit its throat and sent it staggering down between the two lines. Blood from the dying bird sprinkled over the weapons and it eventually collapsed on one of the spears. This was the good omen they had been hoping for and everyone was delighted. Had the fowl died at the feet of a woman she would have been accused of witchcraft and driven from the village.

Snares and game pits are used for catching animals, and when a Mendjim finds an animal in his trap, he breaks off a Y-shaped twig and thrusts it into the nostrils of the animal before carrying it home, where the twig is removed and carefully preserved. Before setting out on the next visit to the traps, he breaks the twig across his forehead and throws the two parts one over each shoulder. This ensures that more animals will be found in the traps.

After I had been with the Mendjim Mey for several months and had gained some influence over them, I was visited by Que-ar-Bar, the chief of another village, who asked for my help in the matter of making medicine to help him hunt. This was the story he told me, speaking in his own language:

"Years ago I married my first wife, who is the sister of Besalla. Recently Besalla encouraged her to desert me, saying that I do not like her any more. She has borne me two children and I still like her, though it is true that I have four younger wives with whom I sleep very often. After all, does not every old man like me enjoy young girls?

"Now the custom of our people is that, when we want to hunt gorilla, our eldest wife must make medicine for us. She takes a small piece of bamboo and lights it in the fire, then she spits on it and rubs the charred end on our foreheads. I have hunted gorillas three times lately, but I failed because my eldest wife was not there to make this medicine. Will you make Besalla send her back to me? If she does not come I shall never again succeed in hunting gorillas."

I promised to do my best, and when Que-ar-Bar had gone I sent for Besalla and the woman. They grumbled a lot, but Besalla agreed to send her back, and the woman said she would perform the magical duties required of her. I met Que-ar-Bar again a few weeks later and he said that the woman had kept her promise and that his luck had returned.

Tribal warfare, of course, had been put down long ago, but many of the older Mendjims remembered the old days. Pomtula, of Arteck, gave me this account of a raid made against the Kaka people, who live to the north of the Mendjim Mey.

"When I was a young man I was a big warrior, and my father was the chief of this village. One day we went through the forest to Toukou in the Kaka country and then on to Bimba, which we burnt to the ground after swimming across the Doume River. The Kakas heard us coming and ran away, but we killed many of their men and captured many girls, whom we brought back here and sold. We brought back the boys too, and kept them as slaves. We ate the men we killed, taking out first the stomach, liver and heart, which of course are the best parts of men or animals. We brought other Kaka men back here alive and gave them to our fathers, who killed them for food. Our fathers tied up these men and killed them by carefully cutting their throats, so that the blood could be drained off and drunk. We also killed and ate some of the women. Everyone tried to get the sexual organs, which are the nicest parts, being full of fat.

"Our chief, my father, commanded us when we went to battle, and he wore a plume of red parrot feathers on his head. We, the Mendjims, were the strongest tribe, for we had guns. Only the N'Jem people had guns beside ourselves. I do not know where they came from, but they were bush guns (flintlocks), not nice guns like yours, and we bought them with ivory. Sometimes our young men went away for months and brought these guns back with them.

"When I was very young, another tribe called the Gart used to make war on us. They came from the west (the Akonolinga side) and they too had guns. They were always taking away our men and women. They joined up with the

Kakas and used them as guides, but we beat them all at last. We hate the Kakas even today."

Oballa had a much more recent account of cannibalism to tell me. "Nine years ago," he said, "the Paramount Chief of the Mendjim Mey came to Arteck and had a row with my father, who told him to get out. The Paramount Chief refused to do so, so my father caught him and tied him up. He cut a hole in each of his forearms, pushed pieces of liana through the holes and tied him to a spiky tree. Then he opened his belly and took out his liver. He roasted the liver and found that it tasted bitter, so he did not eat it, and he burned the rest of the body. The Government found out about this and then sent a lot of policemen to catch my father. They did not kill him, but they put him in prison, where he died last year."

As I had been told, the men of Arteck were jealous of their hunting grounds, and although they were delighted to sell me the animals they caught or killed themselves, for a long time they refused to let me go hunting with them or by myself, and I dared not forfeit their goodwill by defying this ban.

One day, N'Denge came and told me that a pair of gorillas had been raiding a sugar cane plantation owned by one of Besalla's wives, and that Besalla was going to kill them. I hurriedly interviewed him, offered him compensation for the damaged sugar cane, and begged him to leave the gorillas alone while I studied them. He agreed to this, and I got N'Denge and Collonel to build me a hide on the plantation from which I could watch the gorillas without being seen.

I do not like being sentimental about animals, but I must confess that I fell for that pair of gorillas as soon as I set eyes on them. They had both just reached maturity and were obviously in the first year of their life together. The female was pregnant, with about a month to go, and was scarcely half the size of her gigantic lover. Every morning they came out of the bush at about seven o'clock, sat down in the plantation and began to break down all the sugar cane within reach. Usually they only took a bite or two at each cane before discarding it for another, so that, as usual, they ruined far more food than they could eat. One day one of Besalla's wives, ignoring her husband's instructions not to visit the plantation while I was there, put in an appearance and was seen by the gorillas. The female at once made for the bush, but the bull stood erect and beat on the top of his vast belly, whereupon the woman hastily retreated and the bull sat down again to resume his interrupted meal.

Within a week the gorillas had destroyed half the plantation. Besalla was furious, pointing out, quite rightly, that money could not replace his lost food. He insisted that I should shoot them, and threatened to kill them himself if I did not. If my gorillas had to die I preferred to shoot them, for the spears and poisoned arrows of Besalla would have given them a slow and cruel death, so the next time I went to the hide I took my rifle with me. Strangely enough, they did not appear that morning, and when Besalla heard of this he at once decided that they must be ju-ju gorillas. They had known by magic, he said, that I would have my gun with me, and had kept away. Moreover, there was no doubt that they were destroying his plantation in revenge for the gorillas he had killed.

I prevailed upon him to give me another chance, and the next morning he came with me to the hide. This time the gorillas turned up as usual, but when I looked along the sights of my Mannlicher I could not bring myself to kill them. Instead, I fired three times just above their heads, and I was delighted to see the pair of them rush back into the forest. But Besalla's anger had now turned to fear; he refused to believe that I had fired without intending to kill, and was convinced that the ju-ju gorillas had warded off my bullets by magic.

That evening there was a big palaver in the village, and the witch doctor worked furiously preparing all kinds of charms and ju-jus against the gorillas. I hoped that they would not raid the plantations again, after the scare I had given them, but they turned up on the other side of the village two days later. Armed with the charms and ju-jus, as well as with spears and crossbows, Besalla and his men took off to track them down, leaving me disconsolate and unhappy in the village. In the evening they brought back the body of the female. My diagnosis of her condition was correct, and I bought and preserved the almost fully developed foetus, which I sent to the University College, London. The young bull, however, had escaped the hunters, and so far as I know he never again appeared in Arteck.

By now I was sending a constant stream of animals out of the Mendjim Mey through the hands of agents to collectors, zoos, museums and other scientific institutions. As the Mendjims got used to me and realized my economic importance to them, the last vestiges of their reserve disappeared, and they began taking me into the forest or letting me hunt there alone. Through their kindness I was able to spend many happy months studying the numerous gorilla families that bred within a few miles of Arteck, and the many other kinds of fascinating creatures that abounded in the forests.

Soon after my arrival at Arteck, a small boy brought me a baby putty-nosed monkey, only a few days old. My bitch fox terrier was still suckling her four pups, and as an experiment I handed the tiny, spidery thing over to her care. She accepted it without a murmur of disapproval, and half an hour later I found it sucking away alongside the pups, as vigorously as the best of them.

Another kind of monkey common in the forest was the debrazza. They are nearly always found near streams and are excellent swimmers. I had one in Yaounde for years and it regularly swam in my duck pond.

Fresh-water prawns and crabs were found in the Mendjim Mey streams, and made excellent eating. The prawns were nearly three inches long, but the crabs were comparatively small, measuring about five inches across the shell.

I found many Red River pigs and occasionally the rare giant forest hog. The latter live in pairs, not in herds like other pigs, and are browsers, not rooters. When it is almost time for her to farrow, the sow makes a pile of leaves and crawls underneath, while the boar stands guard and will attack any approaching man or beast, as I several times found to my cost. The boar is difficult to see in the undergrowth and will not make a sound until he is almost upon you. Red River pigs do not differ much from other members of the pig family, but one of them got mixed up in a bit of witchcraft in Arteck which I have never been able to understand.

I was strolling about the village early one morning waiting for Atanaga to make my coffee, when I heard an old woman calling out from her hut. A young sow Red River pig came trotting out of the forest and walked straight into the woman's hut, where it was caught and tied up. I asked Oballa how this extraordinary thing happened, and this is what he told me.

"The old woman is called Etcheck and she is the mother of Juoute, a lazy man who will not go hunting. I had him flogged for his laziness not long ago, because his family has no meat to eat. But Etcheck is a witch who has power over animals, and this is the second one she has called out of the forest. The first time she called, a buffalo came to her hut and the young men slew it with their spears. Now you have seen her call up a pig, but you are a white man and you will not believe this magic."

The sow was certainly a wild animal—I made sure of that —and I have no idea why it should have surrendered voluntarily as it did. I bought it alive from the old woman, and when it became reasonably docile I sent it to Batouri, where it became the second wife of the famous boar Abock, whose story is told in the next chapter.

In April there were the huge and beautiful leaf toads lying

among the fallen leaves on the forest floor. They have yellow
backs and red sides, closely resembling autumn leaves. I tried
skinning one of them and two days afterwards I developed
sores between my fingers. Besalla said they were caused by a
poison secreted by glands in the toad's head. Mixed with the
crushed seeds of the plant *Strophantis*, this substance, in the
form of a sticky brown paste, was the poison used on arrows
and darts.

Inside a hollow tree I discovered hundreds of fruit bats,
with chestnut-colored fur and fantastic, rosette-shaped noses.
Their bodies were nearly five inches long and they had a
wingspan of about twenty-six inches. Fruit bats used to swarm
on the raffia palms near Arteck once every two or three years,
and the villagers caught them by the score, stringing them
together like onions and smoking their bodies after the viscera
had been removed. I saw one of these swarms myself. There
were many thousands of bats, and their combined weight had
broken down dozens of the big palms.

Some years later, at Bafang, in the northwest, I saw another
swarm of fruit bats, this time on oil palms. They stayed for
two days, and when they left the trees looked as though they
had been torn to pieces by a violent storm. It took them years
to recover. Unlike the Mendjims, the Bamileke people of
Bafang made no attempt to catch them, and they looked at me
in disgust when I asked whether they were not good for food.
In both swarms, every female bat had a tiny baby clinging to
her fur under her leathery wings, so that it may be that the
swarming had something to do with breeding.

One day in October, during my first year at Arteck, thousands of Abdim storks, apparently on migration, came flying
across the forest from a northerly direction and settled in the
trees. These large black and white birds are venerated by the
tribes in the north of the Cameroons, who consider it a good
omen if they roost on their huts. The storks are therefore
without fear of man, but the Mendjims thought of them only

as food and did great slaughter among them before they took off again and disappeared southeast.

Among the very rare animals I caught were several giant water shrews, which are about the shape and size of a small otter, but with the tail flattened vertically. Several attempts have been made to get these animals back to Europe and America alive, but I do not think anyone has yet succeeded. My own specimens died within a few weeks of capture, in spite of everything I could do. Though I bought other giant water shrews from the villagers, I always let them go again, because it seemed impossible to keep them alive.

Of the many baby animals caught and brought to me from time to time, perhaps the most lovely was a trio of genet kittens. These are small, catlike, spotted animals, which live almost exclusively in the trees, preying on birds and small mammals. Though they are pretty and playful, they do not make good pets, for they do not become wholly tame and can never be trusted. They are too small, of course, to do you much harm, but their bites and scratches can be deep and painful.

More than six months passed before I made friends with the Mendjim Mey Pygmies, whom the Mendjims call Bomanjock, or elephant men. They are seldom more than four feet six inches tall, and are of a lighter color than the average West African tribesman. They have a primitive language, they make and use a few weapons and cooking utensils, and they wear loincloths of skins; but they have no art, no decorations or ornaments and no agriculture. In fact, their way of life is not much more advanced than that of the gorilla.

Their little huts, shaped rather like an Eskimo's igloo, consist of saplings tucked into the ground with others attached to them laterally, and covered with huge leaves like tiles. Encampments of these huts are never occupied for more than a week or two and are always near streams, which are used as paths so that there is no trail leading to the encampment. The Pygmies live entirely by hunting and they are as clever at it as any animal, crawling up through the undergrowth to within a few feet of elephants and spearing them to death. In a later part of this book I have described how I saw this happen.

Organized gorilla roundups in the Mendjim Mey took place only once or twice during my stay there. The Mendjims preferred to hunt gorilla families with crossbows and poisoned darts, after disposing of the Old Man with spears, and like the Nvelle people they mutilated the animals terribly. They could not understand why they should deny themselves the savage delight in cruelty, and for a time the skins they tried to sell me were too badly cut to be of any value. But when they learned that I would not buy skins that were punctured all over with spear thrusts, they took care to kill as cleanly and efficiently as they could, and though there were times when they could not restrain themselves, for the most part their gorilla hunts became no more cruel than the slaughter of cattle in British abattoirs.

This, of course, took time, and the first Mendjim gorilla hunt I saw was horrible. One evening in November, Besalla came and told me that a family of gorillas was making its beds a few hundred yards behind the village and that his hunters were going after them in the morning. He invited me to come and watch, but extracted a promise from me that I would on no account use my rifle. We all got up a five o'clock in the morning, but it was wet and misty and Besalla said that in such weather the gorillas would not leave their beds until after dawn.

We left the village soon after it was light, our party consisting of N'Denge, Collonel, myself, Besalla and five of his hunters, each armed with a spear, a crossbow and a quiver containing about fifty poisoned darts. We soon found the gorillas' beds, which were still warm from the heat of their bodies, and fresh tracks leading into the forest. The gorillas had gone off in a single file and Besalla thought they were returning to a patch of *Aframomum* further on where they had been feeding the day before.

I was asked to wait while Besalla and his men tracked the gorillas, and only a few minutes after they left me I heard the animals screaming and barking. Besalla came back to say that the Old Man had been driven off and that two of his men had gone after him, while three other gorillas had been treed. He asked me to come and watch, but warned me again that I was not to shoot.

When I reached the tree I found a three-quarter-grown male, an adult female and a much smaller one moving about in a state of great agitation in the branches above. Besalla's two remaining hunters were cutting away the undergrowth around the base of the tree, while he stood guard, and when this was done they began to beat on the trunk with the shafts of their spears. The young bull gorilla started to come down, but when he got almost within reach of the spears he went back up again.

Besalla then took up a position some twenty feet from the tree and said that he was going to shoot at the young bull, so that his angle of fire was about forty-five degrees. I watched his target through my field glasses, for I wanted to see what happened when the gorilla was hit, but Besalla missed with his first two or three shots. The crossbow clicked again and this time the gorilla clapped his hand to his thigh, and gave a grunt. He broke off the dart with his hand, and when a second dart struck his shoulder he attacked it with his teeth, grunting and screaming all the time. There were further clicks of the crossbow, and the gorilla was hit in the stomach and back, but many of Besalla's shots missed altogether.

Meanwhile, the other gorillas had also been hit and they were all infuriated, tearing at the branches with their teeth and hands. To my astonishment, the bull tore off a dead branch and flung it at the hunters below, after peering about to locate them accurately. The female was bouncing up and down on the branch, with the intention, Besalla declared, of breaking it off and dropping it on our heads.

About half an hour after the shooting began, the gorillas started to retch and groan, supporting themselves with their feet and hands. Then they began to vomit and sway about in agony. Their muscles relaxed, they swayed more and more, as though they were drunk, and finally two of them died and came tumbling down out of the branches. The third and smallest one crawled along to a fork in the tree and died there, where it was impossible to reach it.

The dead female, I found, had a crippled right foot and a diseased and withered left forearm, the hand being bent inwards and the elbow rigid. Besalla said that the disease was called Chully-Chang and that it was caused by the poison of the liana or vine known as Nqua-Zock.

The young bull had a bad wound on the inner side of his right wrist, which looked as though it had been inflicted during a fight with another gorilla, probably an Old Man with whom he had disputed leadership of the family. In each of his shoulder blades there was a strange and inexplicable hole, about the size of a sixpenny piece.

The hunters who had gone after the Old Man returned as I was examining these animals, one of them with a broken arm. This was his story:

"We followed the big gorilla and when he discovered that he could not get away from us he climbed into a low tree, which is what we hoped he would do, so that we could use our poisoned darts. I fired one dart and my companion fired another. Both of them hit the gorilla and he began to come down the tree. When he was about eight feet from the ground, the other man threw his spear at him and ran away, but I waited until he was nearer and then stuck my spear in his belly and held on to it. The gorilla screamed and twisted round the tree, but I held on and he let go of the tree and fell on top of me, breaking my arm. He tried to crawl away, but the other man came back and speared him again and again until he died. My arm will soon get better, for we will make 'country medicine' for it. Many people have their arms broken, but they always get well again."

When I saw the man the next day his arm was covered with mashed up leaves and supported by a wooden splint reaching from his armpit to just below his elbow, while he grasped a two-inch piece of wood to prevent his hand from growing stiff.

Some eighteen months after this I was in need of "country medicine" myself. I had been feeling unwell for several days and eventually I became so bad that I had to go to bed and stay there—a rare event in my life. The pain that had been gnawing at my stomach grew agonizing—I thought I had been poisoned—and although I dosed myself lavishly with all the few simple remedies I had with me—quinine, aspirin and Epsom Salts—I grew steadily worse. Atanaga was frightened and insisted that I should get carriers to take me on a hammock to Batouri, where there was a European doctor. I readily agreed to this, but before the hammock was ready I felt too bad even to move. In any case it would have taken weeks for me to get to a doctor, or a doctor to me, if one could be found who was willing to make the journey. All I could think of was that I wanted to die. At last, in desperation, I asked Atanaga to see if the village witch doctor could help.

He went off and returned a little later with a most revolting looking brew made, he announced, of "leaves and herbs," and somewhat resembling half-cooked porridge. I was to drink it all, the witch doctor said. With a tremendous effort I managed to swallow about an eighth of the thick, sticky mess, and half an hour later it worked. Nothing was left in my stomach, not even, I believed, the things that should have been there. I vomited like a seasick elephant off and on for the rest of the day, and at the end of it I felt as though I had been gutted. It was a surprise to realize that my heart, liver and intestines were intact. But I slept that night for the first time in days, and next day I felt better. By the end of the week I was as right as rain, but I never did find out what the brew was made of. "Leaves and herbs" was all the witch doctor would say.

What I did find out was that Atanaga had been responsible for my illness in the first place. He had got himself involved in some "woman palaver" and poison delivered surreptitiously by the offended husband had somehow found its way into my food instead of his.

Altogether I stayed in the Mendjim Mey for over three years, to the mutual benefit of myself, the Mendjims, science and, incidentally, the Government, which was delighted to find that at last the Mendjims could pay their taxes. Even the women profited, for with my own men and with carriers coming and going, much more food was needed, and they increased their plantations to sell us vegetables. It was not always easy to deal with these wild, independent tribesmen, who were in turn wise and childish, savage and gentle. But I had only to threaten to leave them to have them falling over themselves to please me.

Early in my stay with them, they noticed and applauded the simple justice I used to settle disputes among my men, and soon they were bringing their own problems for my judgment. The African loves justice and gets as much satisfaction and delight out of wise jurisdiction as a Briton gets out of a Cup-tie Final. They came to me so often for this purpose that I had to set aside Sunday mornings for my casual and quite unauthorized courts. Later I discovered that many of the disputes they brought to me had already been settled, sometimes months, sometimes even years before, but they dearly wanted to know whether my judgment tallied with theirs.

But I was growing tired. One day I realized that I had not been out of West Africa for twenty years—a record for any

European in that part of the world—and I decided that a few
months in England would do me no harm. I came out of the
Mendjim Mey, settled up my affairs in Batouri and Yaounde,
and a month later sailed for home.

10. Shootman's Woman

At the time, I could not understand why I should be thought crazy for taking a young wife back with me into the bush, but my friends in the Cameroons told us bluntly that we were both out of our minds. Life in the remote forests of West Africa is certainly full of danger. There are venomous snakes, scorpions and centipedes; leopards, gorillas and savage wild pigs; sudden violent storms and floods; malaria, sleeping sickness and countless other hideous diseases, many of them still unnamed. There is the constant menace of insect life, with swarms of lively parasites, termites that secretly honeycomb the timbers of a house and driver ants that have been known to overwhelm and devour a sick and helpless man.

We were to live five days' march from the nearest European and a good deal further from any doctor. Our medical supplies were limited to quinine, iodine and aspirin. Somehow we came through it all unscathed, but it was not until years later that I realized how foolish I had been to take an English girl, fresh from a London suburb, to live under these conditions with a primitive tribe who were almost certainly cannibals. It did not strike me then because I was as familiar with the dangers of the forest as a Londoner is with those of Piccadilly traffic and, I suppose, equally indifferent to them. As for my wife, her faith in me overwhelmed any misgiving she might have had. I cannot overcome my astonishment that she should have taken all these things in her stride and accepted so much without a murmur.

Hilda and I met and married during the short holiday I spent in England, and our honeymoon was spent on the voyage back to Africa. We landed at Douala and went by train to Yaounde (a journey of one hundred and ninety-one miles; taking about twelve hours), where the European population was agog to see the woman who was willing to share my reckless, wandering life. But it was their warm friendship and not their curiosity that found expression in the hectic round of dinners and parties to which we were invited, while preparations were made for our journey to the Mendjim Mey where we were to make our home. For this I planned a roundabout route so that Hilda could see something of the country and so that I could visit Maton, the French coffee planter near Batouri who was one of my oldest friends, and to whom I sent all my specimens from the forest for dispatch abroad.

Atanaga turned up as soon as he heard of our arrival, and we sent him off to Maton's with the bulk of the luggage. For this journey, three hundred miles further into the interior, we were offered a lift by two young planters who were traveling up to Batouri in an ancient Ford sedan. We had arranged to leave Yaounde early in the morning, expecting to arrive at Maton's before dark, but in Africa white people soon adopt the native indifference to the clock, and my two friends did not turn up until one P.M. This meant we would not reach Maton's until very late, even if the old car did not let us down. I did not much like the look of it, but our lively companions were so full of confidence that I agreed to carry on.

For a while all went well. Sitting with Hilda in the back of the car, I was fully occupied in answering all her eager questions about the country we were passing through. At Ayos, on the bank of the Nyong river, we came to a Government hospital devoted to research into trypanosomiasis, the dreaded sleeping sickness carried by flies, fleas, bugs and leeches, which is one of the most debilitating and fatal diseases of tropical Africa. During the 1914–18 war, when this was German territory, British prisoners of war were interned in this hospital. Now groups of native patients were sitting outside, most of them with large white numbers painted on their dark skins to record their identity and details of their treatment. This is a common practice in West Africa; it saves the hard pressed doctors a good deal of paper work and ensures that no mistakes are made.

A district particularly rife with sleeping sickness had been chosen as the site for the hospital, for on the other side of the river was an extensive swamp where parasites carrying the disease bred in countless millions. Because of the swamp the continuation of the road we had come along was nearly two miles downstream. The ferry was a primitive affair consisting of three dugout canoes which were connected by stout beams supporting a wooden platform. There were twelve native paddlers, chosen from the local population for their splendid strength and physique.

Three of us got out of the car while our driver urged it cautiously up a crazy ramp of loose planks onto a ferry, which thereupon curtsied deeply to its heavy guest and shipped several gallons of muddy water. We climbed on after it and sat down on the running board of the car, while the paddlers, waist-deep in water, pushed us off and then jumped into their positions, two at either end of each canoe. Twenty yards from the bank, the swirling current caught us and sent us spinning off down the river, while the paddlers dug furiously at the water with little apparent effect.

At this point the river was a mile wide, broken by reeking mudbanks and scores of tiny islands covered with brilliant green vegetation. Whenever we approached an island the paddlers made a supreme effort to get into the quiet water behind it, and thus, in fits and starts, we edged across. Eventually we reached a point about two hundred yards upstream of our landing point, but between us and the bank was a deep channel where the water raced along with tremendous force, and in this the ferry spun and dipped until we began to get dizzy. To our dismay we were swept past the landing point, but before we had got far the paddlers, streaming with sweat and spray, had us out of the main stream. Keeping close to the bank they paddled us back against the milder current until at last we grounded. The men were out instantly into the water, pulling the ferry squarely onto the mud, and ten minutes later the ramp was again in position and the car safely ashore. The crossing had taken us nearly an hour.

The road on this side of the river was deep in liquid mud. Our driver drove at top speed partly because he enjoyed it, but also so that there might be less risk of getting bogged down. This was wise, no doubt, but saplings and branches had been laid crossways to bridge the worst patches of the road, and when we hit them at forty miles an hour we all rose involuntarily and violently a good two feet into the air. The country became mountainous with long stretches of dense forest, broken at intervals by native villages and their adjoining fields, where the women worked amongst the maize, banana and yam plantations.

Before we had gone far we noticed that the outer cover of one of the tires had developed an alarming bulge. We stopped and put the spare wheel in its place, but this looked even less secure than the other. Darkness was falling when, with a report that shook the countryside, the tire capitulated and pitched us all into the bush. We got an old hurricane lantern out of the car and by its dim, smoky light inspected the damage. Fortunately, only our dignity was hurt, but there were no more spare wheels. A passing native took word of our plight to the next village, and shortly afterwards the headman arrived with a crowd of his young men, all of them delighted with this little break in their routine. With their help we soon had the car back on the road, but it was an hour before we had the cover off, the puncture sealed, and everything coaxed, squashed, screwed and cursed back into place again. Meanwhile, Hilda bravely sat through her first lesson in tropical torment, with the heat, flies, ants and mosquitoes as her eager tutors. Solemn, finger-sucking children and mangy dogs stood staring curiously at us from the shadows.

After a hurried supper out of a picnic basket we once more started on our way, but at a considerably reduced speed. The road was so narrow that our wheels brushed the undergrowth on each side and our headlamps were capable of only a dim yellow glow. Moreover we had no wish to meet the elephants which might be roaming this part of the forest. The old car could never have been reversed fast enough if we were charged. It was nearly midnight when we reached the village of Abong Mbang, with still one hundred and fifty miles to go, and we decided to stay there until next morning. I knocked up a native trader I knew and he sleepily gave me the key to a small vacant house he owned close by, where we prepared to make ourselves comfortable for the night.

This proved to be difficult. The house had not been used for months and there were several gaps in the roof where long-forgotten storms had stripped the palm-leaf thatch. Windows, walls and furniture were thick with dust and cobwebs, and the house would have made a happy hunting ground for an entomologist. The only hunting that took place that night, however, was conducted entirely by the other side. We had no bedding or mosquito nets, and as we lay down on the hard, native-style bamboo beds we were too tired to think of the legions of sandflies and mosquitoes that were even then buzzing excitedly in anticipation of the feast. When we got up before dawn next morning the four of us were a dreadful sight, covered from head to foot with spots and blotches, marking the sites of their orgies.

Hilda suffered worst, for her skin was more sensitive than

ours, but it was she who came to the rescue with an enormous bottle of eau-de-cologne, which helped to relieve the irritation. She had also made the interesting zoological discovery that cockroaches have a taste for artificial silk. This had hitherto escaped my attention since none of my garments were of that material, but during the night Hilda's celanese underwear, folded up neatly on a chair, had been reduced to shreds. Cockroaches almost three inches long are common in the tropics; their appetites and digestions are prodigious.

Our troubles were not yet over. We had not counted on so protracted a journey and we had finished the contents of our picnic basket and thermos flasks the day before. We had nothing to drink and no vessels suitable for boiling water from the local streams. Our companions went hungry and thirsty. Hilda and I shared a tin of Ideal Milk, which we drank neat, and we still remember the awful sickly sweetness of it. But our only thought was to get to Maton's as speedily as we could. Our rumbling stomachs made traveling even more uncomfortable than it had been on the previous day, and the only pause in the journey was to stop and stare for a moment at the old German fortress of Doume, a grim brick structure where the Germans for so long defied the British and French forces during the war. We reached Batouri shortly before noon and went straight to Maton's.

His plantation consisted of about three hundred well-kept acres of coffee, pineapples, bananas and groundnuts, and where the land bordered on the pretty Kadai River he had built his house. This was an oblong structure containing his own large bedroom, a fine cool sitting room, and a spare guest room which was almost always occupied, for Maton was one of the most popular men in the French Cameroons, and no one passed through Batouri without spending a few days with him. Connected to the house by a short covered walk was a secondary building, where he kept his girls, his kitchen, his stores and his pet pigs, the first and last occupying rooms at the opposite extremities. There were several outbuildings, including a tiny thatched bungalow where Hilda and I were to stay, and there were extensive well-kept gardens, where roses, hibiscus, lilies and a great variety of shrubs flourished throughout the year.

Maton was a short, lively man, with a dark, close-cropped moustache and laughing brown eyes. He was untidy in his person and was seldom seen wearing anything more impressive than a grubby singlet and crumpled khaki pants. He was waiting on the verandah to greet us, and he welcomed Hilda with a characteristic charm and courtesy that went at once to her heart. In spite of his weaknesses, he and Hilda later became firm friends.

Standing behind him in the shadows was his native woman Iyendi, one of the most remarkable women I have ever known. Maton bought her from her father when she was about fourteen and took her to live with him. Few French bachelors—and they were nearly all bachelors out there—were without their native women, and they made no secret of it. The same thing happened across the border in the British Cameroons, but the British have consciences, and they did their best to conceal it from one another. Iyendi bore Maton several children, all of whom he worshipped.

He sent the eldest to be educated in France and before he died of sleeping sickness a few years later, he had seen to it that thy were well provided for. Iyendi grew old prematurely, as all African women do, and she was, moreover, excessively ugly. She wore brightly colored cotton dresses and a silk scarf over her head, and she was always spotlessly clean.

She was devoted to Maton, and he thought the world of her. Until the nineteen twenties he had traded in rubber. Then the market collapsed, along with a good many other things in those bleak, hopeless days, and in common with most traders he found himself bankrupt almost overnight. In one way or another most of them succumbed to this blow. A few shot themselves, some took to drink and many drifted back to France or to other territories and other occupations. At first Maton went to pieces, but Iyendi was able to accept their downfall as just another of those natural calamities which go to make up life for the African, and in particular for African women. She was an ignorant, illiterate tribeswoman, but she remained superbly faithful to Maton. She nursed him when he was drunk or sick, she encouraged him when he had reached the depths of despair, and out of her simple wisdom she was able to show him how to save himself.

Starting again from scratch on a totally undeveloped concession of land, they toiled together half naked in the sun, clearing the bush and planting a few score coffee trees, which Iyendi rightly judged to be a profitable crop, while they fed themselves on whatever fruits and vegetables they could spare the time to grow. At Iyendi's suggestion they planted groundnuts too, and I believe she was the first woman to introduce them to that part of Africa. Slowly they fought their way back to prosperity, Iyendi taking most of the management of the estate and its growing labor force into her own capable hands, while Maton attended to the business end.

A wife of Maton's own race might have done as much, but Iyendi's devotion to her master went beyond the comprehension of any European woman. She calmly bowed to the fact that her haggard, wrinkled old body was no longer capable of giving him pleasure, so she set about finding him the comeliest virgins of the district, and saw to it that they pleased him. In the daytime she kept them busy about the house and garden, and fiercely watched over their chastity. At the time of our visit Maton had six of these girls, none of them more than eighteen. I had warned Hilda what to expect, and consequently she showed no surprise when dinner was served that evening by a smiling, happy little group of native girls, whose only concession to modesty was a diminutive bunch of leaves fore and aft, and whose full young breasts swung gaily over the dishes they placed before us.

After dinner, Iyendi took Hilda aside and began to talk about African women and her own people, the Kakas, in particular. She had noticed that European women could not carry things on their heads, and she insisted on demonstrating her own ability to do so, carrying in turn a pineapple, a bottle of Maton's beer, and finally an aged umbrella, while she trotted nimbly up and down. Then she called over one of the youngest girls and showed Hilda a most peculiar custom which is, so far as I know, confined to women of the Kaka tribe. The girl produced from her mouth half a dozen small stones, weighing about two ounces altogether. All Kaka women carry such stones under their tongues, even when they are eating or asleep, though I cannot imagine why they are never accidentally swallowed.

The stones are usually small pieces of quartz and are called Telembe by the Kaka people. Girls begin carrying them when they reach the age of seven and they are sometimes exchanged as a sign of friendship. The number varies considerably; I once found a girl who kept thirteen of them under her tongue. A dying woman will distribute her stones among her daughters, so that they are handed down from generation to generation. Every girl knows her own Telembe stones. I have several times taken them from a dozen girls and mixed them up, but their owners were always able to identify them. They have no apparent function, and no one knows, least of all the Kakas themselves, how the custom originated or why it is kept up. Perhaps these little pieces of quartz once had some monetary value and the mouth was chosen as the safest repository, so that in an emergency they could be hastily swallowed and recovered at leisure next morning, an old trick of South African diamond thieves.

Another theory concerns the migration of the Kakas from their original home far to the north, whence they were driven by slavers along with other tribes. During their long trek over the deserts, water was too precious to waste on the women, who took to sucking stones to alleviate their thirst and who, for some reason, retained this habit after settling in the forests. Hilda was given a number of Telembe stones, which she still has in her possession.

There was excitement in store for us that night. I was pleased to find that Maton still had the three pet pigs that I had caught and sent to him during my last stay in the Mendjim Mey forest. They were Red River hogs, a wild forest species, heavily built, with long, reddish-yellow hair and massive heads. Like most wild pigs they are savage, dangerous creatures, capable of disemboweling a man with their long curved tusks, but they tame easily and make wonderful pets.

My dogs had found the first of them, a tiny piglet which had somehow become separated from its dam and from the herd. When I rescued it from the dogs it responded by attacking me fiercely, butting at my ankles with its snub nose and trying to bite my toes, but since it was scarcely nine inches long the only effect of this was to amuse me. I picked it up and laughed aloud in its face. It squealed with fury at this insult and struggled violently, but when I had fed it, the angry blaze in its tiny eyes softened—clearly I was not such a bad fellow after all. I had no wish to leave the piglet in the bush, where it would have provided a small but tasty morsel for a passing leopard, so I took it back with me to Arteck and decided to make a pet of it.

This proved embarrassingly easy. Within a few days the pig would not leave me, trotting at my heels wherever I went. It was a male, and I named him Abock, the Mendjim Mey word for a local small red rat, which he closely resembled. I put up with his surfeit of affection for as long as I could, but since he insisted on following me into the bush when I went hunting and was consequently always in danger of being lost,

I packed him off to Maton's, asking if he could be looked after there.

Abock was a resounding success at Batouri, especially with Maton's children. They made a great fuss over him, supplied him with a blanket and a wickerwork basket, and took him to sleep with them in their bedroom. They had no difficulty in housetraining him, and in this as in many other things he behaved exactly like a dog, even sitting up in a clumsy, hoggish way to beg for tidbits from the table. Red River hogs are big animals, and Abock grew rapidly until he reached one hundred eighty pounds and stood twenty-six inches at the shoulder. Maton decided he was too big for the house, and henceforth he was banished to the adjoining stable, where he was living at the time Hilda and I arrived.

Meanwhile, I had caught two females of the same species, and these Abock took to his bosom with appreciative and affectionate grunts. The three of them were let out during the day and allowed the run of the plantation. They used to make a tour of the laborers' quarters to beg for food, and often went as far as the village, two miles away, where there was always a welcome for them from the natives. Sharp at five thirty every evening they reappeared, and the children brushed them down and searched them for ticks. Afterwards Abock gave the children rides on his broad back, but if too many got on he would suddenly shoot off like a rocket, spilling the laughing youngsters in piles of tangled, naked brown limbs as he went.

European domestic pigs are difficult to raise in West Africa, and Maton had the idea of using Abock to produce a crossbreed which might have all the hardiness of the Red River pig, together with the edible qualities of the European species, but he was never able to obtain a suitable female.

After Hilda retired that night, Maton and I sat up into the small hours talking of old times and discussing plans for the future. About two thirty a.m. we were startled from our reverie by an unearthly rumpus in Abock's stable. Maton grabbed his rifle and I a torch, and we rushed across to see what was going on. The window of the stable had been carelessly left open by one of the laborers, and through this we beheld an astonishing scene.

In the far corner of the table, snarling and spitting, crouched a big male leopard. Holding him at bay was Abock, his sturdy buttocks quivering with rage, his red hair standing bolt upright, making him look enormous. In the opposite corner were the two sows, who were giving their lord and master vocal encouragement. An instant after we had taken all this in, and before Maton could use his rifle, the leopard hurled itself at the hog, and the two animals rolypolied across the floor, ending up with a crash against the door and breaking it open. The leopard had had enough and hared off into the darkness, holding his tail stiffly upright out of harm's way. Domestic animals of this caliber were clearly outside his experience of natural history. But Abock had not done with him yet, and when the leopard disappeared from our sight, the pig was scarcely two feet behind him.

There was nothing Maton and I could now do to help the courageous pig, and in any case Abock had looked perfectly capable of dealing with the situation himself. And so it proved. Half an hour later he came back to be welcomed as a hero by his ladies with little snorts of admiration and loving nuzzles. He was still trembling all over and covered with blood, most of it apparently not his own. There was a good deal of leopard hair sticking to the blood around his nose. Abock's own thick, coarse hair, we found, had saved him from severe lacerations, and although there was a deep wound down the side of his ugly head, he was not badly hurt.

Although pigs are such heavily built, clumsy-looking animals, they can move like lightning when they want to, as the leopard had learned to his cost. Next morning Maton's men found its body among the coffee bushes and we went to examine it. The nose had been ripped off completely and the intestines protruded from a long gash which Abock's powerful tusks had ripped down the side. The skin was too badly damaged to be of any value, but Maton gave me the skull, which is now in the Powell-Cotton Museum at Birchington, Kent.

We could have wished for nothing better than to relax for a few days on Maton's lovely estate, where the coffee trees, in full bloom and redolence, looked as though they had been sprinkled with snow. But there was no time for idling. Our final destination was Arteck, deep in the virgin jungle, and we were prepared for an indefinite stay. Accordingly, our baggage was of considerable proportions. There were camp beds, mattresses, crockery, kitchen utensils and large supplies of foodstuffs such as tea, coffee, flour, salt and canned food.

In addition, there was all the paraphernalia of the hunter and collector: rifles and cases of cartridges, killing bottles for insects and large bottles of preservatives for embryos, the latter carefully packed for me by experts at the University College in London. Skinning knives, machetes for cutting through a dense undergrowth, formalin and alcohol were other important items. Lastly, there was a heavy wooden case full of five and ten centime pieces. These small-denomination coins had holes through their centers, and the natives wore them on strings round the neck or waist. Paper money was useless: it would have been destroyed in no time by the damp or by insects.

We were to travel for days through difficult country where there were no roads and where the only form of transport was by native carriers. All our goods had therefore to be broken down into fifty-pound packs, the accepted load for a carrier, and when the task was eventually completed we found that we would require forty men, as well as our cook, gunbearers and other servants.

Finding suitable combinations of these articles of a convenient shape to carry, and within the weight limit, was not an easy task, and I was pleased to have the drudgery of it broken by a visit from an old and welcomed friend. This was Besalla, the great hunter of the Mendjim Mey, who had been at Bimba, on the fringe of Mendjim Mey territory, when he heard of our arrival. He at once sent the news across the forest to Arteck, voiced by the big village drums. By the same means, Oballa, chief of Arteck, had sent a message back to me, which Besalla had come to deliver.

Besalla welcomed me warmly. Oballa and the men of his "town," he said, were overjoyed to hear of my return and they had already started to build me a house. They had heard that I was bringing my wife with me and that she was also going to stay with them at Arteck.

I clasped him about his broad bare shoulders, telling him how pleased I was to be back. Then we turned and faced Hilda.

"Is . . . is this Besalla?" she asked nervously.

"It is indeed! And a fine fellow you'll find him."

"Yes, Fred, so you've told me. But what has he done to his teeth?"

"His teeth?"

"Why are they filed to points like that?"

This was something I had certainly forgotten to mention before. All men of the Mendjim Mey filed their teeth, and Hilda knew well enough from her reading that this was a cannibal custom. In the old days the Mendjim Mey were continually at war with their neighbors, the Kakas and the Makas. When prisoners were taken, the young girls were kept as wives, and the others, old women, men and boys, were killed either by decapitation or cutting their throats, and then cooked and eaten.

According to Besalla, cannibalism had been dropped many years before, and the Mendjim Mey ate gorilla and chimpanzee meat as the nearest substitute. That was why they still filed their teeth: human and anthropoid flesh is said to stick to the bones and can be more easily removed with pointed teeth.

A few years before I became familiar with the tribe, one of their chiefs had been hung for eating a small girl, but that was the only recent evidence of cannibalism I ever found among them. There was, however, one sinister fact which Hilda herself was to notice during the coming months. Wherever else we traveled in the Cameroons, there were always many wrinkled, gray-haired old people to be seen squatting about the villages; but in the Mendjim Mey we seldom saw a man or woman past their prime. We suspected that when they were too old to hunt or work they were taken quietly off into the bush, slaughtered and eaten. Hilda once asked N'Dimo, our houseboy in Arteck, why there were so few old people to be seen, and his reaction seemed to be significant. He blushed furiously (even the blackest African can blush) and dashed off without a word.

Poor Hilda! There were so many things I had taken for granted and never bothered to tell her about before we left England. She had to discover for herself what it was like to live in the forest with only a shaky contact with civilization. Only the excitement of it had seemed important to me: the thrill of hunting, the fascination of the animals and of strange native customs, the wonder of seeing new lands and finding rare specimens. It was my great good fortune to have chosen a girl who quickly adapted herself to these conditions and who was able to share my own enthusiasm for collecting and studying wild animals.

Besalla also brought news that there were plenty of gorilla —N'gi—in the forest around Arteck, and that one had actually been seen just behind our new house.

With Besalla's help, the business of packing was speeded up and we were soon ready to leave. The Mendjim Mey country lay almost due south of Maton's, but the only track leading directly there was impassable to all but animals and an occasional tough native traveling fast and light. To take Hilda and forty carriers through that way was out of the question. Instead, we had to go back towards Yaounde, along the road we had already come, and then turn south at a large village called Beri to a narrow forest trail.

More old friends of mine, including my gun-bearer Collonel and two expert skinning men of the Mendjim Mey, turned up before we left. Maton brought out his decrepit old lorry and we all piled in on top of the baggage and were carted off to Beri. That was as far as Maton could take us, and after assuring himself that we would have no trouble getting carriers, he shook hands and drove off. He was the last white man we were to see for over six months.

The chief of Beri lined up sixty of his young men from which I could make my choice. I picked out the sturdiest of them, and from these again I chose eight of the best as a team to carry Hilda's tepoy, a bamboo hammock with a covered top, in which she could be carried when she found the going too tough.

Africans claim that they cannot live without women, and as usual the carriers insisted on bringing an adequate supply of them. Since the women could not leave their small children behind, they had to be brought too, and the company I led out of Beri that morning was therefore of embarrassing proportions. The noise was unbelievable. The villagers tacitly accepted the setting out of our expedition as a general holiday, and the entire population turned up to see us off. I placed myself at the head of the column, with Collonel, Besalla and Hilda immediately behind. Then came the long line of carriers, wearing only brief loincloths tied up tightly for the march, and balancing the heavy loads on their heads. Around them straggled the women, many taking tiny naked babies on their broad hips, and all with calabashes, kerosene tins and other essential household utensils they would need en route.

There was the utmost confusion: everyone was talking and shouting excitedly and when I gave the order to move off, the carriers started singing, the women hooted and patted their lips, as Red Indians do, and all around us the villagers were singing, clapping their hands and shouting farewells and good advice. Above this joyful rumpus rose the enthusiastic yapping of the dogs and the shrill bleating of frightened village goats.

Our first stop was Ngalebot, a village about seventeen miles from Beri. Hilda and I found fairly comfortable accommodation for the night in a rest house for European travelers. We were on the fringe of savannah country that stretched far to the north, and I decided to take her on a short hunting trip before turning south towards the Mendjim Mey. This would give me an opportunity for getting antelope for the museums and a supply of meat for the carriers. Like that of most Africans, their diet was deficient in protein, and meat would keep them well and happy during the arduous days ahead. This was to be Hilda's first hunting trip, and as it turned out it very nearly proved to be her last.

We went as far as Nyassi, where we told the carriers to wait. Taking with us only Collonel and six skinmen, we crossed the Doume river in leaky dugout canoes and passed through a mile-wide belt of forest before reaching the savannah. Under a clear blue sky the grasslands stretched as far as the eye could see, broken only by tiny hills, perhaps thirty feet high, and the typical growth of stunted trees. A little way from the edge of the forest were two of these hills, each with a few small trees at its foot, and between them, browsing in the yellow grass as he went, strolled a fine male bushbuck, looking for all the world as though he owned the place. The animal was upwind, moving away from us, and, taking Collonel, I began tracking it, leaving the others where they were.

When we had got as far as the second hill I glanced back over my shoulder and was astonished to see Hilda and the skinmen waving frantically at me. I was so intent on my quarry that for a minute or two my only reaction was anger that they should risk alarming the creature, and I moved forward several yards before it struck me that they were trying to draw my attention to something else. Looking round again I saw what they were pointing at.

Behind me, between the two hills, were seven buffalo, which had come up silently and were stalking me just as I was stalking the antelope. It has been well and often said that buffalo are the most dangerous of Africa's big game. They are mean, vicious, quick to attack and incredibly cunning and persistent in following up a victim. The herd was stamping their feet and tossing their great heads, working themselves up for a charge. Collonel and I did a sprint for the nearest cover—a clump of bushes at the foot of the nearest hill—and our sudden movement triggered off the charge. Two bulls and a big cow detached themselves from the herd and came thundering towards us. I fired twice at the first bull. The animal sagged to its knees and slowly rolled over, its legs jerking in the air. The two others pulled up a few yards beyond it, looking back at their fallen comrade and tossing their heads uncertainly. Then they saw Hilda and charged off towards her.

The skinmen instantly disappeared, in the miraculous way Africans have in such situations. Some of them dropped flat in the longest grass and the others crouched behind whatever bushes they could find. Hilda was utterly bewildered; to her, running or hiding seemed equally futile—as indeed they were —and while she hesitated the buffalo were almost upon her. When I squinted along the barrel of my Mannlicher and saw my wife and the buffalo in the same line of sight, I was so gripped with sheer cold fear that I gasped aloud. I fired three times in rapid succession. The first two bullets struck the leading animal deep in the forequarters, smashing the side of the shoulder girdle. It collapsed on to its chest, but its momentum sent it skidding along the ground, ploughing a deep furrow in the earth with its horns, and it came to a standstill barely ten paces from my wife. The third shot tore a long red gash along the flank of the other buffalo, which bucked wildly with pain and went careering off safely towards the right. The rest of the herd decided they had had enough and stampeded back the way they had come.

The buffalo that had so nearly killed my wife was still twitching and I ran up and dispatched it. Hilda was white-faced and trembling, but the boys, who could think of nothing but meat, were delighted.

"We shootman Massa done get fine fine woman," roared Collonel, dancing round the buffalo. "Missus done bring we plenty good luck."

I gave "shootman's woman" a hug. We had had quite enough hunting for one day, and leaving Collonel and the skinmen in charge of the carcasses we returned to Nyassi. I sent more men to help Collonel and before evening they were back with the flesh and skins. Most of the meat was at once cut up, smoked over small fires, heaped with damp green leaves, and carefully stored away to be beaten on the journey. There was sufficient left over for the carriers and their women to feast themselves that night.

Next morning we were up before the sun, and with the cold, damp mist rising to our waists, we turned south once more towards the Mendjim Mey.

11. Jungle Housekeeper

Carriers on the march are always singing improvised songs to keep up their spirits and to ease their loads. The lead may be taken by anyone to whom a suitable idea has occurred, and the others join in with a chorus which is modified in tone and volume to underline the mood and meaning of the soloist. The nature of the safari, its purpose and hoped for results, the people in it, their complaints and anxieties are common subjects for these cheerful calypsos. My own men were happy to have me back and proud to be carrying "shootman's woman," and they expressed their happiness in song.

"Yea, yea, yea, yea. Company soyar, company soyar (our company is coming)."

And then, from somewhere down the line, a solo voice:

"Massa get some fine fine woman."

Chorus: "Company soyar."

"He go get some fine fine pickin."

"Yea, yea, yea, yea. Company soyar."

And with pointed emphasis: "Massa go pay we plenty money."

"Company soyar. Yea, yea, yea, yea. Company soyar."

As usual poor old Wo-Wo came in for some goodnatured mockery from the safari wag, and the chorus was drowned in laughter:

"Wo-Wo Foot walks quick too much!"

"Yea, yea, yea, yea. Company soyar!"

Towards evening, when they grew tired, there were more hints directed at me.

"All we people stand (start) for tire."

"Company soyar."

No one was happier than Atanaga, who had bought a new and very sophisticated young wife called Eli—short for Elizabeth—out of the proceeds of our last trip. Both of them were dressed up to the nines, Atanaga in a trilby hat, long khaki pants and singlet, and Eli in a pink silk dress. Both wore white shoes which gripped their broad, flat feet so tightly that they limped with pain. With these unsuitable but immaculate garments they assumed an air of infinite superiority over the naked villagers, but they soon found that a muddy jungle track is no place for new clothes, and in order to preserve them without losing their sartorial dignity, they dressed just before we reached the villages, and stripped again as soon as we had gone beyond. In the forest the clothes were carried on their heads, with the white shoes on top.

Sometimes Hilda walked, but when she grew tired or found the jungle to much for her, she rode in her tepoy. Once I plucked a wild white lily from the side of the track and gave it to her, for I knew she loved flowers. Her pleasure was instantly perceived by the carriers, and every day afterwards they brought her sprays of orchids, hibiscus and Flame of the Forest to decorate the tepoy. I can never speak too highly of the courtesy and kindness shown by all these simple people towards my wife, particularly during that arduous journey. It was true that the track to the Mendjim Mey had grown easier since I first went there, for it had been much used and improved by carriers bringing out my animals. Most of the rivers were bridged, but timber rots rapidly in that climate and the bridges were already falling to pieces. In any case, many of the bridges were simply tree trunks felled across a stream, slippery and wet. Hilda had no choice but to walk across them, the raging water lapping at her feet, but there were always a dozen or so pairs of strong black hands, scrupulously gentle and respectful, ready to help and support her.

The simpler the people, the greater their courtesy. During our long stay at Arteck I often left Hilda alone for days on end, while I went off on hunting trips, and never once during my absence did she feel the least sense of insecurity. Oballa used to set two or three of his spearmen to guard her night and day, and if she wanted to take a stroll in the forest they were always with her to see that she did not get lost, to help her over obstacles, guard her from wild beasts and point out dangers that were hidden from her untutored eyes.

At first the villagers were overwhelmed with curiosity about Hilda, for after we passed Meyoss we entered territory where no white woman had been seen before. She was closely examined by all the village women, who touched and pointed in wonder at her clothes. Everyone wanted to shake hands with her and she suffered all this most cheerfully and with the greatest goodwill. I often had to ask her to get out of the tepoy so that she could be looked at. The occasional cases of suffering and disease appalled her, of course, particularly that of a little boy whose feet were a festering mess, half eaten away by jiggers and covered with "country medicine" in the form of mashed leaves. The boy's mother only laughed when Hilda recoiled in horror at the sight. Most of the babies had strings tied tightly round their thighs and wrists, biting into the flesh and causing great pain, and Hilda set to work cutting them off when I told her that the women put them there to see whether the babies were growing.

Resting in the evenings, we played the gramophone Hilda had brought with her, and to the villagers this was sheer magic. They crowded the doorways of our hut listening for hours in dead silence. When we wanted to stop they clamored for more. This sometimes went on far into the night, until we had to tell them that the music was tired and at last they went off to their beds.

The Paramount Chief of the Mendjim Mey greeted us with gifts of a duck, a fowl and some vegetables, and he painted a glowing picture of our new house at Arteck which, he said, had been built "through his mouth," that is to say, by his command. Every chief en route made the same claim, except for the Little Chief Mendjoum, who was much too excited and anxious to clown to bother with false claims on us. He had a baby son a few months old whom he had called Merfield in tribute to me, and when later he had a daughter he called her "Madame," which was the title by which Hilda came to be known among the Mendjims. Atanaga's wife Eli was called "Small Madame" because she wore clothes and was always giving herself airs. Africans have a nice sense of humor.

With such a large and noisy safari we saw no game, but there were plenty of monkeys and birds about and I was able to show Hilda some elephant spoor, including one footprint which measured twenty-one inches across. The villagers had many kinds of live animals which we bought as we went along—wide-eyed bush-babies and pottos, baby mangabey and putty-nosed monkeys, and many insects and birds. Insects became Hilda's department and took up a substantial part of our collecting activities. She spent much of her time at Arteck wandering along the forest paths in search of rare and gorgeous butterflies or iridescent beetles, and our evenings were spent identifying them with the aid of our many textbooks.

She soon learned the curious and disillusioning fact that butterflies, however lovely they are, prefer animal dung to flowers. The dung of animals like duiker and other antelopes is seldom seen on the forest paths, but leopard and civet cat dung is common, and is always the best place to find butterflies. Newman, the famous butterfly man at Bexley, Kent, bought large numbers of our specimens.

On our third morning's march the weather was dull and overcast, plunging the forest into an unfriendly gloom. Towards evening the threatening storm broke with great rolls of thunder, and lightning illuminated the forest with startling flashes of cold green light. Then came the rain, great weltering sheets of water smashing at the leaves and sending us hurrying to the shelter of an outlying hut. The birds and animals of the jungle were silent, listening to the fury of the storm from whatever shelter they could find. Even the mighty trees, bound and laced together with a tight network of vines and creepers, swayed at the impact of the first great gust of wind, and away behind the hut we heard one of them creak, splinter and come crashing to the ground, tearing a vast hole in the forest roof. As usual the storm ended abruptly and dramatically; the birds that seemed brighter than before flew again among the dripping leaves, and half a mile away a family of chimpanzees set up a chorus of delighted screams as the sun broke through the rear guard of the clouds.

There were fewer villages as we approached Arteck, and for the most part of our last day's march we saw no strangers. In fact I began to think that something was wrong. I expected to find at least a few of the Arteck people coming a long way out to meet us, for the drums were talking all the time and they must have known exactly where we were. The puzzle was solved when we reached a large forest clearing about a quarter of a mile from Arteck. One moment there was silence, save for the usual forest sounds, and there was nothing remarkable to be seen; then suddenly, with the most fearful screams, hundreds of naked Mendjims, gathered from all the surrounding villages, came bursting out at us from the undergrowth, waving their spears and dancing wildly around Hilda's tepoy. Behind the warriors were their women, clapping, hooting, and patting their lips, and beside them more men, singing, shouting and beating furiously on portable drums. The noise was terrible, and grew ten times worse when

our own carriers and their women joined in, yelling and singing as loud as they could. The savage dance around Hilda's
tepoy must have terrified her, at least for a moment. A small
moist hand crept into mine, and when I looked at her she was
as white as a sheet.

"Is it . . . is it all right, Fred?" she asked in a tiny voice.
"Are they pleased to see us?"

"Pleased! They're absolutely delighted. This is their way
of welcoming us."

"Oh, thank heavens. For a moment I really thought they
were going to . . . !"

But I lost the rest of what she said when Oballa stepped
forward and warmly clasped my hand. After I had introduced
him to a now more confident Hilda, all his men and their
women fell in behind and we made our triumphant entry into
Arteck. An emperor could not have wished for more.

Our little house, proudly presented to us by the smiling
villagers, was all we could have desired. It was situated on
rising ground at the end of the village and had three rooms—
a large sitting room, a bedroom, a storeroom and a verandah.
The walls were of baked mud and the roof of dried palm
fronds, all lovingly applied by willing hands. Later on we in-
stalled our furniture, fixed up some shelves and had a little
bathroom built at the back. Another outhouse served Atanaga
for his kitchen, and I turned my old house into a workshop,
which came to be known as my bureau.

We wanted to rest, but kindly though the villagers were,
they would have none of that. They sang, shouted, danced
and beat their drums for hours, and only stopped when Hilda
was inspired to set up in competition with her gramophone.
This proved to be a double-edged weapon. The celebrations
ended abruptly, but the whole village crowded around our
house and, though we played our little collection of records
through and through, they were not satisfied until well past
midnight.

The next evening, only an hour after we had gone to bed, Besalla came tapping on our door to say that there were gorillas about. We got up at once, went out onto the verandah and stood listening, shivering a little in the cold, misty air, until in the night, from the bush just behind the house, no more than fifty yards away, came the grunt of a young male gorilla and a rustling as he settled himself more comfortably on his bed. He was answered immediately by two or three more gorillas from the far side of the village, and all around us the bush was full of little whispering noises as the creatures of the jungle went about their secret business. There, in the heart of the primeval forest, we felt that we had our fingers on the very pulse of life itself.

We were awakened in the morning by a loud noise outside the house. Besalla was standing by the door holding a baby gorilla, which was bound hand and foot with creepers. It got one arm free, and gave Besalla a pinch that made him yelp and then tried to bite him. Village women were standing about laughing at the little thing. I got Collonel and N'Denge to make a temporary cage for it and later in the day, when it had recovered from the shock of capture, I was able to feed and examine it. Gorillas are not easy to sex on sight when very young. The male sexual organs are not visible as in other Primates, though when they are adult the size and general physique of the male are unmistakable. Adolescent and mature females, moreover, have a decided and almost humanly feminine appearance. Closer examination proved that Besalla's capture was a male, and Hilda, who had never seen a gorilla before, christened him Tarzan.

A week later he was joined by another baby male. Some of Besalla's hunters, walking quietly through the forest, encountered a large gorilla family consisting of three males, several females and four or five youngsters. One of the babies had strayed from its mother and the hunters snatched it up. It began screeching and the adults immediately came to the rescue. In the melee that ensued one of the females was badly wounded and the rest of the family made off, with the hunters in pursuit. The main family group escaped, and when the hunters returned they found the Old Man trying to drag away the wounded female, which had since died.

Gorillas never abandon their wounded until they are forced to do so, and I have often seen the Old Man trying to get a disabled member of his family away to safety. Besalla's hunters were charged repeatedly, but for some reason they were not successful in their attempts to spear the Old Man. Eventually, seeing that he could not frighten them off, he gave up and went away. The dead gorilla was bound to a stretcher of saplings and brought back. The baby, securely bound, was handed over to Hilda. He proved himself much more docile and gentle than Tarzan, and we called him Jeeves.

I made a huge enclosure for these two attractive young animals, and in a short time they were both hand tame. Every morning they came into the house to join us at breakfast, and the difference in their characters was most remarkable. Tarzan was always the boldest and most aggressive. He much preferred snatching things off the table to accepting what he was given, and unless his mouth and both hands were already occupied, he grabbed the food we gave poor Jeeves as well.

In their enclosure they had large branches to swing about on, and they seemed to be thoroughly happy there. Jeeves always came to me when I called him, but Tarzan was much more suspicious. If I handed him a banana he would snatch it, stuff it into his mouth and then walk away backwards, looking at me out of the corners of his eyes in a suspicious manner, as though he did not intend to be caught napping.

One morning a hunter brought in a dead female chimpanzee, with a young baby clinging to her fur, still alive. We bought the baby at once and put it with Tarzan and Jeeves. This time the youngster was a female. We called her Jane, and she was much more anxious to make friends with the gorillas than with us. She walked across on all fours to Jeeves and put up her finger to his mouth, which is the chimpanzee way of expressing trust and friendship. Then she tried to hug him, but Jeeves trotted off to the far corner and sat there hunched up, giving her glances of dark disfavor. When I offered her some food, Tarzan dashed forward like lightning and snatched it away. Jeeves always submitted to this sort of treatment and was content to have what Tarzan dropped or discarded, but little Jane was of a different temperament. She promptly snatched the food back again, and Tarzan was so shaken with this unexpected reaction that he did not know what to do.

It never seemed to occur to the gorillas to try to escape, but little Jane sat for hours fiddling away at the bolt on the door after she had seen me opening it. Eventually the three of them became great friends and were most unhappy if we tried to part them. When they came in for breakfast in the morning, Tarzan always went straight to Hilda, while Jeeves came to me and little Jane hugged Atanaga. They all learned to drink nicely from cups, and were very fond of tinned milk, of which we had a fairly plentiful supply. There were always gorillas calling in the forest, and our two used to answer them with a sort of roaring snore.

Most of my old pals had died or had been given away before I left for my holiday at home, but we soon acquired a new collection. Apart from the gorillas and the chimpanzee, we had a fox terrier, two sooty mangabey monkeys, four goats, two tortoises, one blue starling—a really lovely bird—and an assortment of frogs. Among our most interesting invertebrate pets, if pets they may be called, were Goliath beetles, more than four inches long, and several Black Rock scorpions.

Once, when I was away hunting, Hilda added a different sort of creature to our menagerie. She was sitting on the verandah, talking to Eli, when a man came forward carrying a large snake. It was about three feet long and very fat, the body tapering sharply into a short, pointed tail. The head was diamond-shaped, bearing two "horns" just above the nostrils, and the body was green, with purple and yellow markings. The man was holding it by the tail and by the back of its neck, and when Hilda asked him what sort of snake it was he grinned and replied: "Suppose dis beef go chop man, he go die." He was right; the snake was a deadly horned viper, and though he claimed to possess a charm over which its poison could not prevail, the truth was that he was extremely skillful in handling snakes and never got bitten.

N'Denge and Collonel wisely put the viper in a deep pit which they dug behind the house and it lived there for a long time. Two months after it arrived it gave birth to twenty-five living young and this caused great excitement among the people of Arteck. Our villagers were astonished that the babies were exactly like their mother, for they believed that the viper is the mother of all other species of snakes. Weeds had grown up the side of the pit and during the night the parent snake, relieved of the burden of its young, had climbed up and disappeared. The little ones were trying to do the same, and a few of them had almost reached the top when I arrived. Like most poisonous snakes, young horned vipers carry a lethal dose of poison from the time they are born, although they are only a few inches long, and the position was therefore alarming. After a frantic search we discovered their mother lying concealed behind a bush. She was picked up with a noose attached to the end of a long stick and replaced in the pit, which had meanwhile been cleared of weeds, but we were never sure whether any of the babies had escaped. Some of them died a few days after birth, but the survivors flourished on a diet of tiny frogs and, together with their mother, they were eventually packed off to a zoo.

The day after we arrived in Arteck, I discharged the main body of carriers, keeping with me N'Denge, Collonel, Dinga,

Wo-Wo Foot, N'Gombie, Atanaga and a young lad called N'Za, whom I had picked up at Batouri and who was already proving to be an excellent skinman. On the following Sunday morning when I got up, all these men were squatting outside the house, which was a sign that they wanted a palaver. They mumbled among themselves for a moment or two and then Collonel spoke up.

"Massa, all man talk say dey want more money."

This demand surprised me, for my men were well paid— far better, for example, than plantation laborers—and in addition my hunting brought them ample supplies of meat, most of which they sold profitably.

Collonel spoke again. "Massa, we savvy you long long time. Jus' now you be big man. You get plenty cargo, fine fine blankets, fine fine bed, fine fine t'ing for wash (this was a canvas bath belonging to Hilda), an' you done buy fine fine woman. All man 'member say you fit pay dem more money."

So that was it! My fine fine woman, they thought, must have cost me a fortune, and therefore I must have been making far more money than they had supposed.

"Me," I told them, "I no pay no one half copper for dis woman. I t'ief him (stole her)!"

At this they laughed and shook their heads, refusing to believe that such women were to be had for nothing. I went on, "How much time I fit tell you white man no do buy woman? Dem father been dash me. (Her father gave her to me)."

They laughed scornfully at this fantastic idea, and then N'Za the boy said, "Suppose he bin dash you, some time dem woman be no good!"

I reached forward and boxed his ears; whereupon the rest of them rolled over roaring with laughter and the palaver came to an end. They never again mentioned the cost of my woman or their suspicion that if really I had got her for nothing there must have been something wrong with her.

Oballa came along to ask if I would be kind enough to hold

court that morning. I had hardly expected them to want Sunday morning court so soon after my arrival, but I agreed, and so that Hilda would be able to understand the proceedings I asked Oballa to select only those cases in which all the parties concerned spoke Pidgin. Presently all was ready. Hilda and I sat on chairs behind a table outside our house, while the villagers squatted on the ground around us in a semicircle. Knowing from past experience that at least some of the cases would be brought forward just to see how I would deal with them, I began with my usual warning.

"You people want me for judge you' palaver. Make me I no spoil my time for nothing."

An excited whispering broke out, interspersed with giggles which were countered by calls for silence, but for several minutes no one stepped forward. Then an elderly man rose and walked up to our table.

"Massa," he said, "one for my woman make jumba for one for you' people."

"What does 'jumba' mean?" asked Hilda in my ear.

"He means that one of his wives has been sleeping with one of my men," I explained. "Not bad, considering we've only been here a few days."

"You savvy dem man?" I asked the plaintiff.

"Yas, Massa. He be dem man you call N'Za."

I looked around for the young imp. He was standing at the back of the crowd, grinning broadly, but the grin vanished like magic when he caught my eye.

"Which woman was it?" I asked the man.

He pointed to a buxom young wench of about twenty.

"You be woman for dis man?" I asked her.

"What kin' woman?" she demanded impudently. "He no do sleep (with) me!"

The crowd murmured its disapproval of such gross negligence.

"He no get strong," she added coyly.

Roars of laughter from the crowd. The charge seemed odd, for though her husband was about forty, which is old for a Mendjim, he was perfectly healthy and looked anything but senile.

"He foller udder woman, Massa," said the girl.

"No be you been tell me jus' now you' man no get strong?" I demanded. "Then how he fit foller udder woman?"

This was just the sort of score that delighted the villagers. There was more laughter and cries of "Yah, yah, yah." The girl could think of nothing to say.

I called N'Za to come forward and explain his conduct.

"Massa," he said, "Dem woman foller me for house. How I go do (what else could I do)?"

Was this the truth, I asked the girl.

It was a lie, she answered. N'Za had invited her into his house.

"How you been go, suppose you no been want for make jumba?"

Again she returned no answer.

I turned to the husband.

"Dem woman want me for sleep for him too much," he grumbled.

"How much woman you get?"

"Four woman," he said.

Litigation was never protracted in the Mendjim Mey, and now, having heard all sides of the dispute, I pronounced judgment.

"N'Za, I no been tell you no for trouble woman for dis country? I go cut you one dollar for you' book. Dem woman, I go tell Oballa for flog him five for arse."

And to the husband: "Better you sleep plopper woman for night. An' no do foller udder woman."

The three of them walked off, looking sorry for themselves, and there were loud cries of approval from the audience.

Another villager stepped forward. "Massa," he said, pointing to a man standing nearby, "Dis man been marry my pickin. He be pass two years an' he no been pay all dem money."

How much remained to be paid, I asked, and was told "two goats an' one dog."

I looked at the defendant.

"Plopper lie, Massa," he said. "I done finish pay long long time."

Had anyone witnessed the payment?

"I done forget," he said.

"Man no fit forget dis," I told him sternly. "Me, I look you face, you be plopper lie man!"

Oballa now came to me and announced that this case had been brought before him many times, and that he had always given judgment for the father, yet the husband still refused to pay up.

I glared at the wretched debtor. "Suppose you no go pay dem goat for two day time," I said. "Me, I go take you' woman and back him for father!"

Hardly an hour had passed before the man brought along the goats and the dog and handed them over to the girl's father in front of Oballa. Meanwhile several more cases had been brought before me and disposed of, and since by then certain savory odors were emanating from Atanaga's kitchen, we packed up for lunch.

"Fred," said Hilda one morning, "you know those little baby dolls we were given as wedding presents in Germany, the ones we keep on the shelf? Why are the villagers always staring through the door at them?"

I really had no idea, but I had noticed this myself, and I called over two or three of the men and questioned them. After a great deal of discussion it emerged that the dolls had fascinated them from the time we had arrived. They had seen me preserving the unborn babies of gorillas and chimpanzees and they imagined the dolls were my own offspring pickled in the same way! Nothing would convince them otherwise until I let them handle the dolls and feel the texture of the celluloid they were made of.

Hilda was now well into her stride as a jungle housekeeper. Maton used to send us vegetables by carrier occasionally, but for the most part we grew our own. I had brought many kinds of seeds and I planted them myself, although Atanaga gravely assured me that they would grow only if they were planted by women. I suppose this fiction helps to relieve the men of the burden of working the plantations. Atanaga was dumbfounded when our little garden produced cucumbers, tomatoes, lettuce, onions, groundnuts, radishes and beans, all of which grew prolifically. If you threw away an overripe tomato, every seed of it would sprout in a few days. In the front of our house we had a pleasant flower garden, including a rural arch with a creeper growing over it.

For meat we lived almost entirely on the jungle, and Hilda made some very pleasing culinary experiments with giant forest hog, Red River pig (a frequent item on our menu), bay duiker, yellow-backed duiker, water chevrotain, crabs, crayfish, buffalo and even elephant. Often only the liver, kidneys and a few other parts of these animals suited our tastes and digestions. Meat had to be cooked within a few hours of the animal's death, for we had no way of keeping it fresh.

Atanaga, of course, did most of the cooking, but cakes, pastries and puddings were beyond his powers and Hilda spent much of her time teaching him. We had brought large supplies of flour with us, and these were periodically replenished by carriers from Batouri, though we could never depend on their regularity. The first time Hilda showed Atanaga how to boil a pudding, she tied it up in a clean cloth and left him watching it boil. Some time later he came running in shouting, "Madame, come look dem pudding. He done move all him clothes." When she went to see what was wrong she found that the cloth had loosened and fallen away.

We made a lot of bacon out of the Red River pigs and, when Hilda gave Atanaga instructions to cut away the rind, he cut out all the lean meat as well, a misunderstanding attributable, I think, to the fact that she did not understand Pidgin very well at first.

Naturally, correspondence with friends and relatives at home meant a great deal to us both, and particularly to Hilda. Letters, newspapers and magazines came to us through Maton and were brought into the Mendjim Mey, together with food supplies, by a carrier we kept especially for the purpose. He was a young and athletic man who could do the journey, even with a heavy load, in under six days when he wanted to, but that was not often. Sometimes three or four weeks would pass by with no sign of him, and when at last he turned up he would be full of excuses involving sickness, domestic matters, natural calamities and anything else he could think of. We were always on the point of sacking him, but somehow, when he did eventually arrive with letters from home, we were so pleased that we forgot our grievance and let him off.

During the twelve months we spent together in the Mendjim Mey we had only one European visitor—Father Wilhelm from the Roman Catholic Mission at Doume. A few years earlier, the good Father had sent a native evangelist into the Mendjim Mey and this man, using a village hut at Arteck as his church, had ineffectively begun the task of converting the Mendjims. In an attempt to overcome their indifference, he gave them an awe-inspiring description of Father Wilhelm and warned them what to expect of his wrath when, one day, he would come to visit them. In the minds of the simple people of Arteck, the separate identities of Father Wilhelm and of the Almighty gradually got confused; fear of God was fear of Father Wilhelm, and his long-delayed arrival was awaited with great trepidation.

Like so many of his calling, Father Wilhelm was indeed a remarkable man, and his visit was a startling episode in our life at Arteck. We knew he was on his way, but one evening, some time after dark, Hilda and I were sitting quietly on the verandah, staring sleepily at the stars, when she suddenly sat up and said, "Fred, was that a bicycle bell I heard?"

"A bicycle bell?"

"Yes. And somebody singing. Listen."

Sure enough, I caught the sound of a tinkling bell and someone singing lustily to the accompaniment of it.

"Why, of course," I told Hilda. "It must be Father Wilhelm. He always rides a bicycle."

"In the jungle?" Hilda asked incredulously.

"Well, only where the paths are reasonably wide and even. He carries it over streams, across bridges and around fallen trees and that sort of thing, and he gets on again wherever the path permits. But I never really expected to find him coming here. Let's go and see."

We walked down to where the path entered the forest and in the bright moonlight presently beheld a most astonishing sight. Careering round the bend came Father Wilhelm, wobbling violently as his cycle struck irregularities in the ground. Most of his face was hidden by a vast black beard and a shabby white sun helmet was tipped over his eyes. His cassock was tucked up above his knees, so that it did not interfere with the pedals, and in his right hand he flourished a wicked-looking spear, while the other was engaged in steering the machine and pinging incessantly at the bell. He was pedaling furiously and between his gasps for breath he bawled what seemed to be a French hymn of very militant temper. It was quite dark in the forest, and his only illumination was a fitful acetylene lamp.

He greeted us warmly in French and hurriedly explained that the spear and the noise were intended to frighten away wild beasts, particularly leopards, of which there were many in Mendjim Mey. It was not his custom, he said, to cycle through the forest at night, but his timing had gone wrong and he had been overtaken by darkness before he could reach us. In the circumstances there had seemed no alternative to pushing on.

We took him into the house, where Hilda and Atanaga quickly produced an excellent meal of pork, curried tinned salmon and fried potatoes, spinach and finally banana pudding. He told us that his visit was more for our benefit than for the Mendjims, whom he seemed to regard as well-nigh hopeless from the spiritual point of view, and he gave us the only reliable firsthand news of the outside world we had heard for over six months. Next morning he rounded up the villagers and in Pidgin harangued and bewildered them for an hour from the improvised pulpit in the little church. Then he was off again, and as we watched him cycle away, with his hairy white knees protruding sideways from beneath his cassock, we could not but wonder at the power and intensity of his faith. Apart from ourselves, he was at that time, to the best of my knowledge, the only living European who had ever entered the Mendjim Mey.

A few days later Hilda went for a walk on her own and came running back to me shouting that there was a naked white man in the forest, carrying a spear. I thought at first that it must be either Father Wilhelm, who had somehow lost both cassock and cycle, or one of the wandering European gold prospectors whom I had encountered in other parts of the Cameroons "looking for money for water," as the natives say, but when I went to see I discovered that the man was in fact a Mendjim—a total albino with a skin as white as mine. These freaks are not uncommon among the forest peoples: the Little Chief Mendjoum was a partial albino, and an albino baby was born at Arteck while we were there.

Most of our time was spent attending to our pets and specimens. Every day the village kiddies brought us packets of cicadas, beetles and tiny frogs, done up in huge leaves which were folded and pinned down with splinters of bamboo. But in the afternoons we usually found an hour to spare for tennis, which we played on a clearing near the house, with a rope stretched across to serve as a net, or swimming in the big pool I had made in the stream. N'Denge made a screen at the pool for Hilda to undress behind. For good measure he built a little seat inside it and on the first day adorned it with a spray of white lilies. The only drawback was that he disturbed a nest of ants and Hilda was stung and bitten all over before she managed to get into the water.

I know now that there is a dreadful disease in tropical Africa called Bilharzia which is caught by contact with infected water. Doctors, I suppose, will be horrified to learn that we bathed in an open stream. Neither of us had ever heard of Bilharzia at that time, however, and we certainly never caught it. In fact, our only concessions to life in the tropics were that we slept under a mosquito net, took daily doses of quinine, and always boiled and filtered our drinking water.

Later on we brought up three sturdy children under the same conditions, much to the astonishment of our friends in the town, whose offspring were nearly always sickly and pallid. Trudie, Gordon and Brian ran half naked with our servants' children and ate much the same food as they did. Among the delicacies highly prized by the natives are fried ants, and Trudie, who is now twenty, remembers with delight how she used to join in the great feasts of them that took place whenever they swarmed. After all, was that so very different from children in England collecting and eating periwinkles?

Our only fear was of jiggers, and Trudie learned to walk on the firm surface of a native bed, so that her feet would not come in contact with infected ground. When eventually she was old enough to wear sandals and was allowed on the ground, she still trotted up and down within the same limits that had been imposed upon her by the bed.

Driver ants were a different proposition, and Trudie narrowly escaped disfigurement by them when she was barely twelve months old. It began at four o'clock one morning when we were awakened by our dog, which was dashing hysterically around the room, banging into the walls and furniture. When I jumped out of bed to see what was wrong I immediately felt as though I was standing on the points of innumerable red-hot needles, and I did not need to light the lamps to know that we were being invaded by driver ants. Shouting to Hilda to follow me, I took Trudie from her cot and dashed out of the house. Outside, Atanaga helped us to rid ourselves of the ravenous insects that still clung to our bodies, while the other servants went to rescue the animals. Some of the birds, whose cages were fronted with gauze, had escaped unscathed, but our chameleons, a ground squirrel and several leaf frogs had been eaten alive. Only their skeletons remained, picked dry and white.

For hours we tried to stem the advancing hordes of ants, using hot ashes, burning newspapers and coal tar as well as various native methods like burning certain leaves. When daylight came it looked as though we had won and we returned to bed, standing the legs of our cots in small tins filled with paraffin to protect us in case the ants returned. I slept for about an hour before I was awakened once more, this time by Trudie crying. I jumped out of bed again, disturbing thousands of ants, and saw to my horror that Trudie's cot was black with them. The mosquito net covering her was held up by four strings from the ceiling and they had found their way down them. In her sleep the child had loosened the net where it was tucked under her mattress and the ants had already got inside. Again we all fled from the house. Trudie had been bitten on her face, hands and feet, but not badly. Had we awakened a moment later she might well have suffered serious and permanent injuries.

Driver ants visited us twice when we were in Arteck and we never knew when the long black streams of them might come trickling out of the forest. The only thing we could do when that happened was to get ourselves and our animals out of their way as quickly as we could, but once we were gone they were welcome to invade the house, for they cleared it most efficiently of cockroaches and other insect pests.

These voracious ants march only on sunless days or at night, always at the start of the rainy season, and some collectors have got up in the morning to find every bird and animal in their cages eaten alive. Even animals as large as pigs and antelopes are not too much for them. They do not construct permanent nests but live in temporary quarters, and we had one of these for a long time at the bottom of our garden in Arteck. We tried all manner of things to get rid of them, but without success. The curious thing about driver ants is that the workers, soldiers and females are all totally blind, and I believe they locate their prey mainly by sound. At a distance of a few yards from them your presence is ignored, but if you stamp your foot they immediately make for you. Their marching columns are so long that they may take three or four days to pass a given point, and the progress of those countless millions of tiny feet wear little furrows in the ground. They seem to have no natural enemies and even the ant-eating pangolins leave them severely alone.

12. Good-Bye Gorillas

There were so many gorillas in the Mendjim Mey that it was almost impossible to hunt anything else without coming across them. Besalla told me that there was a solitary buffalo roaming about near the river, and since my men had had very little meat for some weeks I went after it, taking Collonel and N'Denge with me. We found the buffalo's spoor and began tracking it round an abandoned plantation, where the bush was vile and progress painfully slow. After an hour or so N'Denge tapped me on the shoulder and whispered that he could hear a gorilla moving about nearby. Pushing on, we came to a tiny clearing where we stood three abreast, studying the bush ahead. There was a very strong smell of gorilla and I caught a glimpse of something dark moving towards us, but the vegetation was too dense for me to see what it was or to keep it under observation for more than a split second.

I have repeatedly emphasized that for all their apparent truculence, gorillas are inoffensive creatures and will not attack a man who stands his ground, but this is a generalization to which there are exceptions. Gorillas vary in temperament as much as we do; some are extraordinarily brave, others as timid as deer; and sometimes the behavior of solitary bulls is quite unpredictable. This lesson was to be forcibly brought home to me.

Bending forward slightly so that we could see better, and still keeping shoulder to shoulder, the three of us cautiously approached the wall of vegetation on the other side of the clearing. When we were within a few feet of it, there was a terrifying roar and a monstrous black shape burst out upon us. I am not clear exactly what happened after that. I have a faint recollection of pressing the trigger of my rifle, of feeling the weight of a huge gorilla right on top of me and of seeing Collonel and N'Denge go hurtling to either side. Then I was buried in leaves and bits of branches and everything seemed confused. When I struggled up, the gorilla was standing on all fours behind me, giving vent to short, sharp coughs that turned into prolonged screams of rage as waves of anger overwhelmed him, and making sweeping lunges at me with his right arm. Then, as I recovered my rifle and raised it, he dashed off, but before he had covered five yards a bullet struck him in the back of the neck. He toppled over, but was on his feet facing me again in a moment, and a second bullet took him squarely between the eyes.

Collonel was dazed, with blood trickling from his nose, but apart from severe bruises and scratches, none of us was seriously hurt. The dead gorilla was a fine Old Man, his coat grizzled with age and quite silvery in places. This color is common in elderly males and may look pure white at a distance if struck by a shaft of sunlight, giving rise to reports, even from reputable zoologists, of the occurrence of "white" gorillas. From his teeth I judged that the animal was past his prime, and I imagine that he had been exiled from his family by a younger and more vigorous bull.

N'Denge went off and brought the rest of my men and we carried the gorilla back to the village. While we were skinning it, Oballa came and told me that during the past few weeks so much damage had been done among his plantations by gorilla families living close to the village that he had decided to round them up. Having seen enough of the horrors of gorilla roundups I tried hard to dissuade him, but he argued that the animals could not be allowed to prejudice the village food supplies, which was fair enough, and that there was no other way to get rid of them quickly. We almost had a row about it, but he refused to give way and I had to content myself by repeating my warning that it would be useless for him to try to sell me the skins if they were mutilated.

News of the intended roundup was sent to the other villages in the area by drum, and spearmen began drifting in soon afterwards, bringing their women, who carried calabashes of food on their heads. The drumming went on all night, so that it was impossible to sleep, and towards three o'clock in the morning, with the drums beating a furious crescendo, all the people marched around the village shouting and singing. Afterwards Hilda and I dozed fitfully until six, when we got up and after a cup of coffee went out to see what was happening.

A large family of gorillas had been located and a circular strip of about five feet wide had already been cleared around them, while the fence was going up rapidly. The witch doctor was prancing about waving a pad of "medicine" tied to the end of a long stick toward the doomed animals, presumably with the intention of keeping them where they were until preparations were complete. We joined the women, who stood behind the circle of waiting spearmen. From deep in the bush came the confused barks, screams and belly-beating of the terrified animals.

"They won't come out yet," I told Hilda, "but when they do they'll come with a rush. Keep behind me if you see one of them coming through near us."

"How will they get them out?"

"Some of the spearmen will go inside to break up the family group when the fence is finished. Then the big bull will try to lead them out and once he has been dealt with the others will be easy. Are you sure you want to stay and watch? It will be very unpleasant."

"Well, I suppose I'd better stay, now that I've come. But shoot the poor things, Fred, if you can. That will be better than having them speared."

"I'll try, of course, but once the bull has been brought down the others will scatter and try to break through the fence in all directions."

The women had begun their offensive of noise, hooting, shouting and rattling tins. Renewed screams from the gorillas told us that the spearmen had gone inside and presently we could see the undergrowth on the other side of the cleared strip being tossed about violently as the gorillas came towards us.

The first one to emerge was the Old Man, a magnificent bull. With only his head and shoulders visible, and the great bulk of his body concealed by the undergrowth, he screamed defiance at us. His mouth, wide open and armed with long formidable canines, showed pink and glistening in contrast to the deep black of his hide, and the long matted hair on his arms and shoulders fairly shook with fury. Still out of range of the spears, he hesitated for a moment or two, but then, hearing the spearmen coming towards him from behind, he suddenly charged across the clearing.

A volley of spears flew out from both sides; many of them missed, and a few glanced off him. Two dug deep into his right shoulder and a third into the small of his back. He paused just long enough to knock that one out, as you or I might deal with a gnat, and then charged again, straight towards us. The spearmen and the women scattered, leaving us directly in his path; I swept Hilda behind me and when the gorilla was within ten yards, I fired three rounds from my .45 revolver straight into his chest. He died literally at our feet.

The rest of the family were close behind him and at the sound of my shots they panicked and dashed for the fence.

Two young males were halfway over when, with spears thudding into them from all sides, they collapsed and fell back to their deaths. A young female, badly wounded in the belly, succeeded in getting over, but in her pain and fear she ran straight into the village. Some of the men and a lot of the women chased after her and to my dismay, instead of making for the forest on the other side, where she might have been safe, she ran into one of the huts.

Then followed a most disgusting scene. Knowing that the poor creature could not escape, the women danced round the hut, jeering and laughing at her. Hilda and I followed them and I knew that they had reached such a pitch of frenzy that if I didn't interfere, the gorilla would die a savage and cruel death. Before I could do anything Besalla came up, and when he saw the look on my face he pushed the women and spearmen aside, entered the hut and killed the gorilla as mercifully as he could.

Six gorillas were killed in that roundup and goodness knows how many broke through the trap and escaped, but we had not lost our hairy neighbors altogether. Roving bands of gorillas soon took the place of those that had been slain or driven away. Presently they were raiding the plantation again and in the evenings they could be heard calling to each other from their beds.

That was the cycle of gorilla and native life in the Mendjim Mey. Gorillas were regularly hunted for food, but they continued to raid the plantations until the villagers, roused at last from their usual lethargy, killed comparatively large numbers of them and drove away the rest. For a short time the plantations were secure, then more gorillas moved in from other parts of the forest and it all began again. Thus, both gorilla and human populations were maintained at the level appointed by that delicate, complex and inexorable system of laws which we call the Balance of Nature.

* * *

The vanishing hippopotamus of the Mendjim Mey was a puzzle I never managed to solve. There are no hippos in the Mendjim Mey, at least there ought not to be, for though the country is interlaced with rivers, these are comparatively small, and the forest comes right down to the water, so that there is no suitable bankside vegetation for hippos to feed on. Consequently, when, one day, I found fresh dung and the tracks of a big hippo near the Boumbi River, about a mile from Arteck, I was almost as surprised as I would have been to find a hippo wallowing in the Serpentine. I had no idea where the beast could have come from, for the nearest hippo country was a hundred miles away, south of Assubam. The Boumbi River, though deep, is never more than fifty yards wide and is choked with rotten tree trunks and branches, offering no suitable cover for so large a beast.

This intrigued me and I began hunting the animal and making inquiries among the Mendjims. The Boumbi River and its tributaries were fished almost daily by the men and boys, but none of them had ever seen the hippo. Its territory consisted of a stretch of river where there were some half a dozen small, swampy patches of grass on which it apparently fed. Otherwise the banks were covered with dense forest, and the hippo had made wide pathways through the undergrowth as elephants do.

Every day for nearly three weeks, I and seven of my men hunted this animal. The fresh tracks we found were always to and from the river, so there was no question of its lying up in the swamps. One day it got into the plantation of a village near Arteck and played havoc among the crops, so the villagers dug a pit in the forest pathway. The hippo fell in, but somehow it got out again and from then on it never used the same path twice.

Apart from Besalla and one or two others, none of the Mendjims had ever seen a hippo and they knew nothing about these animals. They believed that it lived somewhere in the river, spending the day at the bottom, but they had no idea that it would have to come to the surface at regular intervals in order to breathe. The fact that it was such a big animal, which they knew from its dung and tracks, that no one had ever seen it and that it had defeated my efforts to track it down, led them as usual to believe that it was some sort of ju-ju beast. It was, indeed, remarkable that the animal could conceal itself so efficiently from the eyes of my expert trackers.

The vanishing hippo continued to haunt the Mendjim Mey, as I heard by report, for some years after I left there. I had judged from its tracks that it was a bull hippo, and I shall never understand what it was doing in the Mendjim Mey.

Hippos, however, have a reputation for roaming about in unexpected places for no apparent reason. The most famous of these wandering animals was Huberta, who for two years toured parts of South Africa where no hippos had been seen in living memory and was feted and protected wherever she went. Huberta's story even reached the pages of *Punch*, and thousands of people all over the world followed the newspaper reports of her daily progress.

*   *   *

Towards the height of the rainy season Atanaga fell ill. It began when he came to us saying that he had worms and asking for treatment. We gave him some Santonin tablets which Maton had sent with a recent consignment of supplies, but leter on we found that he had been taking the advice of numerous villagers and was swallowing all manner of native concoctions. Then he caught a chill and went to bed with a slight fever. At first we thought nothing of it, but when Hilda took his temperature and found it to be 105 we were seriously alarmed. Atanaga and his wife Eli had spent a great deal of money on fancy clothes, so that they could show off in front of the almost naked villagers, but neither of them had seen fit to bring so useful a thing as a blanket. We gave him one of ours and tucked him up as comfortably as we could, but the next day he seemed worse.

I got him out of bed and gave him a steam bath, which is usually successful in bad cases of fever, and dosed him liberally with aspirin and fever tea brewed from the blades of citronella grass. In the morning we were surprised to find that his temperature had dropped only one degree. He was complaining of severe pains in the lower part of his chest, and had a dry hard cough. We spent the morning thumbing through our medical book and eventually decided that his symptoms fitted only one disease—pneumonia.

There was very little I could do about it except to keep him warm, but I tried cupping him—a practice which was still in vogue out there—and that seemed to ease him a little. But now he had begun to fear that he was going to die and he told me that this was because he had underpaid an old woman for some plantains and that she had cursed him for it, and warned him that he would never return to his home in Yaounde. The old woman, he said, had certainly put a witch into him and, since in these circumstances European medicine would obviously be useless, he begged us to allow the village witch doctor to come and treat him.

For a time I held out against his request, but on the fifth day his temperature and pain had not abated, and at last I yielded to his pleading and sent for the witch doctor. This person, a man of about forty, wore none of the insignia which Europeans popularly associate with his profession. Normally it is impossible to distinguish a witch doctor from any other villager; the paint and the ornaments so dearly beloved of fiction writers and film producers are in fact only worn on special occasions.

Our witch doctor brought with him a monkey-skin bag and a large gourd. In the bag were a clay pot, parrot claws, dried rats, some leaves, pieces of bark, a crescent-shaped knife and a small bushbuck horn with the tip cut off and the opening covered with a lump of black beeswax. The gourd was half full of bark and some ashes, and the bones of fowls. He carefully examined his patient and announced that someone had introduced into him at least one powerful witch and possibly several. Prognosis was grave, but he was prepared to do his best.

He began by boiling the bark and leaves in the clay pot, and while this was brewing he examined Atanaga's left shoulder blade, where the pain was worse. He took the skin between his forefinger and thumb and with the knife made two cuts about half an inch long. Then he rubbed them with ash from the gourd, placed the horn over the wounds and sucked out as much of the air as he could, sealing up the opening with beeswax. He left the horn in place for about five minutes and then released the vacuum by piercing the wax with a splinter of bamboo. The horn came away from Atanaga's skin and was then held over a leaf and explored with the bamboo. A few blobs of congealed blood fell out, but the witch doctor shook his head gravely and said that the witch itself had escaped.

This treatment was continued and an hour later poor Atanaga had sixteen cuts in various parts of his body. The result was always the same—no witches! The witch doctor, looking very severe and sad, rubbed his hands in the liquid brewed in the clay pot, producing a soapy foam, and liberally anointed Atanaga with the rest of the stuff. Turning to Hilda, who had been an interested spectator of these proceedings, he said that in spite of his efforts the witches had got away, but that he would return tomorrow and try again.

He came next morning and began cupping and cutting Atanaga in various parts of the body. At last, he poked about in the horn, two tiny objects fell onto the leaf and he let out a cry of joy. These were the witches maliciously introduced into Atanaga's person by someone who understood witchcraft. Had they remained there, Atanaga would certainly have died.

In spite of the witch doctor's protests, we insisted on keeping these witches. One of them was sent to the Powell-Cotton Museum, and the other lies beside me as I write. I am sorry to disillusion anyone who romantically clings to some sort of belief in magic, but our witch doctor was a fraud, at least on this occasion. My witch was simply a tiny blob of black wax with the end of a bird's quill—the sort of thing you find remaining in the skin of a plucked chicken—stuck on the top. There is no doubt that he had concealed them in the horn before he began.

Atanaga complained of renewed pains in the head the next day, and again the witch doctor came, this time giving him a broth made from a stewed rat, parrot claws and various leaves. On the eighth day his temperature suddenly fell back to normal, precisely as our medical book forecast in cases of pneumonia, but of course he was convinced that the cure had been effected by the witch doctor, and we did not try to disillusion him. Atanaga was afterwards so thin and weak that we sent him to his home in Yaounde to recuperate.

Meanwhile I had made a discovery that excited me tremendously. One of the village kiddies who collected small creatures for me had brought along some tadpoles in a tin can. Nothing remarkable in a child finding tadpoles, you may say, but in this case the tadpoles were three inches long, the biggest I had ever seen. I began to hope that at last I had found the Giant or Goliath Frog, which had been the object of several unsuccessful expeditions I had made in the past. On one occasion, just before I met my unpleasant client Vincent, I spent two fruitless months wandering about the forest in search of these enormous amphibians, which exist nowhere else in the world. Hilda and I tended the tadpoles as carefully as if they had been sick children. We found where they came from and caught many more, but they always died and I was never able to discover the adult frogs. Later on, dissection proved that they were not the ones I was looking for, and another two years were to pass before I eventually found the true Giant Frogs in the Yabassi district of the Cameroons. The queer thing was that none of my friends would believe me until they actually saw them.

"What's this rubbish I hear about you finding frogs weighing over four pounds, Merfield?" The question came from Harry Francis, one of a group of friends with whom I was enjoying a drink in Douala.

"It's not rubbish at all," I replied. "I've got a dozen of them."

They all laughed. "We've had enough of you, Merf," said another of them. "Gorillas, giant eland, cannibals and all the rest we can swallow. We know that's true. But frogs over four pounds—never!"

I went outside and sent one of the servants back to my house, telling him to bring the large tin drum he would find on the verandah. When he returned I placed the drum on the floor, and gently pried open the lid. Like a very powerful and efficient jack-in-the-box, an enormous frog shot out and hit Harry Francis squarely on the chest, almost knocking him over. When the pandemonium died down, I recovered the frog and showed it to them. I tried to buy Harry a drink, for he looked as though he needed one, but he seemed to think that in the circumstances the privilege should be his.

"Now tell us all about the beastly things," he said, when we had quieted down again.

"There's not much to tell really. You know I've been looking for them for years. They were quite easy to find once I had discovered that they lived in a particular part of the Yabassi Forest. Fast-running, rocky, hill streams are the sort of thing they like, and you can see them sitting about on the rocks in the daytime. Unfortunately they pop into the water and disappear as soon as they see or hear you, and for a long time I couldn't catch them. Then I tried at night. It was quite easy to see them; their eyes gleamed brightly in the light of my lamp and they seemed dazzled by it, so I managed to net them without much trouble.

"Then I learned that when they are disturbed and jump into the water they creep into comparatively small holes under or between the rocks. I tried to get one of them out, but when I put my hand in the hole he forced upwards with his hind legs and my hand was jammed against the roof. I got free after an effort, but I left a lot of skin behind, and it was impossible to get the frog out without killing or severely injuring it."

To satisfy my friends, I brought out the frog again, put it in a bag and weighed it on the scales of a nearby store. This specimen just reached four pounds six ounces. Its body length was twelve inches, and when the hind legs were stretched out behind, nearly double that. The giant frogs never tried to bite me, though they were immensely strong and two hands were needed to hold them. They lived on all manner of small living creatures—snails, toads and smaller frogs, mice and even large rats, all of which were caught and swallowed whole. In the Natural History Museum, London, a mounted specimen is shown in the act of swallowing a large rat. Their method of doing this was fascinating, in a horrid sort of way. They caught the rats by the head, holding them fast with the row of tiny teeth they have in the upper jaw, and then, sitting upright in the water, they use the front paws to stuff the wretched creatures inside.

I kept them for several months in a pool surrounded by a high fence of galvanized iron, for they were capable of jumping prodigious heights and were almost impossible to catch once they got away. Then the late Professor Heck of the Berlin Zoo arrived in the Cameroons and delightedly bought the lot. I heard from him later that he had not been able to keep them sufficiently moist on the journey home, and that they had all died. I do not think that *Rana Goliath* has ever been exhibited alive in England.

Another rare animal I got was a subspecies of the Red Colobus monkey—*Colobus ferrugineus preussi*, to give its full scientific name. It began when I noticed a native in Yabassi carrying the skin of a monkey I had never seen before. I bought it from him and, since I could not identify it, I sent it to the late Captain Guy Dollman, of the British Museum of Natural History. He wrote to say that the animal up to then had been known only by one skin, which was in the Berlin Museum. It was collected by Dr. Paul Matschie as far back as 1900, and no other specimen had since been found.

That was all the encouragement I needed for a new expedition. The man who had sold me the skin had bought it from another native who was a stranger to him, so that did not help me, but after some months, exhaustive inquiries led me to a little village called N'Dogofas, high up in the mountains thirty miles north of Yabassi, and in the surrounding district I found the elusive Colobus.

These monkeys were impossible to catch alive, for they lived high in the inaccessible branches of tall trees, and never seemed to come to the ground. Even when frightened or disturbed, they did not drop down into the undergrowth as other monkeys do. Shooting them from the ground was difficult, for they were hard to see and moved about rapidly. Living in large family groups, and never coming near human habitations, they favored high rocky country, broken by fast-running rivers. The females have unusually large menstrual swellings, a phenomenon which was investigated in my specimens by Dr. Osman Hill, who is now Prosector of the Zoological Society of London. At last I was able to secure a dozen specimens and sent them to the British Museum and Ubersee Museum, Bremen. While engaged in writing this book I went with Mr. Miller, my collaborator, to the British Museum to examine gorilla skulls, and we were delighted to find that my

Red Colobus skins are still there, and in an excellent state of preservation.

*   *   *

Hilda's introduction to the Pygmies of the Mendjim Mey did not take place until some time after she arrived, for the little men of the forest were extremely shy. Sometimes, during her evening walks or her butterfly hunts, she would catch a glimpse of them darting like frightened antelopes across the forest paths, disappearing without a sound into the undergrowth on the other side, but they would not come near her. Then the time came when I thought she should make a deliberate effort to win their confidence, and I went out with her looking for them and carrying tins of salt to give them as presents, for there is nothing they value more highly.

On our first few expeditions we drew blanks, but one day we came across a large family of Pygmies moving along an elephant track on their way to new hunting grounds. They vanished among the leaves as soon as they caught sight of us, but I told Hilda to stand still and I called out to them to come back so that I could give them the salt. For a long time there was no sight of them, and I thought they were going to ignore me altogether, so we put the salt on the ground and withdrew a few paces. Presently a small, wrinkled brown face peered at us from behind a shroud of vines, and then its owner stepped out onto the track. The little brown man gravely picked up the salt and, looking over his shoulder, said something to the rest of his hidden family, and they all came out to join us.

Like the villagers, the Pygmies were deeply interested in Hilda's clothing and her white skin, but they, too, soon got used to seeing her wandering about the forest, sometimes with a butterfly net in hand, sometimes rooting about among the undergrowth in search of beetles and scorpions, and they came to accept her as an interesting, friendly and entirely harmless innovation. They no longer hid or ran away when they saw her; if they were busy hunting they greeted her with a smile and a nod; if not, they stopped and delightedly accepted the little presents she always took with her in case she should meet them.

But Besalla and the other Mendjims were jealous of our friendship with the Pygmies and we had to be careful not to offend or alienate either side. Pygmy families are always more or less under the thumb of a local village chief or other leading native, who exploits their hunting skill and on whom they are entirely dependent for weapons, salt and tobacco. Besalla once used this influence over the local Pygmies to cheat me out of a pair of valuable ivories, but at least the incident served to give me a closer acquaintance with Pygmy life and hunting methods.

The bull elephant that carried those ivories had been roaming near the village for several weeks and I decided to go after him. Besalla consented to come with me—rather too eagerly I thought—and together we began tracking the animal. This took much longer than I had expected and towards six o'clock in the evening we had still not caught up with him and it was getting dark. Besalla said he knew of a Pygmy camp in the area, and not wishing to make the long journey back through the forest after dark, I agreed to go there and seek shelter for the night.

As usual there was no track leading to the Pygmies' camp and we had to wade along the bed of a stream to reach it. Our reception was not as cordial as I could have wished, for though at first the little men were happy to see me, their faces fell when they learned that I was hunting elephant in what they considered their reserve. Nevertheless they readily agreed to let us spend the night in one of their tiny, leafy huts and we were asleep in a few minutes after we had crawled in through the low entrance hole.

In the morning Besalla behaved strangely and was obviously uneasy about something. When I questioned him he said that the Pygmies were angry with us for hunting the elephant, but I knew him well enough to suspect that this was not the whole truth. He went so far as to suggest abandoning the hunt, assuring me that the elephant would now have gone too far to be found. Why not leave the elephant to the Pygmies, he asked. After all, I would only give away the meat to my men, and I could always buy the ivories from the Pygmies for a very low price.

Then, seeing that I was suspicious of his attitude, Besalla tried a different line. He reminded me that when I first came to the Mendjim Mey I had been most anxious to see how his people hunted gorillas; would I not be equally interested in the Pygmy method of hunting elephants? If so, that could easily be arranged. I agreed to this proposal, not only because of my admitted interest in the Pygmies' technique, but also to discover what Besalla was up to, for I was certain he had some sort of nefarious scheme in mind.

Standing some way from me, Besalla had a long conversation with two of the Pygmies. Then they seemed to reach an agreement; the two little men nodded vigorously, looking towards me, and Besalla came over and said that they had agreed to take me hunting elephant with them, but that I must promise not to use my rifle unless in an emergency. I gave them my word, and we all started off through the bush. After half a mile I was utterly exhausted, for I just could not keep up with the Pygmies. They moved through the jungle at an astonishing pace, seeming to slip like shadows through tiny gaps or weak points in the vegetation that I would never even have noticed. Again I was struck with their ability to do this without making a sound. It was almost as though the leaves themselves moved noiselessly aside to let them pass.

Besalla was faring no better than I, and we lagged so far behind that at last I feared that we had lost the Pygmies altogether. Besalla gave a long, low whistle, and in a second or two our guides reappeared, looking surprised at our weary faces. Besalla told them that it was impossible for us to keep up such a pace and they suggested that we should stay where we were until they had found the elephant. We gladly agreed to this plan, and sat panting on a fallen tree for perhaps half an hour when, without so much as a rustle to warn us that he was near, one of the Pygmies suddenly reappeared and beckoned to us to follow him.

We crept along after him for a considerable distance until we came to the second Pygmy, standing almost invisible among a tangle of lianas. Fifty yards away was a patch of jungle much more dense than the rest, and in this stood the elephant. Only his vast gray backside was visible to us. The Pygmy tapped me on the chest and pointed to the ground, indicating that I was to stay where I was. Then he stooped and ducked into the bushes, disappearing once more.

I studied the jungle between us and the elephant closely, trying to follow the Pygmy's progress, but there was not the quiver of a leaf to show where he was. I gave that up and turned my attention to the elephant, watching him through my binoculars. The great beast seemed to be dozing, and his only movement was to shift his weight occasionally from one hind leg to the other.

Suddenly I saw the Pygmy and I gave a little jump of astonishment, for the man had risen from the bush so close to the elephant's left hind leg that he could easily have touched it. I saw him make a quick deft movement, and the blade of his broad-headed spear glinted as he drove it home into the elephant's belly. The poor beast gave a terrifying scream, and went crashing away from us through the forest, trumpeting with fear and pain. The Pygmy had speared it and disappeared again so quickly and silently that the elephant could never have known what sort of creature had attacked him.

It would not have been possible for me to go after the wounded animal in that bush, and I had to be content with the Pygmy's assurance that it would soon die, though I was pretty sure that its death would actually be slow and agonizing. We returned to camp and the next day the Pygmies announced that they had found the elephant dead and invited me to inspect it. I found that the spear had been driven deep into the intestines, just in front of the hind leg and that the elephant had broken off the protruding shaft.

Back in Arteck, Besalla's plan became clear. If I had shot the elephant it would have belonged entirely to me. I would have sold the ivories and parceled out the meat among my men, so that Besalla would have got no more than the others. But the Pygmies were very much under his control, and when they brought in the smoke-dried meat he was able to get it for what it was, a bargain price.

The Pygmies haggled with him for nearly a week, inspecting and rejecting various numbers, quantities and combinations of spearheads, knives, salt and tobacco. Now Besalla had an attractive young daughter, whom Hilda and I knew very well and who was about twelve at this time. During the week one of the Pygmies saw her and asked for her in exchange for the meat and ivories. Besalla held out against this for a long time, simply in accordance with African business traditions and not through any filial affection for the girl, but eventually he agreed and she was handed over. I don't know whether she understood what was happening to her, but she went off with the Pygmies without a murmur, and of course there were no fond farewells of any kind between father and daughter before they parted, for Besalla thought no more of it than if she had been a goat. Hilda and I never saw the child again.

*   *   *

We had known for more than four months that Hilda was going to have a baby. I was anxious that she should be attended by a European doctor during the birth and we therefore decided to leave the Mendjim Mey. Trudie was born in the comparative security of a small hospital at Yaounde, but owing to the death of a patient in the next room from an infectious illness, the doctor advised us to leave a few days after she was born and the only other shelter we could find was a native hut. Afterwards the responsibility of a family imposed a more settled but no less colorful life upon me, but every now and then I would find a native with a skin or carcass of an animal I had rarely seen before and I could not rest until I found where it lived and brought it back, alive or dead.

When this happened Hilda always understood, though it often meant loneliness and hardship for her. Giving me a little squeeze, she would bid me go after the animal, knowing that I would never be happy until I had found it. We came across gorillas again many times in other parts of the Cameroons, but nowhere were they so plentiful as in the Mendjim Mey.

When the Second World War broke out and the French in Europe capitulated, Hilda and the children were evacuated to the British Cameroons, but I stayed behind and luckily the French declared themselves for General de Gaulle. After general mobilization there were only a handful of Europeans in the French Cameroons who understood native ways and could control the tribes, and because of that I was asked to accept a commission in the police. I spent the war years as *Monsieur Le Commissaire* in the towns of Yabassi and Bafang, and owing to wartime conditions I virtually governed the place. The French Government were kind enough to award us an Order of Merit and a Colonial Medal. I wonder if any other Englishman has ever become a French policeman? Hilda and I have many stories to tell of these years, but they must await another book.

All these things still lay ahead of us as we struggled out of the Mendjim Mey, with Collonel and N'Denge, grown even gentler than before, helping and sometimes carrying Hilda on their backs across streams and over rickety bridges. Just after we had left the Little Chief Mendjoum at the village of

Jebada we heard a familiar sound. Hilda and I let the carriers move on ahead of us and, when the last of them had passed and we stood alone in the forest, we listened together, for the last time, to the grunts and barks of our neighbors, the gorillas.